The Chinese in
Silicon Valley

Pacific Formations: Global Relations in Asian and Pacific Perspectives
Series Editor: Arif Dirlik

The Chinese in Silicon Valley

Globalization, Social Networks, and Ethnic Identity

Bernard P. Wong

ROWMAN & LITTLEFIELD PUBLISHERS, INC.
Lanham • *Boulder* • *New York* • *Toronto* • *Oxford*

ROWMAN & LITTLEFIELD PUBLISHERS, INC.

Published in the United States of America
by Rowman & Littlefield Publishers, Inc.
A wholly owned subsidiary of The Rowman & Littlefield Publishing Group, Inc.
4501 Forbes Boulevard, Suite 200, Lanham, Maryland 20706
www.rowmanlittlefield.com

P.O. Box 317, Oxford OX2 9RU, UK

British Library Cataloguing in Publication Information Available

Library of Congress Cataloging-in-Publication Data

Wong, Bernard P.
   The Chinese in Silicon Valley : globalization, social networks, and ethnic identity /
Bernard P. Wong.
      p. cm. -- (Pacific Formations)
   Includes bibliographical references and index.
   ISBN 0-7425-3939-3 (cloth : alk. paper) – ISBN 0-7425-3940-7 (pbk : alk. paper)
   1. High technology industries--California--Santa Clara Valley (Santa Clara County)—
History. 2. Chinese--California--Santa Clara Valley (Santa Clara County)--History.
3. Chinese Americans--California--Santa Clara Valley (Santa Clara County)--Social
Conditions. I. Title. II. Series
   HC107.C23 H538 2006
   305.895'1079473--dc22

                                                                    2005012638

Printed in the United States of America

♾™ The paper used in this publication meets the minimum requirements of
American National Standard for Information Sciences—Permanence of Paper
for Printed Library Materials, ANSI/NISO Z39.48-1992.

Contents

Contents

List of Tables

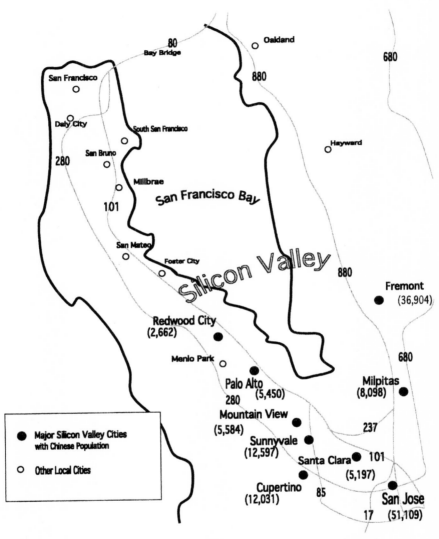

Major Silicon Valley Cities (with Chinese populations indicated)
Source: U.S. Bureau of the Census, United States Census 2000.

Acknowledgments

I want to thank all those who assisted me with my fieldwork in Silicon Valley, my students and colleagues, friends and family, for without them the writing of this book would not have been possible; if I was to find the door open to my research, the social connections had to be there. I want to thank particularly Michael Chang, Connie Yu, Victor Lee, Aiwen Lee, Richard Duong, Tony Tsang, Chilling Yeh, Jean Lee, Wellington Cheng, Sheikie Tao, and LiAnne Yu. All provided valuable information about the high-tech community in Silicon Valley and also introduced me to other research contacts.

While doing my fieldwork I had the opportunity to meet a number of important entrepreneurs and experts in the high-tech industry. I therefore owe my profound academic debt to Dr. David Lam, Dr. Alex Leung, Dr. Chester Wang, Dr. Wufu Chen, Dr. Milton Chang, and Wayne Liu: each provided me with valuable insights and feedback.

Danfei Wang and Dr. William Yang generously gave their time and energy to help analyze the data. Charlen Fong and Nadine Selden of the *San Jose Mercury News* gave me their insightful comments on my initial research findings; and I am also grateful to Susan Squires and Gary Waymire who asked many probing questions and helped me to focus my initial research.

Finally, I would like to express my gratitude to Dr. Michael Siu who has helped me in a very special way, to Lynne Murata and Jesse Keyes who were of great help in editing the draft of the manuscript, and to Matthew Aaronson who designed the map for the book. Thanks, too, to Kärstin Painter and John Shanabrook for their expert editing and guidance of the manuscript through production.

1

The Asian Century and the Rise of Globalization and Transnationalism

This work addresses the significance of the development of the newest Chinese community in the San Francisco Bay Area: the Chinese community of vibrant Silicon Valley. The Silicon Valley Chinese community is being developed out of the reinforcement and constraint of several factors: a growing global economy, burgeoning new technology, and the cultures, traditional or otherwise, of both newcomers and their host. The formation of the newcomers' identity and community is a result of globalization and transnationalism, and it involves the crossing of national borders, acquisition or nonacquisition of citizenship, and flexible accumulation of talent and capital. These newcomers, therefore, can no longer be seen as helpless victims of circumstance, burdened by their ethnic culture. Instead, they are agents and creators of a syncretic culture with hyphenated collective identities.

Many theories of global economic development and international migratory movement have lost their relevance. The World Systems theories of Immanuel Wallerstein (1974, 1980, 1990) focus only on the relationship between empires and their colonies. In a similar vein, Andre Frank (1967) anticipated the connections between Latin American and European colonizers. The linkages between colonies or former colonies and past or present colonial powers have understandably been the center of intellectual discourse for many years. However, major changes in Asia that include reconfigured societies, the emergence of Asian economic power as a hub of manpower, talent, and skill, and the development of Asia into a major center of consumption and manufacturing have only recently gained notice. This is of particular significance in U.S.-Asia/Pacific economic interactions. The burgeoning importance of the Asian sector can be seen when we note that large air carriers have carried more transpacific than transatlantic passengers in recent years. And even when economic conditions in both the United States and Asia are sluggish (as they were in 2001), optimism for the future of Asia's contribution to the world economy is still strong. This is particularly true when China is included in the economic equation. Many economists believe that China has room to grow, and that its economy could climb annually in the range of 10–12 percent. Economists also believe that other areas of Asia such as Hong Kong (economically distinct from mainland China), Taiwan, and Korea have the potential for further growth.

The restructuring of the U.S. economy is closely linked with conditions in Asia and its people. Many of the high-tech manufacturing plants that serve the U.S. economy are situated in Asia, while highly educated Asian immigrants power many of the research and development offices in Silicon Valley. It is not difficult, therefore, for many scholars to believe that the twenty-first century will indeed be the "Asian Century," and furthermore, that the United States and Europe will come to depend on Asia and Asians in order to maintain their affluent lifestyles. In the globalization models of Wallerstein (1974, 1980, 1990) and Andre Frank (1967), the engine of global economy is powered by wealthy European nations. However, in the modern economy, the Asian contribution cannot be underestimated. Some popular writers like John Naisbitt (1995) and others even hypothesize an eventual Asian dominance of the world economy. The concept of "Asianization" has accordingly been used to highlight the cultural influence of Asians in the economy of the modern world. Among Asians, the Chinese, who have emphasized higher education for centuries, have been frequently depicted as important players in the U.S.-Asian economy (Kotkin 1993; Weidenbaum and Hughes 1996; Seagrave 1995). In Silicon Valley, Asian Indians and the Chinese have been recognized as a driving force behind the valley's high-tech industry. Together with the Indians and Chinese, Pakistanis, Vietnamese, Malaysians, and other Asian groups constitute additionally an important segment of the population of the San Francisco Bay Area.

THE ASIAN WORKFORCE IN SILICON VALLEY

California has undergone a major shift in its population composition in the past ten years, reflecting the rise of Asian influence in the Golden State. Though statistically still the largest racial group, whites are no longer in the majority. The U.S. Census of 2000 indicated a significant dip in the white population to less than 50 percent of California's total population of 33,871,648. In contrast, there has been a noticeable surge in California's Latino and Asian populations (see table 1.1), and Asians now account for 11 percent of all Californians.

Table 1.1.   Percentage of Ethnic Population in California: 1990/2000

White	1990:	17,029,126	57.2%	2000:	15,816,790	46.7%
Hispanic	1990:	7,687,939	25.8%	2000:	10,966,556	32.4%
Asian	1990:	2,613,599	8%	2000:	3,648,860	10.8%
Black	1990:	2,092,446	7%	2000:	2,181,926	6.4%

Source: U.S. Bureau of the Census, United States Census 2000; *San Francisco Chronicle* March 30, 2001, A1.

In the San Francisco Bay Area there has been a corresponding increase in the Asian population in every county. However, the most significant increases of Asian population can be found in Silicon Valley. Here the high-tech boom has attracted many Asians. Chinese and Indians in particular form the largest racial group of the Silicon Valley non-white population. Cities in this area, Santa Clara, Fremont, San Ramon, Pleasanton, Milpitas, San Jose, and Menlo Park have all experienced tremendous growth due to the influx of Asian workers. Indeed, it is often said that the high-tech industry has been built by IC (Indians and Chinese). Their predominance is evident. While Asians overall make up 11 percent of the state's total population, in the nine counties of the Bay Area (Sonoma, Napa, Solano, Contra Costa, Marin, San Francisco, San Mateo, Santa Clara, and Alameda) they account for 19 percent of the total county population (see table 1.2). These nine counties have a total population of 6,783,760; of this number, 1.3 million are Asians (United States Census 2000; *San Francisco Chronicle* May 24, 2001, A1).

With the concentration of such a large Asian population in one area, there has developed a booming infrastructure of diverse Asian communities. Asian supermarkets, restaurants, and gift shops are plentiful. Among the Asians in the Bay Area, the Chinese are by far the largest group, with a population of

Table 1.2.   Population of the Nine Counties of the San Francisco Bay Area

Alameda	1,443,741
Contra Costa	948,816
Marin	247,289
Napa	124,279
San Francisco	776,733
San Mateo	707,161
Santa Clara	1,682,585
Solano	394,542
Sonoma	458,614
Total Population of the Bay Area	6,783,760

Source: U.S. Bureau of the Census, United States Census 2000; *San Francisco Chronicle* April 9, 2001, A13.

468,736 (see table 1.3). This means that 48 percent of the Chinese population in California (980,642) lives specifically in the San Francisco Bay Area. While some of these work in ethnic businesses such as Chinese restaurants, grocery stores, and gift shops, others work as professionals, and still others work in the high-tech industry in Silicon Valley.

As previously noted, Asian Indians and the Chinese have become a signif-icant labor force in the high-tech industry of the Bay Area. They are particu-larly visible in the residential neighborhoods of Union City, San Jose, Milpi-tas, Fremont, Santa Clara, Sunnyvale, and Cupertino (*San Francisco Chronicle* May 24, 2001, A1; August 10, 2001, A21). The profile of these Asian residents is that of the high-tech worker: many are the computer scientists, engineers, software specialists, or business managers who have been recog-nized as an important driving force behind the Silicon Valley phenomenon. According to Ana Lee Saxenian (1999), 29 percent of Silicon Valley startups during the period from 1995 to 1998 were run by Chinese or Indian migrants. In 1998 these two ethnic groups headed 2,775 Silicon Valley high-tech firms, employing 58,000 people. Thus, Asians constitute an important segment of the white-collar as well as the blue-collar labor force. According to Ken McLaughlin and Ariana Eunjung Cha of the *San Jose Mercury News* (April 16, 1999), the white-collar force is comprised of about 60 percent white and 31 percent Asian workers. Among the blue-collar workers and technicians, the workforce is about 57 percent Asian, 21 percent white, 18 percent Latino, and 4 percent black. Thus, in both white-collar and blue-collar high-tech em-ployment, Asians play an important role. In high-tech companies, however, there are proportionally more whites than Asians among the ranks of CEOs. A *San Jose Mercury News* survey of Silicon Valley's top public companies in-dicates the same disproportion: of the top 150 public companies, 89 percent of the chairmen and CEOs of those companies were white, 10 percent were Asian, and 0.6 percent were black (April 16, 1999).

Nationally in 2000, Chinese Americans numbered 2.43 million, represent-ing the largest Asian group. San Francisco meanwhile still retains the title of having the largest Chinese population in California, with 152,620. In the rest

Table 1.3.   Asian American Subgroups in the San Francisco Bay Area: 2000

Asian Indian	143,306
Chinese	468,736
Filipino	321,333
Japanese	74,505
Korean	56,724
Vietnamese	146,253
Other Asian	78,992

Source: U.S. Bureau of the Census, United States Census 2000; *San Francisco Chronicle* May 24, 2001, A6.

of the Bay Area, there are 316,116 Chinese, with many now residing in Silicon Valley. Among Chinese Americans, some are born locally while others are immigrants from Taiwan, Hong Kong, mainland China, and elsewhere. In terms of visa status, the Chinatown-connected Chinese tend to arrive as relatives of permanent residents or under the sponsorship of U.S. citizens through legal kin-related connections. In contrast, the high-tech Chinese tend to arrive in the United States as H-1B visa holders who are qualified to fill the United States' need for special talents and professional skills or expertise. (The holder of an H-1B visa is legally allowed to engage in temporary work or business.) According to the *Zhongguo Daily* (January 17, 2000), of the quota of 110,000 visas allotted in 2000, most of which were given to high-tech immigrants recruited by American corporations, Asian Indians occupied the first place among H-1B visa holders, those from mainland China ranked tenth, while Chinese from Taiwan ranked fifth. The Chinese and Indians have become the high-tech workhorses for the industries of the South Bay.

The success of these immigrants, as will be demonstrated herein, depended (and continues to depend) on many factors, opportunity of time and place being foremost. This group of Asians came at the right moment, and as engineers and technicians they filled an incessant demand for high-tech labor when the restructuring of the U.S. economy was creating an infant information technology (IT) industry. There were cultural factors as well. And in light of the success of these two Asian groups, immigrant culture can no longer be viewed as baggage to be packed, unpacked, and transplanted. Ties with the past and one's land of origin do not vanish. The predominant patterns of transnational migration allow recent immigrants to keep abreast of their social and cultural ties while traversing national and cultural borders. Furthermore, these traditional social ties can be utilized as important human and cultural resources that, aided by technology and other new economic assets, result in trans-Pacific social mobility and a parallel ability to establish roots in a new land.

As I focus on the role of Chinese immigrants in the development of the Silicon Valley high-tech industry and in the creation of a new immigrant community, I will address a number of interrelated questions:

1. What is the nature of the transnational Chinese community in Silicon Valley?
2. How do members of this community achieve their entrepreneurial success in the high-tech business sector, in the global economy in general, and in Silicon Valley in particular?
3. How have globalization, localization, and technological development influenced their social lives and cultural identities in this new land of opportunity?

4. What are the interaction patterns between the Chinese and the larger society?
5. What are the social costs of their transnational lifestyle?

The theoretical framework of this work is guided by a number of theories. The first are those theories related to the study of globalization (Wolf 1982; Hannerz and Lofgen 1994, 1979, 1996; Appadurai 1996; and Basch, Schiller, and Blanc 1994, just to cite a few). These authors correctly point out that the human community has been influenced by forces emanating from its own territorial confines. Eric Wolf (1982, 16) asks a rhetorical question: Has there ever been a time when human populations have existed in independence of larger encompassing relationships, unaffected by larger fields of force? Ulf Hannerz argues that there has been an increase in the interconnectedness of world communities, by which he cautions that the local could be influenced by the global (1996, 19). Arjun Appadurai goes as far as to say that globalization has changed the world and created disjunctures between economy, culture, and politics (1996, 33); while Basch, Schiller, and Blanc suggest that economic activities, ethnic and social relations, technological change, and national development have to be analyzed from a global perspective (1994). In the study of the Chinese diaspora, this global perspective is particularly relevant. Adam McKeown (2001), Bernard Wong (1997), and a host of other authors have indicated that migration and ethnic relations will not be understood properly until they have been analyzed from such a perspective. Nation-based ethnographies and analyses, it is suggested, obscure the dynamic aspects of human activities, because immigrants do not pack up their native culture and disappear into another. The former model of immigrants shedding their traditions, values, and cultural traits and assuming the values, institutions, and social interactions of a dominant culture is no longer realistic. As will be demonstrated in this study, that model of assimilation (Gordon 1964) does not fit social reality. Though it was this assimilation model that inspired the discourse of the melting pot of America, many social scientists have lately found this kind of unscientific assertion to be the farthest from the truth. Researchers on different American ethnic groups, from Polish Americans and Norwegian Americans to Greek Americans, continue to find the persistence of ethnic cultures in America, even after a hundred years of so-called melting.

Nor is it appropriate to assume that ethnic groups are merely an extension of the old world cultures from which they derived, as though nationality groups in the United States are merely copies of their old national cultures. People are dynamic, and they interact with new social and economic environments. Thus the tradition of nation-based ethnicity research is off-target. As social actors, transnational migrants often act under the reinforcement and restraint of both the new and the old countries. These are some of the extraterritorial factors of ethnic identity. Social ties between transnational migrants and their home cultures, for instance, continue. Similarly, diasporic communities are formed with local as well as external input (B. Wong 1986). The transnationals of our time are known for their frequent travel across national and cultural boundaries, and for maintenance of multi-stranded social ties with members of their former and new communities. Furthermore, the global circulation of skill, labor, technology, and financial resources is characteristic of the new communities formed by these transnationals (Basch, Schiller, and Blanc 1994; Sassen 1996a, 1996b). Since the modern economy is a global economy, parts of a product may be assembled in one nation by using skills and materials from many other nations. Similarly, the movement of people, ideas, talent, and technology is often associated with this global economy. Appadurai (1996) and others have convinced us that we do live in an interconnected world. This is particularly the case in the study of Chinese transnational migrants in Silicon Valley. Hence an approach that integrates localized research with knowledge of the globalization activities of the transnational migration will probably yield a more complete understanding of the internal linkages in the community, and of the global connections between the Chinese diaspora and the outside world. Since the 1980s, transnationalism as a way of life has been noticed by journalists as well as scholars, as transnationals have navigated between localities, countries, and continents in search of a better life. Many immigration scholars of Chinese communities have characterized transnationals as the people of an ungrounded empire (Ong 1999; Ong and Nonini 1996). But not all transnationals are noncommittal toward their national state. While it is true that opportunistic multiple-passport holders or "flexible" citizens do exist, it is difficult without empirical data to generalize this to all transnationals. As this study will show, for example, one cannot underestimate the motivation and commitment of the new transnationals in Silicon Valley. Circulation and navigation are not ends in themselves. They are merely the means transnationals use to achieve their final goal: establishing roots in a desirable land. For these reasons, data from Silicon Valley indicate that transnational activities and global strategies need to be integrated with local community information in order to achieve a comprehensive understanding of the actors and players of the social script.

The second group of theoretical components from which the framework of this work is built comprises those concepts derived from the study of social networks in a global context (Portes 1996, 1997; Portes, Castells, and Benton 1991; Castells 1996b; Marcus 1998; Kotkin 1993; Ju 1996; B. Wong 1988, 1998a, 2001b, 2001c).

Chinese transnationals, as will be demonstrated in this work, are not fleeting strangers. They are here because of existing ties, and many have cross-boundary ethnic networks and connections with both their homeland and local community. Among the connectors or nodes in the net are family members, kinsmen, friends, colleagues, and alumni. These individuals are deeply involved in social connection maintenance. Some of these connections, or *guanxi*, are developed and activated in public and semipublic settings such as alumni associations, professional organizations, neighborhoods, social clubs, and locality of origin associations, while other connections are simply based on blood ties. In studies of the social networks of the overseas Chinese, emphasis has traditionally been placed on kinship, friends, and fictive and ritual kinship contracted through surname, district, trade, and dialect associations, to which are also added civic, political, and professional associations. These intersecting, web-like social bonds are created, formed, and transformed continuously for different goal-seeking activities, and the connection of an identical language, dialect, or hometown are no longer a prerequisite. There are now other over-riding concerns; ideology, social mobility, and professional interests have become more important than the traditional principles of kinship. Indeed, scholars of network studies have pointed out that networks can be used for market and labor opportunities (McKeown 2001; B. Wong 1988, 1997; Ramu 2001; Allan 1996; Barnes 1954). Only recently, however, have scholars specifically noted how networks can be used for the creation and maintenance of ethnic identity and imagined diasporas (Werbner 2002; Mayer 1961; Hannerz 1990). For instance, Mayer distinguishes between two kinds of social networks among labor immigrants in East London, South Africa. One is an encapsulated ethnic group that maintains close-knit networks spanning both town and country. This group is culturally conservative in its leisure activities. The other is made up of non-encapsulated immigrants who form wide-ranging, loosely knit networks of friends made in town, and who explore new forms of consumption and entertainment.

In many Chinese communities there are traditional immigrants who want to maintain ties with their hometown acquaintances and friends, and who often isolate themselves from outside influence. But in the Silicon Valley Chinese community there is another type of social network that is formed by people who know each other from work, school, a professional association, or from shared social and political activities, and whose common interest lies in gaining a place socially, economically, and politically in the new country. Members of these social communities network to engage in a struggle for multicultural citizenship in America, a struggle that includes consensus building with other transnationals, forming coalitions with Asians who have similar goals, working against racial profiling and discrimination, and campaigning for equality in America. Moreover, there are nonlocalized social networks through which transnationals increase their ability to reach out to other coethnic groups in a larger region or in different parts of the world. The following chapters will examine the creation and use of such social networks by the Chinese in Silicon Valley in both a local and a transnational context. Doing this will enable us to gain a better understanding of the social reality of the Chinese in Silicon Valley, a reality defined by economic activities, ethnic identity, and community life.

The third group of intellectual components that guides the theoretical outline of this book is drawn from the study of concepts of ethnic identity and diaspora communities in general (Barth 1969; G. Wang 1999, 2000; B. Wong 1998a, 2000; Wang and Wang 1998; Wing Chung Ng 1995; Fong 1994; Chen 2001). Ethnic identity is a social construct. According to Barth (1969), what defines the ethnic identity of an ethnic group is the social boundary which is generated in its interethnic interaction, and this identity is therefore fluid. In other words, context often dictates the assumption of identities. The formation of identities is also influenced by extraterritorial as well as exogenous factors. U.S.-China relations, the global economy, and China-Taiwan relations, for example, can have an impact on ethnic identity and its maintenance (B. Wong 1978, 1982, 1986). The global economy, and the emergence of the People's Republic of China (PRC) as a world power, have also affected the assumption of the ethnic identity of the Chinese.

Closely related to the concept of identity is the concept of diaspora. Some believe that there is only one Chinese diaspora with a single identity. Some argue that there are diverse Chinese diasporas around the world. To begin with, the term *diaspora* needs a clarification. Traditionally, a diaspora (Safran 1991) is a dispersed people who have been forced out of a homeland and exist, strictly speaking, without a nation-state. The most undeniable diaspora, according to Jonathan Okamura (1998), and existing for centuries, is that of the Jewish people. But in contemporary usage the concept of diaspora has changed. Contemporary diasporas are the result of transnational migration. The old paradigm of diasporas as dispersed ethnic, religious, or national communities has been altered. Modern scholarship shows that diasporans can maintain their connections with each other and with their homeland though "mediascapes" (Appadurai 1996). Additionally, contemporary diasporans can intensely participate in the social and political life of their host culture (Werbner 2002), and they may engage in struggles for citizenship and equality in their host country. Scholars have shown that diasporans may also engage in debate on issues relevant to identity, civic responsibilities, loyalty, and relations with co-diasporans and other ethnic minorities (Werbner 2002; G. Wang 2000; Lyman and Douglas 1973). Some scholars even emphasize the concept of "cultural citizenship" (Rosaldo 1989; Ong 1996b). Many diasporans in contemporary America have demanded that civil rights, respect, and recognition be extended to them due to the fact that they are residents who contribute to U.S. society. At the same time, they maintain their cultural identity and celebrate their cultural differences (Lynn Stephen 1996). In the case of the overseas Chinese, there is no one single ethnic identity assumed by a single Chinese diaspora (B. Wong 2005). Some of the overseas Chinese may be "essential outsiders"; in other places they may be "pariah entrepreneurs" or "flexible citizens of ungrounded empires." In still other countries, they may be deeply involved in contested ideology and citizenship and in localized struggles for cultural citizenship. Gungwu Wang (2000) advocates that the overseas Chinese be studied in the context of their respective national environment. Some studies (McKeown 2001) intimate that the Chinese diaspora in America is in a middle ground between hybridity and essentialized identity. From my fieldwork on the Chinese in the United States, I have found that there is a spectrum of ethnic identity among the Chinese. Individuals may assume one or many identities simultaneously, some of which are hybrid or hyphenated identities. The admonition of Wang is not only laudable—it is also the correct path for anthropologists who pursue the emic (insider) approach and who want to ground their theory on fieldwork.

Hybridity and hyphenated identities are found in many diaspora communities (Lessinger 1996; Mortland 1998; Werbner 2002). Pnina Werbner shows that Pakistanis in Manchester belong to several diasporas—Asian, Muslim, nationalist Pakistani, and Punjabi. In this sense, they belong to a hybrid diaspora. By examining the issues of diversity and complexity of diasporic identity, I will seek to uncover the multi-strands of identities. The Chinese in Silicon Valley, as will be seen, are not a homogeneous community in terms of class, locality of origin, or political ideology. Their diaspora is a transnational diaspora. It is not a homogeneous and harmonious *gemeinschaft*, but rather a heterogeneous community in which economic competitions are conducted and debates about identity and civic obligation are frequent and contentious. However, the Chinese community in Silicon Valley is not to be perceived as a disorganized hierarchy of many fleeting strangers. There are indeed social ties that link its members internally and globally.

Conceptually, this book will examine how globalization has impacted the formation and use of social networks for economic pursuit and in the development of an ethnic community in a technological society. Theoretically, this work hopes to clarify a number of questions about the paradox of globalization and localization, the formation of ethnic identities in plural societies, and the influence of technology on modern life.

Ethnographically, this book intends to debunk a number of misconceptions. First, participation in the global economy does not signify the noncommitment of the Chinese to their adopted land. Second, the use of social networks indicates that *place* is important. Social networks are tools that can be utilized to achieve social equality and to fight racism. Third, the movement of the new Chinese immigrants can no longer be understood as taking place in a one-directional fashion: it is often nonlinear, circular, or zigzagging. Similarly, the circulation of capital and talent is conditioned by social and economic circumstances in a global context. The departing and receiving countries of these transnational immigrants may change in time. Places of work and places of residence may not coincide. In Europe, for example, it is possible for people to be members and residents of the European Union (EU) and at the same time citizens of their own ancestral or sending countries. Thus, the British in France or the Turks in Germany may prefer to keep their citizenship in the United Kingdom or Turkey. However the profile of the Chinese immigrant in the United States context does not follow this pattern. The majority of the Chinese who participate in the global economy or the Asia-Pacific economy prefer to retain citizenship in their adopted country (the United States) rather than in that of their ancestral land (the PRC, or Hong Kong). This phenomenon of immigrants committing their loyalty to a host country also differs from the overseas Chinese elsewhere. Therefore, the prevalence of flexible citizenship or noncommitment to one's adopted country is not applicable to most of the Chinese in America.

In the face of globalization, the question of why citizens become more loyal to their adopted nation-state rather than to their country of birth must be deciphered. The stereotypical idea that the overseas Chinese have a "bamboo" network (Weidenbaum and Hughes 1996), and that they are the "lords of the rim" (Seagrave 1995) who are linked up together as an "ungrounded empire" due to their common ethnicity (Ong and Nonini 1996), are too simplistic to have validity. As this study will show, the Chinese of the Pacific Rim are a diverse lot. The fact that they are identified as *Chinese* does not necessarily mean that they share the same networks. While pivotal to any relationship, these social networks or *guanxi* have to be formed and cultivated. Informal egocentric social circles formed for particular goal-seeking activities, such as social networks, like many other social groups, come to exist and dissolve depending on activity, sentiment, and interaction. Chinese social networks are similarly contingent on space, time, and circumstance. From my research, it is clear that a ready-made bamboo network unequivocally uniting all Chinese does not exist. Furthermore, the meaning of what we might call "Chinese-ness" also needs to be defined. The stereotype that all Chinese immigrants are successful entrepreneurs has to be debunked. To categorize all Chinese high-tech personnel working in Silicon Valley as entrepreneurs is unrealistic. As this work demonstrates, it cannot be true. There is no cultural propensity to warrant entrepreneurial success to every Chinese person. Ethnographically speaking, there is indeed a need to depict the true nature of the Chinese community in Silicon Valley, and to dissect this community's social, economic, and political reality.

Politicians as well as social scientists have long predicted the decline of the nation-state as a consequence of globalization. However, it is apparent that globalization may not necessarily weaken the power of nation-states. Nor does globalization diminish local and cultural differences. This book will show ethnographically how globalization and localization have simultaneously burst into fruition in the context of a newly developed community in Silicon Valley.

THEORETICAL ISSUES AND SUMMARY OF THE CHAPTERS

This book deals with the pertinent issue of how globalization has made a dramatic impact on new migration movements, community formation, ethnic identity, and social and family life. Globalization has changed the face of the world, and it has impacted theories of international migration, identity formation, and diaspora. This book also represents an attempt to provide ethnographic details of the inner workings of a transnational community, and to explain the social reality of a new kind of diaspora in the high-tech Silicon Valley. Although a number of ethnographic studies have been conducted in Silicon Valley, none have dealt specifically with the activity systems of its Chinese community of entrepreneurs and engineers. AnaLee Saxenian's *Silicon Valley's New Immigrant Entrepreneur* (1999) is a structural analysis of Chinese and Indian entrepreneurs in the region. In this respect, it is a pioneering study that attempts to quantify the presence and contribution of the immigrant entrepreneurs. From an urban sociological perspective, Castells and Hall (1994) are interested in the global and technological aspects of the IT industry. And a recent study by J. A. English-Lueck is an anthropological exploration of the everyday lives of people who live and work in high-tech Silicon Valley (2002). Additionally, there are journalistic accounts in both Chinese and English about luminaries and social and political developments in the valley (Zhang 2000; Teng 1998; Bronson 1999; Barsook 2000; Sexton 1992). A number of dissertations have been written on Silicon Valley's economic complexity. For instance, Karen Hossfeld discusses the employment practices of factories (1988), and Edward Park examines the general issues of race and ethnicity in the postindustrial economy of Silicon Valley (1994, 1995). All of these works contribute much to our understanding of the place. However, none of these focus on how Chinese Americans in the high-tech industry participate in the local and the global economy. These works also do not deal with the impact of globalization on the Chinese in Silicon Valley. The reciprocal relationship between the global and the local is the central theme of this book, and it is essential to an understanding of the formation of the Chinese ethnic community as well as the high-tech industry in Silicon Valley in general.

Chapter 2 continues the description begun above of the nature of the Chinese community, and it presents relevant history and demographic statistics to show that community's heterogeneity. The chapter provides a general background for this book, and it will argue that globalization affects not only the migration of the Chinese to Silicon Valley—it also complicates the formation of identity, and has a special impact on the relationship of the Chinese diaspora with the larger society. Interactions between Chinese high-tech professionals and the larger society have generated special issues and concerns pertaining to the day-to-day existence of individuals in Silicon Valley. Chapter 3 then describes how the Chinese use their resources and social networks to participate in the global economy. We will find that globalization does not cause the disappearance of informal social relations; on the contrary, globalization encourages and requires the use of social networks which are, nowadays, created within organizations like alumni, civic, and professional associations. Chapter 4 discusses in turn how the Chinese are establishing roots in Silicon Valley. Chapter 5 examines the impact of globalization on the Chinese community. This chapter will show that globalization and localization go hand in hand. Chapter 6 depicts the social cost of this globalization. It focuses on the impact of globalization on the family life of the Chinese Silicon Valley transnationals. Chapter 7 goes on to discuss the impact of globalization on the ethnic identity of the Chinese. Issues of identity formation, hybridization, and diaspora will be discussed under the aspect of this impact. Finally, chapter 8 sums up the major findings of this study, and discusses their relevant theoretical contributions.

METHODOLOGY

This work was developed with data from fieldwork and relevant written sources in Chinese and English, including local Chinese newspapers. Fieldwork activities included observation, participation, and interviews conducted from 1998 to 2003. The fieldwork techniques followed, two of which are discussed in greater detail below, included (1) participant observation, (2) in-depth interviews, (3) collection of life history materials from interviews and published sources, (4) use of census, statistical, and biographical data, (5) use of relevant written materials published by local authors, local organizations, and local newspapers, and (6) use of a group of master informants to check accuracy and to assist in the analysis of data.

Participant-Observation

Much of my information regarding the social life and economic and professional activities of the Chinese in Silicon Valley was obtained from observation and interviews with people in their workplaces, their company cafeterias, at meetings of various professional associations, and sometimes at the homes of informants. Observations were made in various computer software and hardware companies ranging from large multinational corporations to small family-run businesses. Since my research interest was in high-tech professionals and entrepreneurs, my fieldwork activities focused on several distinct but related activities. First, I visited major high-tech companies that employ Chinese. These included chip manufacturing, software and hardware companies, and high-tech venture capital firms. Second, I participated in many of the professional meetings, conventions, and job fairs of Chinese high-tech professionals. These included the annual meetings of various professional organizations. Third, I visited the offices or headquarters of professional associations, and I collected the bulletins, directories, and documents published by these associations. Fourth, I participated in the social activities of Chinese professionals in Silicon Valley. These activities included dinner parties, receptions, and celebrations given for them by the Chinese consulate or Taipei Economic and Cultural Office. I also went to the wedding and birthday celebrations of Chinese high-tech workers. Additionally, I was able to visit the Industrial Technology Research Institute and Science Park in Hsinchu, Taiwan, in 2000. My visit was significant in that it helped me understand why some Chinese have returned from Silicon Valley to Hsinchu. During my trip I was able to gain insight into the return migrations of these transnationals.

In-depth Personal Interviews

I have conducted in-depth unstructured interviews with one hundred informants from Taiwan, mainland China, Hong Kong, and the United States. Efforts were made to get an accurate presentation, and informants selected were of different ages, occupations, and genders. Interviews were taped and then transcribed. Because the gender ratio in the high-tech industry is highly uneven, most of the informants I interviewed were male. Most of the engineers were also quite young, being under the age of forty-five. In contrast, many of the venture capitalists were above the age of forty-five.

Social acceptance and personal rapport had to be there first before I could make inroads in my research. During the first year I was given financial assistance by a research organization, and with the help of my research assistants I was able to interview thirty-two persons. Through their social network, I then gradually expanded my sample. From 1999 to 2003, I added seventy-eight more informants. Networking was essential in my fieldwork, and most of the informants I met were introduced to me by friends, students, classmates, family members, and their contacts. Some of my informants I met through professional organizations and at special occasions. Additionally, I also used a group of "key" or master informants who helped me check the accuracy of my information and analysis. This group of master informants was composed of the "old-timers" of Silicon Valley, those familiar with the career paths and the social lives of the Chinese engineers and entrepreneurs there, and it included entrepreneurs from Taiwan, Hong Kong, and mainland China, a local historian, as well as a former mayor of a Silicon Valley city. Most of the information I obtained was ethnographic and qualitative in nature. When it became necessary to obtain statistical data, I depended mostly on the U.S. census data of 1990 and 2000. There was no particular reason why I limited myself to one hundred informants, but after four years in the field, and having consulted with my professional colleagues and expert informants, I felt that I had accumulated sufficient data for the purposes of this ethnography. In order to neutralize possible biases, I double-checked with my master informants. My goal has been to produce an ethnography that shows how the global economy has affected the Chinese community in Silicon Valley, both individually and collectively. And at the same time, it has been to depict how the members of this community use their social capital, and their cultural values, connections, and organizations to position themselves to participate in the global economy.

2

The Nature of the Chinese in Silicon Valley: An Ethnic Community of High-Tech Professionals

The Chinese in Silicon Valley are scattered across a vast territory extending from the county of San Mateo to the counties of Santa Clara and Alameda. There is no Chinatown within Silicon Valley, yet the Chinese there form a community in the truest sense of the word. Sharing a common ethnic culture with many cultural and professional ties, the Chinese in Silicon Valley have strong links to the high-tech industry. In fact, there are more Chinese working as high-tech engineers in the stretch of companies between San Francisco and San Jose (the so-called Silicon Valley) than in any other profession there, and they indeed identify themselves as workers in Silicon Valley. When asked the question, where do you work? the high-tech Chinese engineer commonly answers, I work in Silicon Valley.

Place, technology, and cultural heritage all define the Silicon Valley Chinese community. First, the members of this community came from Taiwan, Hong Kong, mainland China, or other overseas Chinese communities. Second, they are tied to Silicon Valley by work and residency. Third, they are all involved in the high-tech industry through their work as engineers, owners, CEOs, programmers, or computer industry techies (technicians). Fourth, these transnational migrants continue to have a strong attachment to Chinese culture. Chinese parentage is another of the commonalities shared by the Chinese in this community. There are of course differences among them in terms of origin, social class, education, occupation, alma mater, the degree of their eagerness to maintain their ethnic culture, and their attitude toward their motherland, but globalization has pulled them together and placed them in Silicon Valley. Globalization has also divided them and separated them into different groups. Thus, globalization has created a unique Chinese community that is made up of heterogeneous elements. Globalization unifies but also diversifies the Chinese in Silicon Valley. Heterogeneity, contrary to the claims of many social scientists (Appadurai 1998; Hannerz 1996), is in fact a characteristic of the transnational world. Although a community results from transnational migration, it is not an island of strangers. Migration scholars and urban studies scholars for many years have insisted that strangers and immigrants from remote areas are social isolates and strangers without ties (Wirth 1938; Redfield 1941). This chapter will show that the community created by transnational migration is heterogeneous and at the same time populated by people with social ties. Thus, *community* is no longer to be grasped as a culturally homogeneous and harmonious *gemeinschaft*. Nor is this an urban community composed of fleeting encounters as argued by the Chicago School (Park, Burgess, and Mackenzie 1925; Redfield 1947; Wirth 1938). Furthermore, social ties and social networks exist, and some of these social ties go beyond the narrow geographical boundaries of cities and nation. This boundary-crossing phenomenon is in fact an essential element in the transnational community.

Community is more than just physical boundary. In fact, the Chinese community in Silicon Valley has no physical boundary such as a Chinatown or other geographic anomaly. The boundary of this Chinese community is rather a social one made up of interactions, and it reflects what Conrad Arensberg defines as essential to such social organizations:

> Communities are the basic units of organization and transmission within a culture providing a minimum of cultural adaptation to nature and the kind of interpersonal relations necessary to assure survival and cultural transmission to future generations. (Arensberg 1954)

The Chinese community is an ethnic community that shares similar interpersonal interaction patterns and at the same time utilizes survival skills. Its boundary is a social and ethnic one, and the concept of ethnicity that defines it is consistent with studies by Fredrik Barth (1969). There are social ties among the members of this community, and these ties, because they are translocal and transnational ties, go beyond a localized area. Common ethnicity is also used for economic and political adaptation and incorporation into the larger society. This phenomenon has been recognized by Robert Ibarra in a study of the Norwegians in Wisconsin (2001, 171). While the dynamics of the ethnic and social networks of the Silicon Valley Chinese will be discussed later in greater detail, it is important to note here that social relations in this community were developed as an adaptive response to the global economy, and that they are tools to survival in the new land. But some basic questions need to be raised here in this introduction to the Chinese community: Why and how did the new Chinese transnational migrants come to Silicon Valley? What are the general characteristics of this high-tech Chinese community? In what way is this community an adaptive response to a transnational movement?

WHERE IS SILICON VALLEY?

The geographic area situated to the south of San Francisco, moving from Palo Alto to San Jose, and winding around the eastern shore of San Francisco Bay to Fremont and then back to Union City is what is known today as Silicon Valley (see map 1). It is a borderless community without an overall municipal or governmental structure governing the region. Initially, Silicon Valley was a sunbathed saddle of land between the Santa Cruz Mountains and San Francisco Bay where flowers and pears and other fruits were grown. In the old days, this stretch of the South Bay was filled with orchards, and locals called it the "Valley of the Heart's Delight." The now-famous nickname, "Silicon Valley" was coined only in 1971 by author Don Hoefler (2000). Gone are the orchards, however, and in their place today are such high-tech companies as IBM, Intel, Oracle, HP, Apple Computer, and Cisco Systems. The Valley of the Heart's Delight is now a valley of silicon chips.

THE CHINESE IN SILICON VALLEY:
AN OVERVIEW AND SHORT HISTORY

The reader should not have the misconception that the Chinese presence started only with the "Silicon Rush" of the 1980s, but while a short description of this group's regional history will not do full justice to the group's hundred years presence in Silicon Valley, for our purposes it will suffice.

The Early Chinese in California

Early Chinese immigrants began to arrive in California in the 1850s. They worked the western frontiers as an untiring force, creating the infrastructure of California through their backbreaking labor (B. Wong 1988). As gardeners, railroad builders, highway builders, fisherman, and miners, the Chinese were everywhere, from Monterey Bay and Santa Clara County in the south to San Francisco in the north. Historical records show that the Chinese helped build the railroads to Santa Clara County. They worked the land as well, cultivating flower gardens, vegetable farms, and strawberry fields. In San Jose in 1887 it is recorded that a Chinatown burned down (Yu 1993), and since the 1860s Chinese have lived in Gilroy, Milpitas, Alviso, Campbell, Cupertino, and Mountain View (Chan 1991; Lai 1997; Lydon 1985; Saxton 1971; Yu 1993).

From World War II to the Present

There have been many changes in this area since World War II, the first being the development of flower-cultivation, particularly chrysanthemums. Even today one can find the descendants of the early Chinese flower growers living here. Then from the 1940s to 1960s, with better education, the Chinese left the blue-collar labor strata and entered the ranks of the middle-class community of professors, doctors, and dentists to emerge as pillars of the Asian community in Silicon Valley.

Beginning in the 1960s, an increasing number of Chinese moved into the valley. The census of 1990 shows that there were 67,432 Chinese then living in Silicon Valley. From 1990 to 1995, the community was infused with an additional 16,025 Chinese immigrants (see tables 2.1 and 2.2). The development of Silicon Valley attracted many new Chinese immigrants from Taiwan, Hong Kong, and China, making the Chinese the largest immigrant group working in the high-tech industry. According to Professor Ana Lee Saxenian, in the period immediately preceding, from 1975 to 1990, Silicon Valley high-tech companies created 150,000 jobs and its foreign-born population increased to 350,000 (1999, 11). But by 1990 the total workforce in Silicon Valley was 1,806,233, and of this number, 274,335 were in high-tech businesses. The census data of 1990 further indicate that 30 percent of this high-tech workforce was foreign-born. Among them, one third were scientists and engineers, with the majority being Chinese and Asian Indians, and in fact, the Chinese population out-numbered that of Asian Indians. By 1990, therefore, 23 percent of the population of Santa Clara County was foreign-born. In fact, the largest concentration of immigrants in the Bay Area today is found in Silicon Valley.

Table 2.1.   Chinese in Silicon Valley by Country of Origin (1990)

United States (California-born)	16,307	24.2%[a]
Other U.S. born	4,878	7.2%
China	15,475	22.9%
Hong Kong	5,223	7.7%
Taiwan	14,637	21.7%
Macau	89	0.1%
Vietnam	6,189	9.2%
Singapore	268	0.4%
Thailand	197	0.3%
Philippines	321	0.5%
Other Asia	1,952	2.9%
Canada	304	0.5%
Latin America	332	0.5%
Other	1260	1.9%
Total	67,432	100%

Source: U.S. Bureau of the Census, United States Census 2000.
[a]Percentage of total valley Chinese population,1990.

Table 2.2.   Chinese Immigration from 1990 to 1995: Santa Clara County

Hong Kong	2,175
China, mainland	7,826
Taiwan	6,204
Total:	16,205

Source: U.S. Immigration and Naturalization Service.

The first of five tech-related waves of foreign-born Chinese migrations can be traced back to the 1950s (see table 2.3). At that time, technology immigrants were sponsored by IBM and other American companies. A second wave of Chinese immigrants, in the 1960s, arrived in California to work for the defense industries. The third wave was related to an infusion of graduate students from mainland China after 1970, when the PRC relaxed its policies concerning studying in the United States. Table 2.3 further indicates that an increasing number of Chinese immigrants came to Silicon Valley in the late 1980s and 1990s. This fourth wave of immigrants was composed of Chinese from within the United States, Taiwan, mainland China, and other overseas Chinese communities. The fifth wave of immigrants came in the decade from 1990 to 2000. These were generally mainland Chinese students who finished their graduate training in the Unites States. After graduation they then sought employment in Silicon Valley. Around the same time, students from mainland China also came to this country on H-1B visas. In a very general way, one can divide all of these Chinese immigrants into three groups according to their country of origin: Hong Kong, Taiwan, or mainland China. More specifically, as will be discussed later, those who came from mainland China also came from different geographical areas like Beijing, Shanghai, Nanjing, and Xian, and there were regional differences among them. The Taiwanese Chinese were composed of many subgroups as well. Some were Taiwanese who were born in Taiwan of local residents. Others were Taiwanese who came originally to Taiwan as political refugees from mainland China or were descents of mainland Chinese who came to Taiwan after 1949. It should be noted that my use of the terms *mainland Chinese, Hong Kong Chinese,* and *Taiwanese Chinese* will be inconsistent with the legal definitions of those terms as used to classify immigrants according to sending country.

Table 2.3.   Five Waves of High-Tech Chinese Migration into Silicon Valley

Date Range	Wave Composition
1950s	Technology immigrants to work for IBM, Intel, Fairchild, and others.
1960s	Technology immigrants to work for the California Defense Industry.
1970s	Mainland Chinese graduate students.
late 1980s into the 1990s	Technology immigrants from Taiwan, China, overseas Chinese communities, and U.S. areas outside the valley.
1990s to 2000	Mainland Chinese graduate students.

Who are the Silicon Valley Chinese, and in Which Valley Communities Do They Live?

At present, four types of Chinese reside in Silicon Valley. The first type is defined by those Chinese Americans who were born in the United States and who have local roots in San Francisco or Northern California. The second is made up of foreign students who adjusted their visas in order to stay permanently in America. This group has been in the United States since the 1960s and is composed of students from Taiwan and Hong Kong. It is centered in the Stanford area. With the growth of Silicon Valley beginning in the 1980s, Hong Kong, Taiwan, and mainland Chinese engineers with advanced degrees flocked to the area, and these make up the third type of Chinese valley resident. Many are also secondary migrants who moved from another area in the United States. The fourth type of Chinese valley resident arrived during the 1970s and after 2000, and came from Southeast Asia or a different part of the world.

Today the Chinese from Taiwan and mainland China are the two dominant ethnic groups in the high-tech industry, and there are more Taiwanese and mainland Chinese with advanced degrees than any other Chinese group. The great number of Taiwanese Chinese is due to the fact that for many years only students who graduated from college in Taiwan could obtain exit visas. Thus for the most part, this group consisted of graduate students who were pursuing advanced degrees in the United States. Mainland Chinese students coming to the United States since the 1980s have also been mainly graduate students pursuing master's or doctorate degrees.

There are strong Taiwan influences in the Silicon Valley Chinese community. People here speak Mandarin, many with a Taiwanese accent, and some even speak Fujianese (a local Taiwanese dialect). Many restaurants and Chinese grocery stores serve Taiwan-style food. There are also churches (with pastors from Taiwan) serving Taiwan immigrants. According to some estimates, there are about two hundred social organizations that are related to Taiwan and are registered with the Chinese Cultural Center of Sunnyvale. In fact, there is a large annual celebration in Sunnyvale of Confucius's Birthday, and it is attended by thousands of immigrants from Taiwan. Fremont also has a large concentration of Chinese from Taipei, and near the downtown district of Mission Street there is a neighborhood called "Little Taipei."

Differences between the Mainland and Taiwanese Chinese exist. Mainland Chinese tend to have more problems in communication skills due to their lack of English fluency and lack of knowledge of Western capitalism and of the American lifestyle. Many lived in China when it was still relatively isolated from the international community, and after they migrated to the United States in the 1990s they were not sufficiently enculturated to American culture due to a lack of exposure. Hence, these high-tech Chinese workers experience difficulties in adjustment. There are also other intercultural communication problems. Having been raised under socialism for many years, many do not understand how to negotiate with their employers for better wages and working conditions. There is also a difference in communication style. Americans value open and direct exchange. Employers, for example, may not appreciate employees who are quiet in professional meetings and self-effacing about their achievements. Some Mainland Chinese employees may stress their loyalty to a firm by staying with the firm for a long period of time. American employers may read it differently. They may think that their employees have no better employment prospect and hence are willing to stay with the company. Chinese employees, on their part, may not understand that social and professional mobility may require geographical relocation and the change of companies. Mainland Chinese, due to language and cultural unfamiliarity, also tend to encounter more discrimination in promotion. The "glass ceiling" phenomenon is frequently cited as a mainland Chinese employee's reason for frustration with an employment situation. The glass ceiling refers to barriers that restrict an employee's promotion to higher management levels; it is said to be glass because one can see through it to a desired management position but cannot go through the impenetrable barrier that it represents. Conversely, the Taiwanese Chinese high-tech personnel have better English communication skills, tend to be better educated and older, and also tend to be more knowledgeable about Western capitalism and the American lifestyle.

A third important ethnic group of Chinese in Silicon Valley are the Hong Kong Chinese who speak the Cantonese dialect as their lingua franca. Their English skills are generally better than that of the Taiwanese or mainland Chinese due to their history of British domination and compulsory English-language education from the elementary school period. Paradoxically, the Hong Kong Chinese as a group are less educated when compared to the Taiwan or mainland Chinese. This is because most of the Hong Kong Chinese migrated to the United States to pursue their baccalaureate education, Hong Kong having very few and highly competitive universities. After graduating from U.S. universities, many Hong Kong citizens entered the world of business rather than go on for advanced degrees. It is not surprising then that there are fewer PhD holders among the Hong Kong Chinese. In fact, this is also reflected in the makeup of their respective alumni associations. The Hong Kong Student Association is organized on the basis of its members' high-school affiliation in Hong Kong, while the Taiwanese alumni associations are organized on the basis of members' home universities in Taiwan. The mainland Chinese have both high-school as well as university alumni associations in Silicon Valley.

Not only do the Silicon Valley Chinese differ in their dialects and education background, they also differ in their birthplaces and political aspirations and ideology. At the same time, they also share certain common interests, such as finding lucrative employment and establishing roots in the United

States. They all want to gain permanent residency and have their children educated in the United States. On the other hand, they want to retain Chinese culture. It is interesting to note that these different groups of Chinese do not intermingle socially, instead forming cultural and residential clusters. While they may work for the same company, and therefore may interact professionally within the work environment, they do not have much social interaction after working hours. Thus, there is a distinct social distance among these three groups. In chapter 3 a more detailed examination will be conducted to illuminate the intra-ethnic differences between these groups.

Chinese people live and work in different towns and cities in Silicon Valley, and they are situated in different social spaces. Not all Chinese belong to the same social stratum. Depending on their social and economic positions, some may live in exclusive Los Alto Hills where houses start at $1 million, or in the Menlo Park and Palo Alto areas. Others may live in the southern parts of the valley, in Morgan Hills, South San Jose, and Fremont. Some Chinese are wealthy founders of large corporations, while others have more modest employment as data processors and receptionists. Newcomers from Taiwan and mainland China prefer to live in Fremont, Sunnyvale, and Mountain View where housing costs are slightly cheaper. Fremont still has the space to build new houses, attracting the many newcomers who prefer to live in newer homes. Sunnyvale on the other hand has many apartments for rent, and recently arrived Chinese engineers from mainland China like to live there. The upper- and upper-middle-class Chinese prefer to live in Cupertino, where there are good schools for their children's education. In fact, Cupertino is a favorite place for many Chinese families from Taiwan, so much so that the city of Cupertino is known to many people in Taiwan by its zip code: 95014. When I visited Taiwan in 2000, an old gentleman told me his son's family lived in the Gu City (Shi). I was slightly at a loss with the transliteration of the name of the city. Immediately, he told me that it is a city with a zip code: 95014. For the convenience of visitors to the city, there is a map of Cupertino printed in Chinese. On the reverse side of the printed map, there is information about community services, schools and colleges, recreational centers and parks, shopping centers, festivals, and motels and hotels in Cupertino area.

As mentioned above, strata differences exist among Chinese workers in the high-tech industries, workers who range from CEOs, managers, and engineers, to blue-collar workers doing cleaning, packaging, and assembling. However, a great majority of the Chinese in Silicon Valley are professionals or managers. While U.S. 2000 Census data allowing an occupational breakdown of the Chinese are still not available, Public Use Microdata Sample (PUMS) Files from the 1990 census indeed indicate that most of the Chinese in this community are in the ranks of professional or managerial personnel. Table 2.4 offers an example of the occupational breakdown of the Chinese in Santa Clara according to birthplace or country of origin.

Table 2.4. Selected Occupations of Santa Clara County Chinese (by place of birth)

Occupation	China	Hong Kong	Taiwan
Managerial	7077 (43.44%)	1866 (34.42%)	5657 (38.15%)
Professional	2067 (12.83%)	1188 (21.91%)	3752 (25.30%)
Technical	870 (5.4 %)	400 (7.38%)	1355 (9.14%)
Administrative support	983 (6.10%)	536 (9.89%)	1002 (6.76%)
Total of the above	10997 (67.77%)	3980 (73.6 %)	11766 (79.35%)

Source: Public Use Microdata Sample (PUMS) Files, 1990.

As the table indicates, among the three groups of Chinese, the Taiwan-born Chinese group was the largest in Santa Clara in 1990 with a workforce of 11,766, although my sources in the community suggest that China-born Chinese professionals now outnumber those from Taiwan. My informants estimate that there are approximately 15,000 Chinese high-tech professionals from mainland China working in Silicon Valley today (2002). The Taiwan group of high-tech professionals is approximately 10,000. In addition to the three groups represented in the table, there are also Chinese from Latin America and Southeast Asia.

Today the San Francisco Bay Area is the metropolitan area in the United States with the largest Chinese concentration (468,736). However, the Chinese are concentrated in only four major counties: Alameda, San Francisco, San Mateo, and Santa Clara (see table 2.5). In Alameda County, many high-tech companies are located in the cities of Fremont and Pleasanton. San Mateo County, Redwood City, and Menlo Park also have quite a few computer hardware and software companies, while San Francisco City and County have a few high-tech companies, computer dealers, and repair shops. Many of the so-called dot-com companies in the San Francisco Bay Area, however, went bankrupt in the downturn from 2000 to 2001.

Santa Clara County has the largest concentration of high-tech companies, including the most famous ones. Apple Computer, 3Com Corporation, Applied Materials, Cisco Systems, HP, Intel, Lockheed Martin Missiles and Space, National Semiconductor, Solectron, and Sun Microsystems are all located here. This is accordingly the area where many Chinese work and live (see tables 2.5 and 2.6). In fact, San Francisco County has the largest Chinese population and Santa Clara County has the second largest Chinese population (115,781) in the Bay Area. Within Santa Clara County, three cities have large Chinese populations: San Jose, Sunnyvale, and Cupertino.

The Chinese work force is drawn from Asia as well as other parts of the world, and Silicon Valley is like a magnet attracting these new professionals to the area. In the old days, California attracted principally laborers to build

Chapter 2

Table 2.5.   Chinese Population by County in the San Francisco Bay Area

County	Chinese Population
San Francisco County	152,620
Santa Clara County	115,781
Alameda County	111,006
San Mateo County	48,996
Total:	428,403

Source: U.S. Bureau of the Census, United States Census 2000.

the railroad and the infrastructure of the region. Now, the Chinese come as laborers in the new high-tech economy. In the Chinese community some even call themselves *gao jie hua gong* (high-class laborers), however there is a difference. Among these high-tech professionals, some become entrepreneurs. Evelyn Iritani of the *Los Angeles Times* reported on October 18, 1999, that there were 2008 Chinese high-tech companies in Silicon Valley. The number of Chinese companies subsequently grew to 2,472 in 2002 (Saxenian 2002), with total sales of $16,891 million. Saxenian further estimates that there are 20,000 Chinese engineers working in the high-tech industry. Estimates from my informants range from 20,000 to 25,000. The exact number will only be determined when the latest census data is released.

Most Silicon Valley Chinese are employees working for the various computer hardware and software companies such as those mentioned above. Among the top 150 firms in Silicon Valley, some of them were founded by Chinese, firms that include Solectron, Cadence Design, Yahoo, Network Appliance, Integrated Device Technology, BEA, Nvidia, Channel 84, Avant!,

Table 2.6.   Chinese Population in the Cities of Santa Clara County

San Jose	51,109
Sunnyvale	12,597
Cupertino	12,031
Milpitas	8,098
Mountain View	5,584
Palo Alto	5,450
Saratoga	5,419
Santa Clara	5,197
Los Altos	2,244
Campbell	1,360
Los Altos Hills	1,006
Morgan Hill	464
Gilroy	256
Monte Sereno	176

Source: U.S. Bureau of the Census, United States Census 2000; *Sing Tao Daily* February 4, 2002.

Oak Technology, Clarent, Trident, and Lam Research. Many of these Chinese companies were established by Taiwanese Chinese. Most recently, there have been companies established by Chinese entrepreneurs from mainland China. GRIC, Viador, WebEx, and Sina.com are examples.

These firms are active in many areas of the high-tech industry. Some are in hardware, others in software. Some specialize in web design, e-commerce, fiber optics, video and voice technology, commercial applications of the internet, or graphic design. These firms have also branched out as venture capitalists, incubators, and angel-investors. In the Silicon Valley community, most of the Chinese are related in one way or another to the technology industry. Computer programmers and engineers are in great abundance, and among these technical experts there are those who have risen in the ranks to become entrepreneurs. The concentration of such a large population of highly paid technical personnel naturally has given rise to ethnic supermarkets, retail stores, service businesses, restaurants, department stores, and video shops. In addition to ethnic businesses, there are also, as I have mentioned, churches and other nonprofit organization to serve the newcomers. Among these organizations, the most important ones are the professional and alumni associations, which will be discussed in detail later. Suffice it to say that the presence of the Chinese in Silicon Valley, with their ethnic businesses and social organizations, is quite predominant.

Silicon Valley also sustains a large Vietnamese population, some of ethnic Chinese descent. Additionally, there are other Asian groups: Filipinos, Indians, Japanese, Koreans, Cambodians, Pakistanis, Laotians, Thai, Indonesians, Sri Lankans, Bangladeshis, Malaysians, and Hmong. With the presence of such a large contingent of new immigrants, many Asians feel at home. However, the Chinese have the largest representation because many Chinese high-tech people are particularly fond of this area. A Chinese engineer explained:

> I like to live and work in Silicon Valley more than any other parts of the country. They are so many Asians here. I do not feel that I stand out. I like the diversity in the Bay Area and there are so many Asian restaurants and products available to the Asian consumers. (Informant AB, interview with author, March 18, 2002)

This fondness of the place was echoed by all my Chinese informants.

Besides the perks of working for high salaries, many immigrants like the mild climate and the fact that Silicon Valley has the latest technology, representing in this way the pinnacle of high-tech development in the world. In other words, working here is both a challenge and an opportunity—one is able to be creative because the workplace provides dynamic opportunities to contribute to a new, exciting, and growing field. And of course, many come here because they already have friends or relatives in this region. Dan

Lee, one of my informants, had an opinion of the area that was shared by a majority of my informants:

> When I worked on the East Coast, I always dreamed of coming to Silicon Valley. I always feel that Silicon Valley is friendlier to the Chinese and appreciates the contribution of the Chinese to the United States. People seem to understand the Chinese better. There is more tolerance and more diversity here than in any other part of the United States. There are so many authentic Chinese restaurants here too! (Dan Lee, interview with author, March 18, 2002)

From Chinese video stores to Chinese movie houses, from Taiwanese food to Beijing food, from *liche* nut to tapioca, everything from Chinese culture is available in the San Francisco Bay Area. The ethnic consumer support as well as the cultural support available here for many Chinese engineers and entrepreneurs is substantial. One enthusiastic Chinese engineer said: "Everything Chinese is available. Although I live in the United States, I can have all my Chinese favorite food here. Everything one needs to have, Silicon Valley has!" (Dan Lee, interview with author, March 18, 2002).

GLOBAL IMMIGRATION MOVEMENTS OF THE CHINESE

In the nineteenth century the migration movement of the Chinese followed the international spread of the western colonial powers. Traditionally, the Fujianese, Tiochew (or *Chaozhou*), and Hakka (or *Kejia*) people went to the South Seas and the Indian Ocean as workers in the colonies of the French, the Dutch, and the British (Tien 1953; B. Wong 1987, 1997). Cantonese from Chung Shan (or *Zhongshan*) and Nam Hoi (or *Nanhai*) went to Latin America to work in colonies like Cuba dominated by the Spanish. Most of the Chinese from the Sze Yap (or *Siyi*) and Sam Yap (or *Sanyi*) districts south of Canton came to the United States (Tien 1953; B. Wong 1979). The early Chinese immigrants were recruited principally to work as laborers, miners, and railroad builders in many colonies of the Western powers. The path and rationale of migration of the Chinese in the past can be explained by theories proposed by Immanuel Wallerstein (1980) and Andre Frank (1967). Colonialism and the needs of the colonial administration attracted Chinese laborers, as well as middlemen-entrepreneurs and shopkeepers. Today, however, the paths of the new immigrants deviate from those of the nineteenth century, and these theories cannot explain the new migration patterns of the Chinese. In the modern era, while some immigrants come to the United States via a second country, others come to the United States directly; and after staying in the United States for awhile, some then return to Asia. The movement is therefore not linear, but sometimes shows a circular pattern. Additionally, secondary migration occurs when immigration routes pass through another country such as Canada, England, or Mexico. These second country staging areas serve as temporary stations rather than as the immigrant's goal country.

The Chinese are drawn from all over the world. Some speak Spanish as a second language while others speak Chinese or English as their primary language. Overseas Chinese now live in 135 countries around the world and in 1990 made up a total population of 35 million (Poston, Mao, and Yu 1992). Eighty-eight percent of the Chinese reside in Asia, 9 percent in the Americas, 2 percent in Europe, 1 percent in Oceania, and less than 1 percent in Africa. Outside of Asia, the following countries have the largest Chinese populations: Canada, Peru, the United States, and Australia. All of these have an annual population growth of 9 percent or higher. This growth, according to Poston, Mao, and Yu is not due to the natural growth of the local Chinese population, but is due principally to immigration. The United States, Canada, and Australia still attract Chinese immigrants for a number of reasons: (1) a perceived political and economic stability; (2) the opportunity for better education for children; (3) the existence of established Chinese communities; (4) the existence of kinship and friendship connections; (5) the enticement of the H-1B visas; and (6) the availability of investment visas. In terms of investment visas, the United States is the most expensive, requiring an investment of one million dollars or more, while Canada and Australia require only about $180,000, which some Chinese can afford. As a result there are more Chinese immigrants who have gone to Canada and Australia with investment visas. In the United States a majority of Chinese immigrants enter as family reunion visa holders. They come to join a relative who has previously settled in the United States, and, consequently, many Chinese in the United States believe that only the poor Chinese come to the United States, while the rich Chinese go to Australia and Canada, because the rich Chinese, who are investment visa holders of course, have the investment capital necessary to qualify (B. Wong 1998a, 2001b).

But Chinese migration to the United States has another face. In addition to the large number of family reunion visa holders, there has been a surge in the number of H-1B visa holders. These are most often highly educated scientists and technical personnel. Some of them are foreign students from China, Hong Kong, Macao, Taiwan, and from overseas Chinese communities in Southeast Asia and Central and South America. Some Chinese high-tech workers are also recruited from Canada and England. A majority of the Chinese high-tech personnel, however, are recruited upon graduation from various graduate schools in the United States. Some, in fact, get practice training visas upon graduation in order to work for American companies in different parts of the United States. All these visa holders constitute an important work force for high-tech companies.

GLOBAL ECONOMIC TRANSFORMATION AND
THE CHINESE COMMUNITY IN SILICON VALLEY

Beginning in the 1980s, the focus of U.S. foreign trade gradually shifted from the Atlantic-European region to the Pacific Rim. There was a newfound symbiosis between the Western and the Eastern economies (Fong 1994; B. Wong 1998b, 2001b). Many products, from electronics and textiles to toys, were (and today continue to be) manufactured in places like China, Korea, Malaysia, Taiwan, and Japan. At about the same time, there was also a restructuring of national economics in many advanced industrial countries from a manufacturing base to a service base. This was particularly the case in the urban areas of the United States. In the San Francisco Bay Area, garment and other manufacturing businesses became less important, moving out of the United States and relocating to the low-cost areas of Asia and Central or South America.

High-tech businesses started to gain prominence in the mid-1990s. Computer companies, both software and hardware, proliferated and created a demand for scientists, programmers, and other technical personnel. Many American firms in the San Francisco Bay had to recruit high-tech workers from all over the United States and around the world. In particular, places like India and China became favorites for many American job recruiters. Some recruiters placed ads in trade journals; other advertised in local newspapers in Hong Kong, London, and Singapore. Another method of recruiting needed computer workers was to go to American universities to recruit both American and foreign students. Many students from mainland China, Hong Kong, Taiwan, and other parts of the world were also offered jobs from Silicon Valley companies that promised to obtain employment visas for them. As a result of the employment efforts made by the companies in Silicon Valley, the high-tech Chinese population grew rapidly until the recession of 2001.

From 1995 to 2001, Chinese professionals in Silicon Valley were highly visible in high-tech companies, and today they remain important not only for Chinese and American firms, but also as clients of real-estate offices, banks, restaurants, grocery stores, travel agencies, ethnic businesses like video stores, and ethnic shopping centers such as Milpitas's Ranch 99 and Cupertino's Marina Food. Even American supermarkets like Albertsons have started to market live catfish, bok choy, ginger root, and fish sauce to meet Asian ethnic demand. And since Asians have become an important demographic group, American advertising companies are now eager to target them, with the result that Asian faces are appearing on blue jean ads. Furthermore, Wells Fargo and other banking institutions are eager to attract Chinese customers (*San Francisco Examiner* September 3, 2000).

The Chinese of Silicon Valley also help connect American cities with Asian cities by the creation of "sister cities." Many Californian cities have not only

Chinese residents, they also have sister cities in Asia. Tainan (the ancient capital of Taiwan) is a sister city of San Jose, and Chang-du (China) is in the process of also becoming a sister city of San Jose. Santa Clara has Izumo (Japan) as its sister city. Palo Alto has Palo and Leyte in the Philippines as sister cities, while the sister cities for Fremont are Lipa City (Philippines), Tienjin (China), Tanggu (China), and Chung-Li (Taiwan). Currently, many Chinese cities in Taiwan and mainland China are in the process of establishing their own sister cities in Silicon Valley. In this way the Silicon Valley Chinese play a bridging role between their adopted and mother countries.

Many Chinese universities, it may be added, have alumni associations in Silicon Valley. The well-known ones from mainland China are Beijing University, Jiaotong University, Tsing-Hua [*Qing Hua* in pinyin] University, and Fu Dang University; but Taiwan's National Taiwan University as well as Cheng Kung University also have alumni associations. In fact, an immigration official from the U.S. Immigration and Naturalization Service (INS) once remarked that "Silicon Valley is dominated by a number of prestigious Chinese Universities!" Many outsiders may not realize that the high-tech Chinese in Silicon Valley are the elite in their profession, the crème de la crème, having graduated with advanced degrees from elite universities in China and the United States. Quite a few of them possess PhDs from Harvard, the Massachusetts Institute of Technology, Princeton, Stanford, University of California, Berkeley, the California Institute of Technology, and the University of Michigan. They are often bicultural and bilingual and are the product of two or more education systems. They are therefore poised to play the role of "culture brokers" (Wolf 1966) and bridges in international trade and of actors in the global economy.

There are other salient commonalities among the Chinese of Silicon Valley, for while many Chinese professionals are in the high-tech industry, almost all of these professionals complain about discriminatory treatment in the workplace. They all seem to have experienced the glass-ceiling phenomenon in their profession. There are, as I have mentioned, few CEOs among the Chinese. In fact, Professor Saxenian has found that only 17 percent (2,001) of the 11,443 high-technology start-up firms in the valley in 1990 were headed by Chinese. For entry-level jobs in 1990, Asians were paid 14 percent less than whites (see table 2.7). And this does not seem to have changed in the ten years since the PUMS data were compiled. In 2000, the entry-level pay for an Asian engineer was around $45,000. But in a comparable job, a white engineer would easily make $55,000. The Chinese are better educated but are paid less and promoted less. In conversations with Chinese engineers, two topics frequently come up. One is the availability of jobs. Where are the job openings and what are their perks? Are there stock options? The second is *jian ye* (establishing an enterprise) or *chuang ye* (creating an enterprise).

Table 2.7.   **Average Pay by Occupation and Ethnicity**

	Managerial	Professional	Technical
White	$52,542[a]	$46,965	$36,700
Indian	$52,095	$45,269	$34,659
Chinese	$49,131	$45,517	$36,153
Other	$45,315	$43,496	$34,508

Source: Public Use Microdata Sample (PUMS) Files, 1990.
[a]1989 dollars.

Globalization has not homogenized or equalized social differences (Blim 2005). Ethnic and racial differences continue to exist, and social heterogeneity in terms of social classes, cultural diversities, and intracommunity differences continues to persist. Globalization, of course, has drawn the Chinese from different regions of China and even diverse parts of the world, and the disparity of the origins of the Chinese population are one of the reasons why "not all the Chinese are the same." Sinologists as well as anthropologists have found that members of a national state are not necessarily homogeneous. Thus the regionalism that persists in China (Gladney 1999) continues to persist in Silicon Valley. Furthermore, the linguistic differences among the Cantonese, Hakka, Fujianese, and Shanghainese that Gladney finds rooted in ancient Chinese, as will be discussed later, get their opportunity to manifest themselves again in the diaspora. North/South ethnocentrism as well as political divisions that reflect identical divisions between Taiwan and mainland China are also carried over to Silicon Valley.

THE MANY KINDS OF "CHINESE-NESS"

Amidst similarities, there are diversities in this Chinese community. Between each of the three larger groups, there are differences. The members of these larger groups eat different foods, read different newspapers, watch different TV programs, speak different dialects, wear different clothes, and possess different political ideologies. The Hong Kong Chinese prefer to eat their own Cantonese-style cuisine, while the Taiwanese Chinese have their own special kinds of coffees, teas, and tapioca drinks. The Taiwanese Chinese also prefer Taiwanese cooking, while the mainland Chinese like to eat Beijing-, Shantung-, Sichuan-, Shanghai-, or Zhejian-style food.

Although in Silicon Valley the dress code is rather informal, insiders can identify a Chinese resident's locality of origin by glancing at his or her clothes. The Western clothing worn by the Chinese from the mainland is identified easily, while clothes made in Taiwan tend to follow the current fashions of Japan and Hong Kong. Hong Kong Chinese in their tailor-made suits easily indicate their origins. American-born Chinese, meanwhile, wear popular American clothes represented by the Gap, Banana Republic, and Dockers brands. Formal clothing such as suits and dresses are even more obvious with regard to their manufacturers. In a general way, the Taiwan and Hong Kong Chinese are more concerned about fashions and brand names than those from mainland China and the United States. The differences in clothing style among the different groups of Chinese tend to minimize as time passes. After the Chinese have been in the United States for a number of years, they dress alike as they gradually acquire clothing from similar kinds of stores in the Bay Area.

Beneath outer appearances and aside from food habits, different Chinese speak clearly different dialects at home. Generally, Taiwanese Chinese speak Mandarin and Fujianese, but mainlanders speak *Putonghua* or standard Mandarin. The Chinese from Hong Kong and often the American-born Chinese speak Cantonese. Many of the second- and third-generation Chinese Americans speak only English at home. With regard to reading ability, the foreign-born Chinese from Taiwan, Hong Kong, and mainland China are highly literate. They like to read Chinese-language newspapers, as a result of which the valley's Chinese ethnic press is quite lively and busy. There are many Chinese newspaper reporters and journalists in Silicon Valley, the two most widely read papers in Chinese being the *Sing Tao* [*Xingdao*] *Daily* and the *World Journal*. Each of these newspapers boasts a daily circulation of sixty thousand in the Bay Area. Other Chinese newspapers like the *China Press* (*Qiao Bao*), the *Chinese Times* (*Jin Shan Shi Bao*), the *China Daily* (*Zongguo Yi Bao*), and the *International Daily News* (*Guo Ji Yi Bao*) have daily circulations of about a thousand. Additionally, there are weekly and occasional Chinese newspapers available free in Chinese shopping areas in San Jose, Cupertino, and Milpitas, and in front of stores like Ranch 99. The Chinese from Hong Kong and the mainland tend to read the *Sing Tao Daily* while those from Taiwan prefer to buy the *World Journal*, a pro-Kuomintang (KMT) publication from Taiwan.

The Cantonese-speaking Chinese from Hong Kong watch KTSF (Channel 26 in San Francisco), which broadcasts in Cantonese, while the Taiwanese Chinese prefer Chinese programs from Channel 32, which serves Oakland, San Jose, and San Francisco. The mainland Chinese watch Channel 32 as well as the special programs piped in from Beijing's Central China Broadcast. The two most popular English newspapers among the Chinese of the valley are the *San Francisco Chronicle* and the *San Jose Mercury News*. The Silicon Valley Chinese are thus widely exposed to the news media in both Chinese and English. Many Chinese read two newspapers a day: one in English and one in Chinese.

Like many first-generation immigrants in America, the Chinese are influenced by politics in their homeland. Taiwan's local elections, political debates on China-Taiwan unification (*zhong guo tong yi* [transliteration is my own]), discussions on the Taiwan independence movement (*Tai Du*) and one country–two institutions (*yi guo liang zhi*), as well as local news stories appear in the valley Chinese media and on the talk shows. Taiwan legislators often travel through Silicon Valley to recruit support from its Taiwanese Chinese immigrants; Hong Kong's SAR (Special Administrative Region) chief and other officials travel to San Jose and other cities in Silicon Valley to recruit investors to Hong Kong; and the PRC sends its delegates to speak to different Chinese professional associations so as to recruit talent and investors to China. Not surprisingly, important events in China attract the attention of the Silicon Valley Chinese. The Tiananmen Incident, World Trade Organization (WTO) discussions, the bombing of the Chinese Embassy in Belgrade, China's bid to host the 2008 Olympics, military exercises in Taiwan or China, or presidential elections in Taiwan have embroiled the valley community in heated debates. From time to time, squabbles among Chinese of different political persuasion occur. This should not be interpreted to mean that the Chinese in Silicon Valley are not patriotic to their adopted country. As will be demonstrated later in this book, a majority of the Chinese consider the United States their permanent place of residence. They are committed to the United States and are interested in *lo di sheng gen* (establishing roots). Suffice it to say that first-generation Chinese immigrants are naturally interested in what is going on in their homeland. It is the kind of primordial feeling that Clifford Geertze (1963) refers to. Kinship, friendship, hometown connections, and blood ties all still play a role in the life of these immigrants.

MULTIPLE STRATEGIES OF IMMIGRATION

Chinese immigrants who want to migrate to the United States have a number of options. In terms of visa eligibility, there are four major ways. One is to come here as the immediate relative of a U.S. citizen via the family-reunion clause. Children and siblings of U.S. citizens qualify for this category. The second one is via employment, using the H-1B visa as an option. The third one is via an investment that requires a million dollars collateral. The fourth one is to come here seeking political asylum. By far, the first two methods are the most common.

In terms of strategies for improving one's lot in the United States, there are five. First is to migrate to the United States to find a well-paying job, or to start a business and in this way to establish roots. Second is to migrate to the United States and, after securing resident status, to return to one's home country to pursue a livelihood. Sometimes immigrants realize that their businesses in Asia are performing well, except for the constant worry over political instability. After they have arrived in the United States and investigated a number of options, they then decide to return to their home countries, because after getting their green cards they feel that they have a "back road" (meaning a safe place to return), and can go back to Taiwan, China, or another place in which to do business. A third strategy is for the primary wage earner to migrate to the United States first and establish a home there for her or her spouse and children. The primary wage earner then shuttles between the United States and Asia. The fourth strategy is similar to the third one except that husband and wife, after establishing a home in the United States for their children, then return to their country of origin to conduct business. A fifth strategy is to go to another country first. Some Chinese go to England to study and work. But they use England only as springboard to come to the United States. Similarly, some go to Canada first but their intended final destination is the United States. Thus, even the routes of immigration have become globalized.

The economic boom of the high-tech industry in the late 1990s attracted many Chinese to Silicon Valley. The recession of the late 1980s, on the contrary, pushed many Chinese to return to Taiwan. The recession of 2001 similarly created a return migration to mainland China. Prior to their return to Asia, however, these immigrants would have acquired their permanent residency or citizenship. The recession of the late 1980s affected California more than many other states because California was home to the defense and aeronautics industries. Many of the Chinese high-tech people from Taiwan who were then employed in the defense and aeronautics fields lost their jobs because of the closing of military bases and the defense industries. Meanwhile, Taiwan needed talent from California. The push factor of the recession (job loss) was further strengthened by the pull factor (job gain) of Taiwan. Many Chinese in the semiconductor business were therefore deliberately recruited to work in Taiwan. The recession of 2001 in like fashion pushed many new mainland Chinese engineers to return to their homeland. Again the pull factor of the growing economy of mainland China and of government incentives enticed these Chinese immigrants to return home. The returned migrants, however, did and do not sever their ties to America. They maintain permanent residency, and some have U.S. passports. Some also maintain property and children in the United States.

ISSUES AND COMMON CONCERNS OF SILICON VALLEY CHINESE

In this community of high technology, many of the concerns of the residents are related to work, immigration, and intellectual property. There is, as I've mentioned, uneasiness about the pay disparity between Chinese and white engineers. Some valley Chinese speak of finding jobs in Asia. Periodically, there are also debates between Chinese and whites on U.S. immigration policies and H-1B visas. Intellectual property rights are another major issue that needs to be addressed since Silicon Valley is a community full of inventors, entrepreneurs, and technological wizards.

Pay Disparity

It is conceivable that some of the engineers laid off during recessions in the United States wanted to return to Asia; however, among the returnees, there were also people who were not laid off. There were good reasons for their departure. Some felt that there was subtle discrimination. As shown in table 2.7, pay disparity did and still does exist among the different ethnic groups of the valley. In order to combat such racism and discrimination and to advance their social mobility, the Silicon Valley Chinese resort to a number of survival strategies: (1) change jobs frequently; (2) start up firms of their own; (3) return to Asia to work; (4) organize and use these organizations to fight racism and to promote their interests; (5) use networks and other social resources to organize businesses in Asia and to participate in economic globalization; (6) actively participate in American politics via interest group politics to support politicians who can represent and protect their interests; and (7) build coalitions with other ethnic groups, especially other Asians.

The H-1B Visa: Immigrant vs Local High-Tech Workers

If the Chinese feel a certain amount of discomfort at work because they are targets of unfair criticism and attack, this is particularly the case among the H-1B visa holders, who are described by some as cheap laborers who take away the jobs that would otherwise go to Americans. H-1B visa holders naturally feel that they are not welcomed by some of the local workers. The more this debate goes on, the more the visa holders feel that they are in the middle of a controversy. There are two sides to the story concerning the pros and cons of approving more H-1B visas. Employers such as Microsoft, Intel, and HP are in favor of doubling the issuance of H-1B visas. The immigrants themselves, whether they are Korean, Chinese, Indian, or Russian are also in favor of an increase in visa quotas for immigrant high-tech personnel.

This opinion is not unanimous. There are people who believe that the hiring of immigrant workers will leave minority workers, women, and people with disabilities on the sidelines (*San Francisco Chronicle* October 19, 2000). Some are against increasing H-1B visa quotas for immigrants on the grounds that the visas cheapen wages and encourage age discrimination. These detractors argue that immigrant engineers are always less well paid, and that they are always younger. They go on to say that these cheaper and younger immigrants are displacing older and more expensive American-born engineers. When I posed these arguments to my Chinese informants in

Silicon Valley, however, I found out that they have valid reasons for wanting higher H-1B visa quotas.

First, my informants told me that in Silicon Valley, companies look for certain talents. When the existing pool does not have the right kinds of talent, they have to go elsewhere. My informants said that hiring foreigners for the sake of hiring foreigners does not work. Employees will not save their company any money if they do not meet the company's needs. In certain areas of the industry, companies need immigrant engineers who can do a specific job, and these immigrant engineers are extremely well trained, being the best and the brightest in their field. It is also easier to find PhD holders among immigrants than among American-born graduates. For years, many American students did not go to graduate schools for advanced degrees. Second, some employers believe that immigrants work harder and are more trustworthy. Third, contrary to the contention of many, immigrants have actually created much wealth and larger job markets for America. In 1998 alone, the Chinese and Indian high-tech companies in Silicon Valley employed more than 58,000 people, many of them not Asians, and had total sales of $16.8 billion (*Wall Street Journal* September 21, 1999). The *Wall Street Journal* also notes that that 8 percent of the Forbes's High-Tech 100 (of top companies in the industry) were created by Asians. Between 1983 and 1992, according to the article, immigrants created more than 20 million jobs in America.

Those who visit Silicon Valley cannot fail to see that the prosperity of Silicon Valley has much to do with its immigrant entrepreneurs and professionals. Many experts in the high-tech businesses acknowledge that in certain areas such as fiber optics or voice technology immigrants are superior to the locals. Such immigrants are needed, and they will enhance the businesses of Silicon Valley. All my informants agreed that there is a need for mainstream American society to change its image of immigrants. Though immigrants have traditionally been seen as the lowest of the low in their home country and the refuse of their society, many of these new immigrants are in fact the best and the brightest of their society, as is indeed the case among the immigrant high-tech talent.

High-Class Laborers?

In the past ten years there has been a rapid increase in the influx of high-tech engineers from China into the valley. Some of them have risen to managerial positions and even CEO status. In the popular press, these successful entrepreneurs from mainland China are labeled the "Red Guards of Silicon Valley" (Zhang 2000). Some of the latecomers have been able to find their own niches and have established well-known companies such as Viador in Sunnyvale, GRIC in Milpitas, WebEx in San Jose, Sina.com in San Mateo, and

AsiaInfo Holdings in San Francisco. The CEOs of these companies are Chinese intellectuals from mainland China who mastered the American system and emerged as successful entrepreneurs in Silicon Valley. Of course, not all the Chinese engineers from mainland China are as successful. In fact, many of them feel that they are left out of the system and treated just like low-status manual laborers. They feel that they are only assigned work to be done according to deadlines and specifications. In fact, they feel that they are highly skilled workers and call themselves in Chinese *gao ji hua gong* (high-class laborers). As a result, many are disenchanted with their work in Silicon Valley. As ordinary workers, they can be laid off at any time. During the downturn of the U.S. economy that began in 2000, and encouraged by many job offers from mainland China, these high-class laborers started to return there to seek employment. When I asked one of these engineers why he wanted to go back to China where the pay is lower, he said:

> Although the pay in China is not as good as here in terms of dollars, the money is good and can go very far. Taxes are lower. You are treated with respect. You are not considered as workers but as high-class intellectual [*gao ji zhi zi fan zi*] and leaders of the scientific field. These are the good things. Of course, there are advantages and disadvantages, no matter where you work. There is more advantage for me to return at this moment. For I know for sure I will not be laid-off that easily. (Informant D, interview with author, May 23, 2001)

The above statement reflects the sentiment of many returnees to mainland China. The fact that they return to China does not imply that they have "changed sides again." When they made their decision to migrate to the United States, they actually made a decision to stay in the United States permanently. Their return to China is a temporary move. This is a reversal of the Chinese immigrants who came to the United States in the nineteenth century as temporary workers and sojourners. Today the Chinese immigrants in Silicon Valley are returning to China as expatriates. It is a short-term economic move. The ancestral home, China, has become a temporary home away from their permanent home in Silicon Valley.

The phenomenon of returned migration is also found among the Chinese from Taiwan, Malaysia, and Singapore. They return to their home countries specifically to seek better economic opportunity. One engineer who worked for a Silicon Valley company and a local university in the San Francisco Bay Area told me that he would be better appreciated in Malaysia than in the United States. He said that in his case, his combined income from the university and his high-tech company was the same as his salary in Malaysia. But he said he could live like a "king" in Malaysia with servants taking care of him and his family. Like other Chinese engineers, he intends to come back to the United States to live permanently. In the past several years, the Taiwanese Chinese have gone to China to start new companies or to work for Taiwanese-owned companies in the Shanghai area (J. Wang 2004). Both the responsibilities and pay offered by the Taiwanese companies are said to be good. But again, the trip to Shanghai is said to be a temporary one. It is an economic move to make quick money and try out one's career. These Taiwanese Chinese also plan to return to the San Francisco Bay Area to live in the future. In a sense, Silicon Valley outsources its Chinese American talent to Asia. These returnees feel the same too. They are more appreciated in Asia, whereas they feel that they are treated like high-class laborers in Silicon Valley. However, their current or eventual permanent home is in the United States.

Intellectual Property Rights

Conflicts between individuals as well as corporations exist in Silicon Valley. Some Chinese American entrepreneurs have told me that issues concerning intellectual property rights and business secrets are so common that they should be considered part of life. When similarities in products and designs occur, there is always the suspicion of theft of intellectual property. When an employee changes jobs, there is always the fear the he or she will steal the company's business secrets or copy its designs. There have been cases involving individuals who left a company with stolen designs. One Chinese engineer was accused by IBM of stealing business secrets when he left IBM to work for Oracle. Another Chinese engineer was similarly sued by Intel. A third was sued by Borland when he moved to Symantec (Teng 1998, 547–49).

Corporations may also sue each other. One case involved Avant! and Cadence Design. A similar legal battle was fought between Intel and Cyrix. The former accused the latter of a violation of copyright in the sale of certain products. Most of my informants concede that the situation in China is more problematic than that in the United States. Chinese American firms in China believe that China needs to develop a better system of dealing with intellectual property rights. Traditionally, the concept of intellectual property rights was never strong in China. The Chinese state historically did not have special laws dealing with these violations. There was no historical precedent for intellectual property rights, nor was any provision made for protecting such rights. When the central Chinese government, with all its resources, still finds it difficult to enforce these laws, other provincial and city level authorities will encounter yet greater difficulties. This is partly due to the fact that Western-style commercial law never existed in Confucian cultures. Business transactions were regulated more by ethics and established personal relationships than by strict laws. In dealing with Western societies today, China is gradually adopting international laws that deal with piracy and other matters related to intellectual property rights (Haley, Tan, and Haley 1998).

High-tech Chinese entrepreneurs are keenly aware of the need for intellectual property rights protection. In order to make sure that no one will be accused of infringement of intellectual property rights, some companies prohibit new employees from using old designs or documents that belonged to their old companies. One entrepreneur had this to say:

> I always tell my engineer to make sure that they start with a clean slate. I tell my new hires not to use anything: diagrams, designs or whatever that belong to another company. They start everything with my company. If their designs resembled another company's, I will scrap them. That is the only way to avoid being sued! (Informant DL, interview with author, June 2, 2001)

Other informants agreed with this strategy. All believe that education is necessary among all the Chinese high-tech engineers. In economic globalization, this issue has become particularly sensitive. Multinational corporations continue to have many legal battles with Chinese manufacturers and designers. Piracy and theft of intellectual property have caused the loss of profits. Many patent holders and creators also feel that their inventions and intellectual achievements are not respected.

CONCLUSION

The immigration movement to the United States of educated Chinese has been influenced by a changing global economy. Many traditional theories on immigration are not adequate in explaining this movement. The social fabric and immigrant settlement patterns in Silicon Valley have been influenced by the local as well as the global economy. Members of the Chinese community, as a result of this influence, share a common culture. It is a cultural diaspora (Clifford 1994; Lewellen 2002). This Chinese culture is what is shared by different segments of the Chinese population. However, there are different degrees of Chinese-ness. Furthermore, the Chinese community in Silicon Valley differs from other Chinese enclaves in the United States in terms of occupation, adaptive patterns, and population. It is a community of professionals drawn from different parts of the world. These professionals are highly educated, many have graduated from prestigious universities either in China, Taiwan, Hong Kong, or the United States, and they are the best in their fields. They have come to the United States by different routes, and their ways of coping with the global economy and the larger society are complex. They also possess different kinds of resources, resources that include education, occupational skill, and social and ethnic ties. Their use of social and economic resources will be discussed in subsequent chapters.

In sum, the economy of the Chinese in Silicon Valley differs from a traditional Chinese ethnic economy composed of restaurants, laundries, and gift-shops such as found in America's Chinatowns. Many of the Chinese in Silicon Valley are employed in the high-tech businesses as engineers, programmers, technicians, or professionals. Many work for large American corporations, while some work for Chinese companies. Others branch out as entrepreneurs in the high-tech industry. Although it is a high-tech area, there are also conventional ethnic businesses in the valley established to serve the ethnic population. However, Silicon Valley is best known as the world capital of high-tech and, indeed, it is home to many Chinese engineers and scientists. Their professional lives as well as their daily existence are intertwined with technology and work. Many of their social organizations and informal social networks are directly related to professional advancement and to adaptive strategies in a changing global setting.

The Chinese in Silicon Valley are a heterogeneous population. Their internal differences, while deeply rooted in their motherland, have been intensified by globalization. Place-based and trans-place forms of cultural differences, along with local and regional diversification, are part and parcel of the result of global transformation. This echoes the findings of Dirlik (1997,1998,), Escobar (2001), and Sahlins (1993). Furthermore, members of the Chinese community in Silicon Valley are not to be seen as carbon copies of each other, or as living in full harmony with their coethnics. This chapter has shown that the modernization and globalization of technology creates competition and social tension in the community. Individuals, as members of a Chinese American community in Silicon Valley, are not to be stripped of all their attributes of subculture, class, occupation, and national and cultural origins. On the other hand, the valley is not an island of social isolates. Members of its community are connected by social, economic, cultural, and transnational ties. The Silicon Valley Chinese community in this sense is a transnational community with ties transcending the narrow geographical boundaries of neighborhoods, cities, and nations.

3

Globalization and Social Networks in the Silicon Valley Chinese Community

Globalization is the new economic paradigm for the twenty-first century, and one that affects all societies as they come under the influence of an ever-expanding network of international corporations and IT media influence. Many writers argue that globalization decreases the importance of local culture and traditional institutions (Cameron and Stein 2000; Enriquez 1999; McLuhan and Powers 1992). They argue that participation in the global economy deprives a community of the individual's participation in its affairs. There are even arguments that the news organization CNN, the Internet, and other transnational information organizations will diminish the control of nation-states and downgrade the importance of "place"—or local community (Appadurai 1996; Ong 1999; Krasner 2000; Peterson 1996). Thomas Friedman and Ignacio Ramonet (1999) contend that the homogenizing and Americanizing effects of globalization are clear. While Hannerz (1994), Castells (2000a), and King (1995) did not believe in the effects of homogenization, they contend that globalization does have some impact on local culture and national institutions. Will globalization and a transnational lifestyle lessen the individual's commitment to his or her local community? Will the modern global economy diminish the immigrant's social networks and membership in and connections with an ancestral land? Will ethnic institutions and culturally specific behavior be transformed by globalization? These are questions that I attempt to answer within this chapter.

Contrary to claims about the loss of local difference and idyllic egalitarianism (McLuhan and Powers 1992), or about the nongovernability of transnational migrants and their rootless existence in the face of globalization, I have found that the Chinese transnationals of Silicon Valley have enlarged their social networks, created many new organizations with traditional features, and increased their participation in community and local organizations. The Chinese Americans in Silicon Valley use both formal and informal social networks to participate in the global economy and to improve their well-being in the United States. Globalization does not lessen the importance of place. Localism, local social networks, and traditional institutions are maintained, and even cultivated and used for economic globalization. Globalization and localization go hand in hand. This simultaneous occurrence has been noted by many social scientists (Portes 1997; Vargas-Llosa 2001; Escobar 2001; Evans 1999). Furthermore, the transnational migrant uses these local formal organizations and informal social networks to fight marginalization and the glass ceiling of employment opportunity. This use of Asian-based connections to gain social mobility represents a new twist. Paradoxically, achieving the American Dream may require leaving America. It may require many return trips to the ancestral home, but these return trips serve to connect the local to the global community. Because of such connections, the much-feared "brain-drain" of a country's intellectual resources does not occur. Neither Asia nor the United States loses its talented best. What happens is "brain-globalization."

Immigrants are generally rich in social connections to their homeland (Portes 1997; Yeung and Olds 1999). The Chinese are no exception, and my study shows how complex social connections materialize as social capital. Chinese entrepreneurs use kinship, friendship, and alumni and hometown relationships extensively to reestablish connections with industries and businesses in Asia. Their *guanxi* (a connection formed by social relationships) is used to start and build new companies and businesses, and it serves as a conduit for bidirectional capital flow—from Asia to the United States and vice versa.

The use of kinship and social networks for the transnationalization of business operations in Asia has been well documented by social scientists who study the Asia-Pacific region (Yeung 1997; Olds 1995; Smart and Smart 1999; 1997; Zhang 2000; Peng 2000). Many have also written about the operation of *guanxi* in the PRC in the past twenty years (Kipnis 1997; Yan 1996; Yang 1994; Smart 1998). As noted by these authors, *guanxi* can be based on kinship, friendship, a patron-client relationship, or an alumni or colleague relationship. These relationships, whether based on classmates, friends, colleagues, or family connections, need to be cultivated and maintained. Other cultures have similar kinds of arrangements and use them for goal-seeking activities (Wolf 1966). In the case of the Chinese, the complexity and the utilization of this kind of interpersonal relationship take on a special dimension. *Guanxi* can be used to connect insiders with other insiders or with outsiders. It can be used for financing, employment, and the maintenance of firms. It is used to fight bureaucracy (Pieke 1995), to develop social solidarity among revolutionaries (Kipnis 1997), or to obtain housing and other goals. It is through *guanxi* that many transnational projects are accomplished.

The opportunity structure in the 1990s in the United States, especially in California, was such that many jobs were lost to the recession and to the declining defense industry. Meanwhile, Asia as a latecomer to industrialization still had room to grow because both China and Taiwan were experiencing growth. Production costs were also lower there, and consumers continued to spend money in the marketplace. At the same time, electronic and computer products were being manufactured in Taiwan and China for local as well as international markets. The changing economic environment in Asia in the early 1990s attracted not only Silicon Valley high-tech workers—some corporations moved their production plants to Asia. For the Chinese in Silicon Valley, the recession, the glass ceiling, and job offers in Asia were reasons that propelled them to return to Asia and to become *tai kong ren* (astronauts), or frequently flying business travelers who leave families behind in the United States. Indeed, these astronauts travel so much that they feel they are nomads without a permanent address. A common joke among these businessmen is that their airplane seat is their real permanent address. The demands of this lifestyle, that force them to leave their families behind in the United States, follow a pattern that breaks with traditional notions of immigration.

This pattern of return migration—which is one of great mobility for the sake of economic survival—also requires the use of social networks. Again, social connections, or *guanxi*, become a necessary factor in entrepreneurial pursuits in China and Chinese-owned enterprises (B. Wong 1988, 1998b, 2001b, 2001c). For instance, classmates from Cheng Kung University in Taiwan or a former professor from Taiwan University can play a role in the relocation to Taiwan of an astronaut. Old connections facilitate the astronaut's smooth return to Taiwan.

In the past ten years the living standard and the salary structure in Taiwan has caught up with that in America. Some Taiwanese high-tech personnel, especially those who have suffered from unfair treatment in Silicon Valley, see four advantages in returning to Taiwan. First, they do not have to put up with American racism. Second, some still have relatives and family in Taiwan or mainland China. Third, these returnees will not have to worry about a glass ceiling in their own country. Fourth, they are not limited to working only in technical support, or as a *gao ji hua gong* (high-class laborer). These returnees with PhDs and work experience in Silicon Valley are admired in Taiwan or in China and consequently have more of an opportunity to work in high-level administrative positions or even as CEOs in Asia. Some actually see a brighter future in Asia than in the American high-tech industry. Their connections in Taiwan or mainland China may help them advance their careers further. A small group of these engineers have even returned to Taiwan with their families, deciding to remain there permanently.

Taiwanese or mainland Chinese graduates use their universities as a basis for organization. The largest of these universities is Taiwan University, the second largest, Cheng Kung University, and the third, Jiaotong University, while many mainland Chinese came from famous universities like Tsing-Hua, Beijing, Jiaotong, and Fu Dang. The alumni associations of these universities meet annually and have social programs throughout the year. They are used for goal-seeking activities as well. From interviews I found that family members, consanguine and affinal relatives, old friends, classmates, and colleagues are important sources for "seed money" or employment. Some husband and wife teams run small start-ups. Their former professors from former universities in Taiwan and their relatives who still live there may then help in the outsourcing of products. Colleagues and friends can be partners in joint ventures. Classmates are also sources for employment.

The flow of capital and labor can be bidirectional: Asia to the United States or vice versa. Some Taiwanese Chinese in the San Francisco Bay Area have led a number of American venture capitalists to invest in Taiwan and China. The flow of international capital is also initiated from Asia. In this way capital from Thailand, Taiwan, and Hong Kong support some of the Silicon Valley Chinese firms. San Francisco's David Hsu of Walden International, for example, has introduced investors to Taiwan. The Taiwanese have also invested large sums of money in Silicon Valley. And Taiwanese companies (Acer, MiTAC, UMAX) have opened branches in Silicon Valley.

The movement of capital requires knowledge and a business plan. But in addition to the formal or informal presentation of business plans, it also requires trust, and kinship and friendship ties. Immigrants who posses such social capital therefore have a decided edge over those who do not, because informal social networks greatly facilitate the movement of capital. This flow is promoted by *guanxi*, and couched in cultural idioms like s*hin yung* or *xin yong* (trust), *yee chi* or *yiqi* (righteousness), and r*en chin* or *renqing* (human feeling). Thus, globalization requires the activation of traditional social networks. Global economic transactions can be conducted in a culturally particularistic fashion and in an informal manner. For this reason, globalization and informal business transactions are not necessarily exclusive of each other. Sometimes the more a business globalizes, the more it becomes informalized. Internationalization does not exclude the retention of culture and social ties. In fact, the former needs the latter. An example of this is a family firm that was started in Silicon Valley. In this firm the husband had to use his wife's connections to have his antivirus product manufactured in Taiwan. When the product became successful, he sponsored his relatives to come to the United States to staff his company. He believed that family members work harder and are more trustworthy. He first sponsored his consanguine relatives and later his affinal relatives.

The Silicon Valley Chinese also play an important role in globalizing part of Taiwan's high-tech industry. Many Taiwan engineers who have green cards or U.S. citizenship have helped anchor these enterprises in the United

States. They travel back and forth between Taiwan and Silicon Valley to establish branches of these companies in the United States. But these transnationals have to build more than just economic connections. They must participate in social, political, and public relation activities as well. (In 1997, for instance, UMAX invited California Governor Wilson to attend its inauguration in Silicon Valley.) They also organize sport events such as golf tournaments. As a result, Taiwanese companies may sell their products to U.S. companies. Sun Moon Star and Acer computers, to name only two such products, are marketed through Best Buy, Wal-Mart, Staples, Fry's, and Good Guys (Teng 1998). Conversely, some Silicon Valley Chinese businesses, through kinship, friendship, and colleague connections establish branches in the Philippines, Malaysia, China, Taiwan, and Hong Kong. Stanley Wang's Pantronix and Chuen-Der Lien's IDT are two firms that have done this.

Chinese Americans have also become conduits for American corporations into Asia. Steve Ting of Nortel, and Sherman Ting of Oracle have been sent to China to represent their companies and to conduct business. Mr. and Mrs. K. C. Shih of Silicon Valley have traveled extensively to Hsinchu or *xin zhu* (Teng 1998). Chinese Americans sometimes find it necessary to travel up to eight times a year to Asia. Some are sent by American companies to organize their off-shore manufacturing plants in Singapore, India, Taiwan, and mainland China. The bilingual and bicultural abilities of the Chinese Americans are essential in recruiting and managing American production plants overseas. Although this practice of exporting jobs to Asia was evident in the late 1990s, it has become a controversy and a topic of heated debate in the U.S. Congress and among the public. This was principally due to the recession that began in 2001, when many American corporations found it necessary to lower production costs and maintain their competitiveness by having their products assembled overseas. For instance, IBM in 2004 announced its intent to move five thousand jobs overseas. Similarly, HP has been exporting programming jobs to China and other overseas locations. Some Americans say that this is "exporting American jobs overseas." Others defend the hiring of workers in China and India. Carly Fiorina, former CEO of HP, has said, "There is no job that is America's God-given right anymore" (*San Francisco Chronicle* January 8, 2004, A1). Similarly, Craig Barrett of Intel Corp argues that in order to stay competitive, companies must be concerned with cost and their consumer base. Skilled labor costs are lower in Asia, and the skills and the consumers are there too. The world has changed, and half of the world population is now in China, India, and Russia, according to Barrett, and these potential consumers have been integrated into the global market economy. Barrett continues: "We're talking about 3 billion people . . . The U.S. has a very simple choice to make. We have to decide if we're going to be competitive with these markets" (*San Francisco Chronicle* January 8, 2004). The common sentiment from the Chinese ethnic press in Silicon Valley is that there is nothing wrong with sharing wealth among all the peoples of the world (www.singtaousa.com January 27, 2004). Many Chinese high-tech workers have no objection to exporting jobs to Asia. They do not feel that this practice really hurts the American economy; on the contrary, they feel that it may help enhance profits for American corporations and investors. Some Chinese also see this as advantage for the Chinese high-tech engineers and entrepreneurs, especially those who have *guanxi* in China or Taiwan. Some Chinese in Silicon Valley say that there are many qualified engineers or workers in Taiwan, Hong Kong, and mainland China, and that these workers are as efficient and as competent as those in the United States even though they come at a lower price. It is quite common for a company to pay $60,000–$80,000 per year for a high-tech engineer in Silicon Valley. For a similar technology professional, a company needs to pay only $8,952 in China. Carly Fiorina has argued that the growing protectionist backlash in the United States is not healthy for the American economy. She further suggests that the only alternative to losing jobs overseas is to make a national decision to stay ahead of foreign competitors by improving grade-school education and by doubling federal spending on basic research (*San Francisco Chronicle* January 2, 2004).

In the Internet business, friendship, marriage, kinship, and other formal or informal social relations play a similar role for the American Chinese. Gerry Yang with a friend and classmate from Stanford started the much-talked about Yahoo! Jack Hong, Benjamin Tsiang, and Hurst Lin were friends and roommates, and they started www.sinanet.com, which recently was integrated into Sina.com. Indeed, these high-tech entrepreneurs make significant use of the traditional networks of old kinship and friendship to launch their global economic activities.

INFORMALITY IN THE HIGH-TECH BUSINESS

Fitting with the highly informal nature of high-tech business in Silicon Valley, clothing or dress codes are quite relaxed. It is common to see the workers dressed in casual wear and without the stuffiness of business suits and neckties. Most wear polo shirts and khaki pants with a cell phone attached to their belts. Because their employees work long and unpredictable hours, some companies even allow pet owners to bring their pets to work. To develop further camaraderie, many companies have social gatherings or parties on Fridays. The first two alcoholic beverages are on the company while nonalcoholic drinks are complimentary. Many businesses have a sliding work schedule because workers sometimes have to work overtime at night without compensation, especially when there are special projects. In order to save money, employees are often asked to recruit their friends, relatives, and other acquaintances who are good workers. When workers are successful in recruiting, they are then given a bonus of $1000–$5000, and thus, network hiring is common. But this bonus is cost beneficial for a company when compared to paying a commission of 15–20 percent of the annual salary of a new recruit to a corporate head hunter. Working hours and the recruitment process are thus highly informal and flexible in order to maximize productivity and profits.

Hiring and firing depend on the market and company performance. In general, Chinese firms are more personable than American firms in this respect. According to my informants, a person can be hired and fired in a very short period of time in an American firm. There is a saying that if you walk into the elevator with your boss on the first floor, you can be fired by the time you reach the fifth floor. The moral here is that impersonality rules in the American workplace. By comparison, the Chinese companies tend to be more humane. They do not fire people that quickly or easily. On the other hand, it is known that Chinese high-tech businesses tend to pay their employees less than their American counterparts pay. Furthermore, Chinese firms expect their employees to work harder and to be more responsible. Therefore, overtime in Chinese companies is generally not compensated. Employees are expected to work overtime when projects are outstanding. Bosses will even set an example by staying in the company later than everyone else. They say, "If I can stay longer, you should do the same!" Thus, there is Asianization in the Silicon Valley Chinese firms. Personalism, loyalty, and long working hours are expected. When non-Asians work in these firms, they are acculturated into the business culture of the Chinese. This process of the Asianization of American workplaces has been noted by many, including Robert Naisbitt, author of *Mega Trends* (1995).

That working hours in high-tech business are flexible for engineers is both a blessing and a curse. This is particularly so for Chinese engineers working in Chinese American companies. Chinese immigrants are highly motivated to achieve the American Dream and are expected to work harder. They tend not to complain about long working hours. As for those in administration, since they have more at stake in the company, they feel that they are personally responsible for the success of the company. In turn they hope their employees will think the same. They therefore expect their employees to be loyal and to work hard to assist the company in making the most profit in the shortest possible time. It is not uncommon to see engineers working from 8:30 am until 9:30 pm. Putting in twelve hours of work a day may not earn a worker more money but it will often gain him or her the appreciation of superiors. Many employees have told me that there is trust as well as the expectation that employees will put in their fair share of work.

Employees also expect reciprocity from their employers. They expect that their supervisors will grant them special privileges in case of need. For instance, when unexpected family obligations or responsibilities require it, bosses are expected to allow their employees to rearrange their work schedules or to take unscheduled holidays. Another case is when a company hires married couples. The wives will then tend to leave at about 3 pm to pick up their children and to supervise their homework. They will also do the cooking for the family. For his part, the husband will work until 6 pm and then go home to have dinner. At about 8 pm, husband and sometimes wife will return to the company to continue their work until 11 pm. Sometimes workers work until the morning hours. In the computer business, testing and experimentation may require uninterrupted work, so engineers may stay late until their work is done. Not responding to or reciprocating for kindness, diligence, and responsibility on the part of the employer is considered a lack of *yiqi* (righteousness) in the employer. In such a case, the employee will be offended and will seek employment elsewhere. Although most of these behavioral rules are not written, they are social expectations. Failure to live up to them will invite criticism and ostracism. Some companies are said to be "cheap" and therefore are said to lack *yiqi*.

But there are also shortcomings to working for a Chinese company. One is the absence of stock options. Some of the companies are privately held or are start-up firms that are not profitable. Another shortcoming is that their pay is lower than that of established American firms. Thus, working for an American firm has its advantages. In general, one feels less *ya li bu dai* (stress) because one does not feel pressured to finish a project immediately. In a Chinese company, there is the pressure to get a job done immediately. However, in American-run companies, different rules and work habits apply. Employees have told me that sometimes it is easier to work for such companies because the companies have clear rules, and workers can go home on time after regular working hours.

Globalization also affects Silicon Valley working conditions in other ways. Some engineers have assignments to visit sister companies or branches six times a year which amounts to traveling overseas once every two months. Upon their return from these assignments, the engineers are given compensation time or vacation. Furthermore, because of global time differences, the busiest and most taxing hours for work in Silicon Valley are in the evenings. Many high-tech companies in the valley start work late in the day and hold telephone conferences in the evening with their headquarters or branches in Asia where it is morning. After these telephone conferences, the engineers in Silicon Valley may have to work on some special project or to correct certain mistakes. They then need to stay late or until the job is done. Globalization does not eliminate informality and flexibility. In fact, global competition encourages this kind of informal practice.

ETHNIC BOUNDARIES

Mainland Chinese engineers feel that they are more isolated from the larger society and from each other for a number of reasons. One is their lack of English proficiency, whereby communication is handicapped. Their work schedules are also such that it is difficult for them to have any social life, with the result that their knowledge of U.S. culture and society is limited. Furthermore, there are so many Chinese who work in the high-tech industry, and who speak Chinese and have similar lines of work that sometimes, by circumstance, a Chinese engineer will only socialize and meet people just like himself. These people are said to *ben ze de sheng huo quan zi* (have a small interaction circle), so that they feel extremely isolated. Being a foreigner in Silicon Valley certainly does not help; the engineer's loved ones and friends are often in faraway China. Additionally, most mainland Chinese engineers are unmarried and are under forty-five, which helps explain why they often complain about *ge mo* (their experience of isolation) or feelings of marginalization: they have no family of their own. Therefore it is not surprising that they treasure newfound or collegial friendships and that they support each other. They go out to eat once a week, and many prefer to eat out with their friends during the week rather than on weekends. I was told that eating out during the week eliminates the bother of cooking. On weekends they are busy with personal chores such as cleaning and shopping. Another reason is that restaurants are more crowded on weekends than during the week. Chinese friends from the office may also go to professional meetings together. They network often to solve technological problems as well as to obtain housing, find new employment, and explore opportunities for future businesses. However, this circle of friend when compared to those in their homeland is relatively small.

HIGH-TECH AND INFORMAL DECISION MAKING

Some informants have told me that Chinese entrepreneurs, especially those from Hong Kong and Taiwan, prefer to make quick decisions. Sometimes these decisions are even made without sufficient consultation with colleagues. In dealing with mainland China, the situation is different. Decision making in China is often slow. Chinese bureaucrats take their time and consultation is lengthy. *Guanxi* figures prominently in the decision-making process in China. Many bureaucrats in China worry about two things: whether a superior will accept responsibility, and whether other business partners are trustworthy. They therefore need to find out their business partners' backgrounds, their personality, and their trustworthiness. In dealing with Chinese bureaucrats, Silicon Valley Chinese tend to have an advantage because they know the Chinese system and they have *guanxi*.

In contrast, dealing with American manufacturers or businessmen, the Chinese have learned to trust their white colleagues and their professional judgments. Their managers, lawyers, and accountants are in fact mostly non-Chinese professionals. The rules of decision making also change when dealing with non-Chinese. Contractual obligations are examined in detail, and the legal aspects are scrutinized with care. Thus, there is a multicultural mode of operation in many of the Chinese companies of Silicon Valley. The Chinese who work in these companies have to treat the American Chinese one way, non-Chinese American professionals another way, and the mainland Chinese bureaucrat still another way. Multiculturalism in this case helps globalization.

GUANXI: AN IMPERATIVE LINK

High-tech business operates on a highly personal level, so much so that personal connections are vital in securing contracts in sales and production. In globalizing one's business, the first step is to find *guanxi* (Yan 1996; Yang 1994; B. Wong 1998a, 1998b). As I've pointed out, globalization does not diminish personal and local connections. In the high-tech business there is a need to reduce risk since investment costs are often high. Having people whom you know and having people you can trust is particularly indispensable.

The art of developing connections or *guanxi* is the first thing one has to master before doing business with Asia. This subject has been discussed in a number of publications (Yang 1994; Ju 1996; Yan 1996; Kotkin 1993; B. Wong 1998a, 1998b). In the following discussion I will highlight some of the important steps in building *guanxi* in the context of Silicon Valley. Among the three groups of Chinese in the valley, there are specific kinds of *guanxi* to be formed and used.

The Hong Kong Chinese tend to use dialect, friendship, high-school connections, and kinship to build their *guanxi* in the Hong Kong and the Shenzhen region of China. Shenzhen, China's "Special Economic Zone," is contiguous to Hong Kong. Ease of access to, and its economic connections with Hong Kong has therefore attracted to Shenzhen the investment of the Hong Kong Chinese. Many Hong Kong Chinese who use a middleman to develop *guanxi* follow these steps.

1. A Hong Kong Chinese company representative travels to Hong Kong or Shenzhen (or similar city) to meet his middleman.
2. The middleman arranges for this company representative to meet the representative of another company in an office or in a restaurant.
3. The two representatives invite their bosses to attend a subsequent meeting.
4. More meetings or social activities between the representatives and their bosses take place over a period of time.
5. There is a reciprocal exchange of pleasantries or gifts.
6. More discussion is followed by the final signing of contracts.

These are the basic components for contracting *guanxi* among the Hong Kong Chinese, and it should be obvious that a skilled middleman is essential to its success. Some Hong Kong Chinese may already have direct business relations in Shenzhen, but if they do not have businesses in China, they must have this resourceful middlemen or culture broker (Wolf 1966) to help build *guanxi*. The mediators or culture brokers will then call their business counterparts in Shenzhen and arrange a meeting there between all three parties. The initial meetings of these three parties will focus on the business project, its feasibility, and the backgrounds of the participants. These are "getting to know you" sessions. In colloquial Cantonese, this kind of meeting is called *mo dai* (*mo di* in Mandarin), which means, "finding the bottom." Finding the bottom will take a number of back-and-forth meetings, but when the parties deem each other to be trustworthy, they will consent to meet again with the leaders of their companies.

Thus, if a Silicon Valley firm wants to establish a production plant in Shenzhen, the company's representative has to meet his or her counterpart there. After these initial meetings of the leaders or representatives, the representatives may invite each other to visit their respective facilities and sample the products. If things go well, they will sign contracts and initiate the paperwork. This whole process of establishing *guanxi* will expand to include more bureaucrats and leaders. The process involves the exchange of gifts, favors, and banquets. It may involve reciprocal invitations to restaurants and places of entertainment. Sometimes mutual help in noncompany matters also takes place, such as helping a son or daughter to find a university in America. Or the local host may help his or her guest find valuable antiques from China. These reciprocal transactions will help them to get to know each other better. The process of cultivating personal relationships and social networks is important in all human societies (Malinowski 1961; Mauss 1990; Benedict 1968; B. Wong 1988; Yun 1996; Yang 1994). Social indebtedness or a created social obligation also helps economic cooperation. Once all the parties are satisfied with each other's trustworthiness, they will have the confidence to do business together. The host may then proceed with speed to complete the project. *Guanxi* can expedite tedious paperwork. In some situations, in order to establish a production plant, one needs to obtain the approval of different agencies and organizations in China. A business plant may need approvals from many agencies. A company's speed and efficiency in securing these approvals depends on *guanxi*. Good *guanxi* means good connections in the government or with high-ranking officials and resourceful business leaders. The process of establishing *guanxi* is tedious and can be abused; it can also backfire. For instance, if one's business connections are tainted, or known publicly as corrupt, one may therefore risk business failure. Or the government may bring charges against certain party members, officials, or a company's representatives and send them to jail. If a Silicon Valley businessman has the bad luck of linking up with the wrong people, he can be financially ruined. Hence, in the process of establishing *guanxi*, one needs to have good contacts, good information, and reliable support. Most importantly, it is crucial to make sure that one's *guanxi* is reliable. This perhaps will change in the future when business practices become more regulated and institutionalized, and when business deals are less governed by personal favoritism. Some people believe that Chinese membership in the WTO will help institutionalize mainland Chinese business. There is also the likelihood that business procedures will then be streamlined and paperwork minimized. However, in present-day China, the reciprocal social relations created through gift-giving, exchanges of favors, and mutual feasting are still important for business transactions. Globalization has not terminated cultural-specific behavior in China. This process of creating mutual trust and reciprocity through what has been called "*prestation*" and "counter *prestation*" (Mauss 1990) is essential in business cooperation. This is a form impression management.

As should be apparent, the successful operation of *guanxi* depends on two components: (1) personal trust, and (2) the resources of the middlemen or connectors. Without *shin yung* (personal trust), a person can be "taken" or swindled. A connector could even be an unreliable *pien ren* (con-artist). But the resources of the connector are equally as important. Without the right amount of influence some *guanxi* are unable to deliver. That explains why there is an art in developing the right *guanxi* with the right connectors and the right agencies or businesses. Research has to be done meticulously.

To do business in Taiwan, one must also establish and use *guanxi*. The Taiwanese Chinese from Silicon Valley tend to branch their businesses out to Taiwan. One of the reasons for this is that they already have *guanxi* developed there. Their most important tool then is to reactivate their old *guanxi*. For this they tend to use their classmates or cohorts from high school, university, and the military services in Taiwan. (The Taiwanese Chinese high-tech or business people tend to have classmates in Taiwan since they finished their education there. Additionally, Taiwanese students need to finish military service before they can leave Taiwan for the United States.) Many of these classmates and friends will now be well-placed in business, industry, or government. And should the Taiwanese Chinese not have friends or colleagues in the area they are involved in, they may seek connections through other classmates, friends, or colleagues. In general, business transactions are more institutionalized in Taiwan than in China where the entire process of establishing a business plant or securing contracts depends entirely on *guanxi*. But in Taiwan there are other considerations. Taiwan has more experience with market economies. Although personal factors and *guanxi* are important, the Taiwanese are more aware of business practices in a capitalistic economy. They cannot completely depend on personal connections or *guanxi*. Factors like productivity, efficiency, skill, bureaucratic requirements, and management know-how have to be included in one's business deliberation. However, the human factor is always present. "Who you know" is a consideration, but not the only one. Many Taiwanese Chinese have told me that they do not have to worry about creating *guanxi* in Taiwan at all since every Taiwanese Chinese has at least three circles of friends that may be instrumental to their entrepreneurial activities: friends and classmates from college, family members, and cohorts from the military service.

Many mainland Chinese in Silicon Valley tend to come from families or work places that had good *guanxi*. Some already worked in important organizations or companies before they came to the United States. When they do decide to return to China, they need only to reactivate old *guanxi* through their parents, teachers, classmates, friends, or colleagues. These are the elite of Chinese society. Among the modern Chinese, old friends, old neighbors, old classmates, and colleagues are important connectors who can serve as the mediators or middlemen of *guanxi*, and who can provide a valuable connection to an agency, company or government office. China is a network society; people are linked up with each other through informal social relationships.

In the past, kinship played a most important role in *guanxi*. Today, classmates and colleagues are more important. Individuals treat their classmates and colleagues like extended kinsmen and friends. Every Chinese person has a group of close acquaintances. When the Chinese travel, they always look up old colleagues and classmates who are their friends. The line between private and public is often obscured in this group of friends because these friends have been pulled into an individual's private realm. Some informants told me that often they have to share space and even their privacy with their friends. They frequently have had to live in a school or work dormitory where neighbors share the same courtyard and workers share the same office or workplace. They have been through "thick and thin" together and have seen many political movements and upheavals. They have participated in the same study groups for their exams. Furthermore, their families and culture have taught them that they can rely on their friends and colleagues. These friends in school and the workplace are the ones who later become potential business partners. Friendship can be a basis for economic cooperative ventures. Take T Computer Corporation. Its owner and founder, Lee Da, came from Beijing University to study in the United States. Upon getting his PhD, he started a small company in Silicon Valley. At the initial stage he recruited his classmates from Beijing as employees and investors. He also knew a classmate who knew a government agency that helped fund start-up firms. With the help of this classmate he got some money from the agency. Mr. Lee is a resourceful person. He has good *guanxi* in Beijing, Shanghai, and Shenzhen. Through the connections of his classmates in Shanghai and Shenzhen, he was able to organize branches in these places. In 1999 he had just a handful of people working for him in Silicon Valley. Today he has 160 employees. All the managers of his company branches are connected to him in one way or another: they are either classmates or friends of friends. This is known as being a person with many good *guanxi* (*you heng hao de guanxi*).

We can see that there are similarities between Taiwanese and mainland Chinese *guanxi* operations. First, they both use classmates and colleagues. These *guanxi* are informal social relationships. Second, the practitioners of *guanxi* continue to nurture their contacts with personal visits, e-mails, and phone calls. But the context of operation differs. The Taiwanese Chinese operate in a rather capitalistic and free market environment. It is more open with regard to the areas one can go to. But all my informants, whether they are from Hong Kong, Taiwan, or mainland China, claim that they have more social networks in the old country than in the new. This phenomenon of having more social networks tied together by kinship, friendship, and colleagues in China than in the United States has been confirmed by Christine Avenarius's empirical study of the Chinese in Southern California (2002). Furthermore, all the Chinese in Silicon Valley have told me that they value their old friends even though those friends are not in the United States. This characteristic among the Chinese of treasuring old friendship is also mentioned by Hsu (1971, 1981, 1983). It is perhaps a cultural attribute of Chinese social networks.

The mainland Chinese businessperson functions, as I've suggested, within a more restricted environment. Resources are controlled more strictly. It seems that one needs more *guanxi* when one's opportunities are limited. Without connections or *guanxi*, it is impossible in mainland China to go to certain businesses or agencies. While the Taiwanese Chinese in Silicon Valley normally use classmates, colleagues, military cohorts, friends, friends of the family, and family members to build *guanxi*, the mainland Chinese use family, colleagues, and classmates. Foreigners who do business in China also need to establish *guanxi*. One of the ways of doing so is through Chinese colleagues in Silicon Valley who have already established connections with Taiwan, China, or Hong Kong. In this way the transnational ties of the Chinese in Silicon Valley are important for economic globalization. These old social ties to the old countries are instrumental and active in most business activities in China, Taiwan, Hong Kong, and other parts of Asia. The transnational migrants' social ties have become resources rather than liabilities in globalization. Contrary to our expectations then, it seems that the traditional fabric of social relations is still maintained in the global economy.

THE PHILOSOPHY OF BEING "REASONABLE"

Some Chinese entrepreneurs and investors complained to me that an emphasis on being "reasonable" is often an obstacle in business transactions. For example, an entrepreneur may expect a venture capitalist to immediately approve a project without going through the proper paperwork. He expects this because of friendship. The entrepreneur may argue that he and the venture capitalist have known each other for years and he should get the approval instantly. This is "being reasonable" for him. But a Chinese investor may not give his approval immediately due to the lack of clear evidence of viability or paperwork. The investor may want to consult other partners and to follow the regular business channels. This in itself can cause disagreements. The entrepreneur may accuse the venture capitalist as lacking in *yiqi* (righteousness), *xin yong* (trust), or may say that the capitalist shows a "lack of reason" (*mei you li you*).

In the work environment, an employee is expected to work longer hours during a peak season or in high demand situations. From the employer's point of view, this is considered a reasonable expectation. Similarly, employees also expect bonuses or appreciation as compensation for their work. When these expectations are not met, the injured party may accuse the other of being unreasonable. A squabble may then break out, and firing or resigning may occur. Some workers told me that this could be avoided if there were a clear understanding about compensation and work hours. Chinese firms often operate according to the concept of reasonableness. The problem with this concept is that it is highly subjective. What is reasonable to the employer may not be reasonable to the employee. Conflicts may arise from a business operation based on reasonableness.

The concept of reasonableness is also applied to expansion, employment, and management of the company. Is it reasonable to enlarge the firm? Is it reasonable to go public? Is it reasonable to lend money? Is it reasonable to expect people to work harder? Even though the answers to these questions can seem reasonable, implementation may still need to follow due process. It is reasonable to compensate an employee for travel and extra work, but the process of compensation may still need to go through administrative processes involving pay schedules or official approval.

Reasonableness is sometimes intertwined with emotion. Some workers are emotional when their colleagues or partners disagree with their designs, proposals, or projects. They may feel that it is only reasonable that other people approve their projects right away because they have good track records. However, their colleagues may have genuine concerns about the project. Chinese managers have told me that this is one problem that many Chinese have to deal with. They need to follow the process of examination and approval. Engineers or employees cannot just blindly and subjectively argue about what is reasonable. Many Americanized angel-investors (venture capitalists) particularly feel that this insistence on reasonableness among the Chinese needs to be corrected. The Chinese, they say, need to separate business affairs or procedures from the person (*dui shi bu dui ren*). And some Chinese realize that they need to change these old business habits. In fact, Chinese entrepreneurs in Silicon Valley gradually do seem to be accepting the business systems and procedures of the larger society. Various Chinese professional associations as well as incubating companies are also helping Chinese entrepreneurs and engineers move in the right direction.

Some informants have told me that with the admission of both Taiwan and China into the WTO, they, as businessmen, will have to comply with many standardized regulation and business procedures. They believe that there will be a less personal or subjective interpretation of reasonableness, and that it will become more institutionalized (*zhi du hua*). In this way, globalization will help the standardization of business procedures among the Chinese in Silicon Valley as well as among the Chinese in Taiwan, Hong Kong, and mainland China.

GLOBALIZATION AND THE SOCIAL ORGANIZATIONS OF THE NEW CHINESE IMMIGRANTS IN SILICON VALLEY

Globalization and an increasing demand for highly skilled immigrants in the high-tech sector predispose the organization of the Chinese in Silicon Valley. Established professionals, students from science- and technology-oriented universities in Asia and the United States, and international financiers have been drawn to this region. The global economy and transnationalism have created transnational social spaces and social ties that connect (1) migrants with their home communities and families in their homelands, (2) migrants with colleagues from the same school or workplace, and (3) migrants with other coethnics around the world (Faist 1999; Portes 1996, 1997). In the case of the Chinese in Silicon Valley, the transnational migrant networks created, and the organizations that serve the professional, emotional, social, and economic needs of the transnationals who make up those networks, are reflective of the types of people attracted to the area. These organizations comprise various professional associations, alumni associations, churches, and political interest groups. Conspicuously absent are traditional Chinese lineage and clan associations, and the dialect and regional associations that are abundant in America's Chinatowns.

The Chinese community in Silicon Valley differs greatly from traditional Chinese communities in San Francisco and New York. In both these urban ethnic enclaves, Chinatown–New York or Chinatown–San Francisco, there are overall community organizations, such as the Chinese Consolidated Benevolent Association (CCBA), and family name (clan) and district associations. The overall community and family name associations play an important role in many of the social and economic activities in these enclaves. But in the Chinese community of Silicon Valley, the traditional kinship and hometown associations are not important. Instead, voluntary associations based on common interest, profession, and ethnicity have become significant. Principles of origin, school or college attendance, and political affilia-tion can also be used as principles for social organization.

These Silicon Valley associations are modern in their outlook. The medium of exchange in official meetings is English, and the place for meet-ing is normally a hotel or a restaurant. Officers are elected. The associations generally have websites and homepages. For social activities, they have sports, bridge clubs, or dance parties rather than mahjong and Chinese opera. Some even have Chinese literature clubs and karaoke competitions. Occasionally, the consulate of the PRC or the Taipei Economic and Cultural Office in San Francisco play host to these Chinese organizations.

The social organization of the Chinese in Silicon Valley reflects four major dimensions of the community. First, the community is focused on technology, because Silicon Valley, as we have seen, is synonymous with the high-tech industry. Second, it is a community that is not homogeneous in terms of ori-gins and political ideology. Third, this community reflects the influence of globalization. Its economy is bound by Asia and the world. Fourth, many of the Chinese here come from the same regions and universities in China or Taiwan, and they often have the same professions, which gives rise to social organizations that are based on alma mater, origin, and profession. Further-more, because these associations exist to promote professional interests as well as international business, they are the most important organizations for the Chinese. The establishment of these organizations reflects efforts of the Chinese in protecting their interests and in establishing their roots in America. Most of these associations have professional activities, social activities, and in-formation centers on jobs, housing, immigration, and visa issues. All the im-portant business and professional organizations have websites, and informa-tion is transmitted quickly by e-mail, fax machine, or telephone. In a sense, the Silicon Valley Chinese society is a network society (Castells 2000b).

Numerous scholars have written about the proliferation of voluntary asso-ciations in urban and industrial settings and in immigrant communities. Aidan Southall (1998), Kenneth Little (1965), L. A. Fallers (1964), and William Man-gin (1965) have all pointed out the importance of associations in providing support for newcomers. What is most striking about the Chinese community in Silicon Valley is the globalized aspect of their associations. The professional and alumni associations provide their members with a forum for networking and a link to their home countries as well as to other members in different parts of the world. These associations go beyond ethnic groups, and they are not just potential platforms for economic joint ventures. Nor are they simply for cultural retention and diasporic solidarity. They are important instruments for the branching out of their ethnic group, for the creation of international joint ventures, and for connecting members with their colleagues in Asia.

Many of the Chinese professional associations in Silicon Valley are partic-ularly interested in globalization activities. To this end they have organized many functions specifically to help their members to internationalize their businesses in Asia. For instance, the Silicon Valley Chinese Wireless Technology Association specifically organized a conference on the Culture of Wireless Technology Use in China, in an attempt to show American and European mobile phone manufacturers and designers that they can benefit (and profit) from the Chinese market. They showed how Chinese behavior, values, and expectations influence mobile communications in China today.

Another striking aspect of these Chinese associations in Silicon Valley is their interest in helping their members to establish roots and gain acceptance in American society. Special interest groups have been the path that many ethnic groups have followed toward a fuller participation in American democracy and a greater access to its resources. Highly educated Chinese are sensitive to this tool as well. In the Western world the development and use of political pressure groups and civil societies has historically been a route for the obtainment of equality and civil rights (Castles 1998). The existence of a large immigrant population, living without the support of family and working as professionals and participants in a new global economy, has propelled the rapid development of these modern associations. Many of these associations are accordingly globalized and have branches around the world. As suggested above, there are four kinds of globalized, modern associations in Silicon Valley: (1) professional associations, (2) alumni associations, (3) political interest and pressure groups, and (4) immigrant churches.

Professional Associations

The earliest professional associations in the high-tech industry were the Chinese Institute of Engineers (CIE) established in 1979, and the Asian American Manufacturing Association (AAMA) established in 1980. These are also the two oldest professional organizations in the United States, and both have many branches. Initially the CIE drew its membership from the Taiwanese Chinese. Ninety percent of the CIE's members before 1990 were engineers from Taiwan (Teng 1998, 533). Representatives from the Taiwan Economic and Cultural Office frequently attend CIE activities. However, changes have taken place in the association as a result of the changing geopolitical landscape. In 1993 the CIE, in a bridging role, organized a conference in China at which President Jiang Zemin played host. Currently the CIE has about one thousand members.

The AAMA also has about one thousand members. Originally, it catered to manufacturers and entrepreneurs. Today, quite a few of its members are investors and venture capitalists. While the CIE is Mandarin-speaking, the AAMA is English-speaking, with members from Taiwan, Hong Kong, and other centers of Asian immigration, and its meetings have been held in the United States, Beijing, Taipei, and Hong Kong. The AAMA has three professed functions: (1) to promote exchange among manufacturers, (2) to foster communication with the United States on the contributions of the Chinese to science and technology, and (3) to attract the attention of Southeast Asian investors and manufacturers. The AAMA pays special attention to the global economy, and it has held trade exhibits in Beijing, Taipei, and Hong Kong. In the 1990s the AAMA organized activities about sourcing, and in 2001 it organized a symposium on capital formation and management.

These are just two examples of the functions of professional associations. In recent years, such associations have multiplied in Silicon Valley. Some serve the particular needs of engineers and scientists from different regions of China; some serve specialized areas of their members' professions such as software, hardware, or internet technology. Table 3.1 provides a list of these associations.

Table 3.1.   Chinese Professional Organizations in Silicon Valley, California

Name (and date founded if known)	Total Membership	Membership Target
Asian American Manufacturing Association (1980)	1000	Asian-American professionals
Chinese American Computer Corporation	270 corporate	
Chinese American Semiconductor Professional Association (1991)	1600	U.S. Chinese, mainland Chinese, Taiwan and Singapore Chinese
Chinese Enterprise Association (1997)	not known	
Chinese Information and Networking Association (1992)	1800	Mainland Chinese, Hong Kong and Taiwan Chinese, other overseas Chinese groups
Chinese Institute of Engineers [San Francisco Bay Area Chapter] (1979)	1979	
Chinese Internet Technology Association (1997)	700	
Chinese Software Professionals Association (1988)	1400	
Hua Yuan Science & Technology Association (1999)	400	
Hong Kong Silicon Valley (1999)	not known	
Monte Jade Science and Technology Association [Silicon Valley Chapter] (1989)	300 individual; 150 corporate	Taiwanese students
Asian American Monte Jade (1995)	not known	Second-generation Chinese Americans
North America Chinese Semiconductor Association (1996)	1000	Mainland Chinese
North American Taiwan Engineers Association (1991)	not known	Taiwanese engineers
Silicon Valley Chinese Engineers Association (1989)	3500	Mainland Chinese
Silicon Valley Chinese Wireless Technology Association (2000)	1900	

As indicated in the table, some of the organizations have a large membership. The Chinese American Semiconductor Professional Association (CASPA), to take one example, has 1600 members and was founded in 1991. Its members are from the United States, China, Taiwan, and Singapore, and it has branches in Austin, Texas, Phoenix, Arizona, and Beijing. CASPA organizes a job fair every year for its members with potential employers from Silicon Valley, Taiwan, and mainland China. Its leadership has a global perspective, and the association assists its members in participating in the globalization of the semiconductor business.

Some professional organizations are specifically oriented to helping Chinese engineers who come originally from mainland China. The North American Chinese Semiconductor Association (NACSA) and the Silicon Valley Chinese Engineers Association (SCEA) are just two examples. Founded in 1996, the NACSA primarily recruits students from mainland China, and it has a membership of one thousand. This organization has been quite active in Silicon Valley, organizing at least fifteen professional meetings or seminars in 2001, and it has played host to officials and visitors from mainland China. Most of its social gatherings are also well attended (*Sing Tao Daily*, South Bay Special, September 28, 2001, 21).

The SCEA is a similarly active organization. It was established in 1989, and it recruits Chinese students from mainland China. This organization has professional meetings, dance parties, sport events, annual meetings, and events to celebrate Thanksgiving and National Day. When China was admitted to the WTO, the SCEA held an event to which officials of the Chinese Consulate were invited. It is concerned with promoting the professional interests of its members. In this role, the SCEA once filed a protest against NBC for misrepresenting the Olympics position of China, and it was a strong supporter of Wen Ho Lee (see chapter 4). The membership of the SCEA has grown from 500 in 1989 to 3500 in 2002. It is the largest Chinese professional association in Silicon Valley.

Some of the valley's professional organizations recruit their members from Taiwan. The Monte Jade Science and Technology Association (Silicon Valley) was originally established by Chinese entrepreneurs from Taiwan in 1989. Monte Jade has 300 individual and 150 corporate memberships, and it has financial support from the Taiwan government. This organization promotes technology and capital interchange between the United States and Taiwan, and there are branches of Monte Jade in New York, Chicago, Washington D.C., Pittsburgh, Boston, Atlanta, and Philadelphia. In fact, the association has globalized itself by establishing branches in Canada, Taiwan, and mainland China, and in 1995 Monte Jade created an Asian American Monte Jade. Monte Jade was established mainly for second-generation Chinese Americans. In Chinese, it is known as *xiao yu shan* (the Little Jade Mountain). It sponsors yearly trips to Taiwan and Singapore, and it encourages and assists entrepreneurship among these second-generation Chinese Americans.

Another Taiwanese professional group is the North American Taiwanese Engineer's Association (NATEA) founded in 1991. The NATEA is concerned with Taiwanese engineers in North America and their professional interests as well as the interests of their counterparts in Taiwan. Its goal is to promote (1) the advancement and application of engineering and scientific knowledge, (2) the professional development and entrepreneurship of its members, (3) the high-tech industry in Taiwan, (4) the interchange of knowledge between Taiwan and the international scientific community, and (5) an increase in technical and professional exchanges among members.

Some organizations are eclectic in their approach to membership recruitment, such as the Chinese Information and Networking Association (CINA), whose members are recruited chiefly from mainland China, Taiwan, and Hong Kong. CINA was established in 1992 and it has a membership of 1800. It holds monthly meetings, special events, seminars, and social gatherings. The organization has six committees to address the separate concerns of wireless communication, entrepreneurship, software, fiber optics, entrepreneurship for women, and return migration to Asia.

Chinese associations in the valley are varied. Some of the associations use Chinese as a medium for exchange, some use only English, and some use both Chinese and English. Some are pro-Taiwan, some, pro-mainland China, and some are neutral. Some are for first-generation immigrant professionals and some are for the second generation. But a common denominator among them is their concern for the professions and technology that they represent. Furthermore, their members are all high-tech professionals who are eager to network with each other through the Internet (Castells 2000b). Many social, professional, and technical discussions can be accomplished through the internet, but association members still feel the need to communicate with each other through face-to-face meetings. The associations and their various activities in this way create opportunities for their members to network in order to accomplish their own social, professional, and personal goals.

As table 3.1 indicates, Chinese professional associations can be subdivided by member specialty and locality of origin. Many of these organizations were established by and for new Chinese immigrants and have come into being only in the past twenty years. But the names of the organizations do not say much about their functions and political ideologies; some are pro-Taiwan and some are pro-PRC; some are active in lobbying activities in immigration areas; others are interested in exports, imports, or outsourcing. These associations also reflect the three geographical origins (China, Taiwan, and Hong Kong) of the immigrants that comprise them. However, all of the associations are open to all people regardless of their origin, and the official medium of exchange for the larger associations is English, though in smaller associations the members may use their own dialects. Hong Kong Chinese, for example, prefer to speak Cantonese, Chinese from mainland Chinese speak

Mandarin, and Taiwanese Chinese may speak either Mandarin or *Minanhua* (Fujianese).

These professional associations have conferences, discussions, and regular activities. From my observation, the Chinese, whether they are from China, Taiwan, or Hong Kong, interact as professionals. However, in their social activities many Chinese prefer to interact with people who speak the same dialect and are related to them in some way, such as relatives, friends, or colleagues. Thus, there is a difference between their public and private spheres of activity. Politics also has an influence, as can be seen in the distance between the ideological standpoints of pro-PRC and pro-Taiwan organizations. When it comes to questions of the unification of China, the independence of Taiwan, or political elections in Taiwan, the members of different organizations may have strong views. But in general, in all professional meetings, members tend to shun topics related to the motherland. After the official meetings are over, and in social gatherings, some of the issues may be raised.

But certain issues can serve as rallying points for social solidarity. For example, the case of Wen Ho Lee, discrimination against the Chinese, the glass ceiling, racism, civil rights, and equal opportunity are concerns for all Chinese. They are equally enthusiastic in supporting other Chinese who participate in American politics. The Chinese immigrants who have been in the United States longer tend to see the importance of participating in American democracy via political parties and special-interest groups. They want to make their voice heard in the running of schools, the city, the county, and the nation.

Are outsiders and non-Chinese accepted at these association activities? The answer is yes. In fact, non-Chinese venture capitalists regularly go to association meetings. Some informants attribute the success of Chinese firms to non-Chinese venture capitalists such as Alpine Technology Ventures, Walden International Investment Group, and Advent International.

Alumni Associations

Alumni Associations are active and play an important role in the social lives of the high-tech Chinese who live in Silicon Valley. As immigrant engineers or high-tech personnel, their work schedules tend to be irregular, making it difficult for them to see each other during normal leisure-time hours. Besides nonconventional hours, some engineers also work on Saturdays and Sundays, making their work habits an isolating factor that inhibits their contact with the larger society. Many alumni associations make use of public holidays to organize activities such as picnics or dance parties. In this way the associations bring many former classmates and friends together to chat about their common interests. The members of these associations have all graduated from the same group of colleges, so there is the added attraction of knowing for sure that their old classmates or old friends will be there too, and that they will be able to talk to each other in their own dialect or language. This is important for Chinese engineers who are not at ease in communicating in English. Seeing old friends and comparing notes about their progress in the United States are important activities. Like family, these friends and classmates provide emotional support. Attending these meetings also helps the careers of the alumni as there is always information about employment and business opportunities. Through these friends, alumni also learn about America, where to visit, where to buy a certain product, which car has the best rating, and so forth. They also offer an opportunity for the opposite sex to meet. Among the Silicon Valley Chinese, it is particularly difficult for men in this field to meet women. It goes without saying that within this industry, men outnumber women by a large margin. In such ways, the alumni associations are an important tool for fighting marginalization and loneliness.

But alumni associations not only help immigrants adjust to America, they also foster connections between university classmates in different parts of the world as they assist each other in networking for jobs and other business opportunities. (Many of the larger universities have alumni branches in different parts of the world too.) Besides serving as fund-raising organizations, or helping to connect alumni with their alma mater, the various Chinese alumni associations are culture brokers filling the void of kinship. Indeed, association members use kinship terms such as *tong xue xiong di* (classmate-brother) and *tong xue zhi mei* (classmate-sister) to address each other. This kind of kinship warmth and sentimentality is particularly important for the mainland Chinese, who often feel lonely and isolated in the United States.

Alumni associations are important among all the Chinese in Silicon Valley. For the Chinese from mainland China and Taiwan, the universities they graduated from are used for organizing their associations. Examples of these are the Jiaotong University Alumni Association, the Fu Dan Alumni Association of Northern California, the National Cheng-Kung University Alumni Association of Northern California, the National Taiwan University Alumni Association, the Nanjing University of Overseas Alumni Association, the Peking University Alumni Association in Northern California, the Tsing Hua University Alumni Association of Northern California, and the University of Science and Technology of China Alumni Association. The Hong Kong Chinese, in contrast, use the high schools they graduated from as a principle way of organizing their alumni associations. Examples of these include the Pui Ching Alumni Association, the DBS [Diocesan Boys School] Alumni Association, and the Hong Kong Students Association. Additionally, the Chinese use American universities as a basis for organizing their alumni associations. The most visible of these in the Bay Area are the Stanford Taiwanese Students Association, the Chinese Student Association of San Jose State University, the Taiwanese Student Association of the University of California, Berkeley, and the Stanford Society of Asian American Engineers.

These alumni associations hold social functions such as dance parties, athletic events, and bridge tournaments.

Transforming friendship into kinship is a characteristic of Chinese interpersonal relations (Hsu 1971; B. Wong 1988), and these organizations are no exception, because alumni associations can serve as quasi-kinship organizations. Sometimes friends can become *gan xiong di* (dry-brothers) or, as noted above, *xue xiong di* (classmate-brothers). Within these alumni associations, members may develop informal social ties and a friendship network that can be instrumental for business activities. In fact, the Chinese CEOs of some start-up companies get their initial seed money from old classmates. One CEO even told me that he could not have started his company without his classmates' help. This is what he said about the importance of his classmates from China:

> I know them well and they know me and trust me. They helped me by lending me the money to launch my start-up company. I did not have to go into detail about what I planned to do. They had full confidence in me! There was no need for receipts and contracts. It was based entirely on friendship and trust! (Informant Y, interview with author, May 15, 2001)

His enthusiasm for and trust in his classmates and friends were shared by all the informants I interviewed.

Networking within and between Associations

Professional and alumni associations are important places for networking. Within each association, professional and social events lead to personal friendships and the formation of social networks for goal-seeking activities. For example, friends may help in the purchase of homes in certain desirable neighborhoods by recommending the "right" realtor. And friends may become business partners for future entrepreneurial activities. One entrepreneur, Chun Xia, who founded Brightinfo.com and ThinkMart.com, got his inspiration for starting a company from the CEO Club of the Tsing Hua Alumni Association. Through the CEO Club he learned from other entrepreneurs from mainland China. He said that he gained much inspiration and confidence from these meetings (Zhang 2000, 138).

These formal associations serve then as important information channels of fundraising and fundraising techniques for start-up companies in Silicon Valley. In 2001 the AAMA organized a conference on founding a company. At the conference, speakers from well-known venture capitalist and high-tech companies like Horizon Ventures, Intuit, H&Q Asia Pacific, Advanced Integrated Photonics, the Indus Entrepreneurs, and Wilson Sonsini Goodrich & Rosat, spoke specifically on how to get funding. Attendants of the conference not only learned how to fundraise, they also had a chance to network and get to know venture capitalists in the valley. Dual or multiple membership in two or more associations is not uncommon, and a person can have several circles of friends in several different associations. Nor is it unusual to find cooperation between different associations. For instance, the AAMA together with Cnetwork, NACSA, the Peking University Alumni Association of Northern California, the Tsing Hua Alumni Association, the SCEA, and a host of other organizations, has cosponsored a symposium called "Riding the China Wave." Associations commonly get together to initiate activities of interest to Chinese entrepreneurs and engineers, and the leaders of different associations are invited to each other's annual meetings or conferences so that they can be kept informed about their activities. Thus, at the annual meeting of the SCEA in 2001, the president of the American Chinese Computer Association, a representative of Cnetwork, and a number of other leaders from various Chinese associations attended as VIP guests.

Professional Associations and the Global Economy

All of these professional associations are keenly aware of the importance for their members of having global knowledge and a global business sense, and they seek opportunities to participate in global conferences like those of the Asia-Pacific Economic Cooperation (APEC) and the North American Free Trade Agreement (NAFTA). In fact, globalization is a theme that dominates the activities of these associations. Other writers have noted that many modern organizations such as chambers of commerce and various professional associations are preoccupied with globalization issues. Jennifer Riley, for instance, has observed that globalization and the high-tech industry are two themes that dominate the activities of local Latino chambers of conference in San Diego, San Antonio, Santa Clara, Miami, Chicago, Washington, D.C., and Houston (1999).

Most of these professional associations have conferences on international trade and sponsor international conferences on technology. Thus in 1993, the CIE organized an international conference in China. And in 1995 CASPE played a bridging role in connecting the Chinese in Silicon Valley with the Chinese in Shanghai and Taiwan. Again in 1995, CASPE organized a conference on semiconductor technology and manufacturing in Taiwan, and a similar conference was organized in mainland China in 1997. CASPE also assists Taiwan manufacturers in running advertisements, renting meeting places, and establishing business liaison offices in Silicon Valley.

On May 23, 2001, the Monte Jade Science and Technology Association established a branch in Taiwan. Originally, the association was established in San Jose by Taiwanese high-tech personnel, and since then it has become an important vehicle for the exchange of information on technology, capital formation, and management and business strategies. Members also feel that the association should be globalized. With branches of Monte Jade in Taiwan and other parts of the world, members believe that they will have a head start in expanding their businesses (*Sing Tao Daily* May 23, 2001, C19). Although many members of Monte Jade originally came from Taiwan, they are also interested in establishing a branch in mainland China. In fact, some believe that Monte Jade could facilitate Taiwan and American business in China.

The AAMA also plays a prominent role in the economic globalization of Silicon Valley. It has a committee on international trade and has organized trade exhibits of products by Asian American manufacturers in Beijing (1986), Taipei (1987), and Hong Kong (1988). In the 1990s the AAMA investigated the outsourcing of American product manufacturing to Asia. The association also provides direct advice to entrepreneurs. It often invite economists, high-tech engineers, human resources (HR) specialists, and other economic experts from different regions of the world to talk about economic opportunities in their regions. To take one example, on September 29, 2001, the AAMA, Sina.com, and ten other professional associations sponsored a conference on job opportunities and a "How-to of China/US trade, Venture Capital and Incubation in China." The conference was held in the Santa Clara Convention Center, and strong interest in the global economy was reflected in the enthusiastic attendance. In fact, the conference was oversold and conference rooms were filled to capacity, many ticket holders having been denied entrance due to the lack of space. Those who were not able to gain admission to the symposium had an informal meeting outside the conference room where they chatted with each other about their business experiences in China, Japan, and Singapore while exchanging business cards. It was a great occasion for networking! In fact, I was able to arrange follow-up interviews with a venture capitalist in order to learn more about how his company was providing a bridge between entrepreneurs in Silicon Valley and Israel, Singapore, Japan, and China. Suffice it to say, networking abounds in the on-going activities of these professional and alumni associations.

The professional and alumni associations also have a social welfare and charitable function. For instance, the SCEA coordinated a blood drive and a relief fund drive for the victims of the terrorist attacks of September 11, 2001. Under the guidance of the American Red Cross's Santa Clara Chapter, the SCEA formed a Bay Chinese 9/11 Relief Fund Steering Committee composed of CASPA, the Chinese Enterprise Association, CINA, Cnetwork, the Hua Yuan Science and Technology Association, NACSA, the Peking University Alumni Association of Northern California, the Silicon Valley Chinese Overseas Business Association, the Shanghai Jiaotong Alumni Association, the Tianjin University Alumni Association, and other valley organizations. By networking with other associations to raise a substantial amount of money from the Chinese community in Silicon Valley for the victims of the terrorist attacks, the associations showed their concern for the larger community.

As can be seen, the associations serve as bridges between their local community and Taiwan, Hong Kong, and mainland China. They play host to visiting dignitaries from Taipei, Beijing, Shanghai, and Hong Kong. They also arrange meetings for Chinese entrepreneurs from the motherland and the United States that allow them to exchange business information and to launch joint ventures.

Thus, in Silicon Valley alumni and professional associations have displaced the more traditional Chinese Consolidated Benevolent Associations, and family, kinship, and district associations that have been historically important in the various Chinatowns of the United States. The professional and alumni associations now perform functions similar to those performed by the traditional associations, but they are more modern and urban in their outlook and are formed strictly on the basis of voluntary association. In each of these associations there is an annual election in which members compete for office and are elected by fellow members.

Informal Social Networks and Globalization

The use of social networks in goal-seeking activities is quite common in modern complex societies. Eric Wolf eloquently writes about the formation of cliques and social networks (1966). Robert Dirks even goes so far as to suggest that the use of social networks is highly common in societies with limited resources (1972). Regardless of the merit of this argument, one thing is sure: the use of social networks exists in the United States. One need only witness the "old-boy" networks found in the banking business, on Wall Street, and in politics. Weatherford writes about the informal social relations among politicians in the United States (1988), while John Barnes (1954), Elizabeth Bott (1971), and Graham Allan (1996) discuss the formation and use of social networks in Norway and Britain. Some participants in these networks use friendship, other use kinship and patron-client relationships to cement their social bonds. How do Chinese informal social networks differ from those of non-Asian Americans? Informal social networks exist in all cultures, and it goes without saying that the bases upon which social networks are formed may differ from culture to culture. There are certain characteristics in the formation of social networks that are peculiar to the traditional Chinese, however, such as the use of shared lineage and locality of origin in the formation of family-name and district associations. This practice is common among the Chinese in U.S. Chinatowns (B. Wong 1988). In contrast, the Chinese in Silicon Valley use colleagues, alma maters, and their own common interests and aspirations to form their associations. In this regard, the Chinese in Silicon Valley resemble middle-class Americans who make similar associations.

As we have seen, alumni relationships in Silicon Valley have come to supersede clan and lineage relationships. Thus, the same family name or lineage is no longer an important basis for social relationships in this community: colleagues, present and former, are more valuable. Sometimes these colleagues are treated almost like family members, and children are instructed to address them as "uncle" or "aunt," despite their having no blood tie. Colleagues, in this case, become "fictive kin." A tendency to treat colleagues as kin is traditional in Chinese society. This special type of bond is exemplified in the Chinese saying, "When you are at home, you depend on your family. When you are away, you depend on friends and classmates." As a society that operates according to a Confucian ideology, the teacher-student relationship is important among the Chinese in China as well as in Silicon Valley. Former students and former professors are sometimes in the same social circles. Many Silicon Valley Chinese have teamed up with their former professors to organize business and professional activities.

Old-boy networks based on the alma mater are common in America. But in the case of the Chinese, school and classmate relationships are even more important due to closer relationships. First, in China it is difficult to get into a first-rate university. When one is admitted, one feels an intellectual bond with others who have been admitted. Such students feel that they are of the same caliber as their classmates, and this creates a strong emotional bond: they are a special group that has worked extraordinarily hard in order to get into these elite schools. Second, there are many exams and other hurdles that they have had to go through together. This is particularly the case among the Chinese in Taiwan. As classmates, they studied together for exams. As peers, they had to serve in the military. These common activities brought them closer together.

One of my informants, Mr. A, told me that his professor in Beijing University sent six of his fiber optics students (one of them being Mr. A) to study in the United States. These six students went to different schools in the United States. Upon graduation, Mr. A moved to Silicon Valley. Mr. A later told his other five classmates about the opportunities in California. They all moved to the valley and followed the lead of A in obtaining employment. Mr. A told me that when he started his company, he asked these old classmates from China to lend him money, and they loaned money to him. Mr. A now has a start-up company that is about eighteen months old. He said that his five friends now work for him in his fiber optics company. These friends, Mr. A. said, have been most important in his career (Informant A, interview with author, May 17, 2000).

University classmates are equally important for the Taiwanese Chinese. Such is the case of Mr. W, from Taiwan. He told me that the reason why he was able to expand his business to Taiwan, mainland China, and Japan was because he had good connections in those three locations. When asked how one builds connections in these places, he said:

> It is easy. Every Chinese from Taiwan has some connections. When I studied in high school, I had classmates. When I went to university, I had classmates and

roommates. I studied, played and did exams with them. They were my peers and cohorts. They became very important friends. When I was in the university, I had to do military training. Those who went through military training got to know each other and became friends. At home, my brothers and sisters came home with their friends who also became my friends. So, in my case, before I came to the U.S., I already had four sets of friends from high school, the university, military service and from my siblings. Later when I wanted to start a business in Taiwan, I just called upon them. If they could not help me, they would refer me to their friends who could help me. Many of my classmates became very important in government and in business. Some of them have been doing business in Japan and mainland China as well. When I needed help, I just called them. (Informant W, interview with author, March 19, 2002)

In the case of his import business from Japan to the United States, Mr. W. told me that he had a Chinese business partner who had studied in Japan. This friend could speak Japanese fluently because he grew up there and attended high school there.

When he was expanding his business to mainland China, Mr. W said he had the benefit of several of his fellow alumni who were influential in China. These were the friends who helped him build contacts in China. Thus, it was through friendship, classmates, and alumni that Mr. W was able to build his international business. "Business is about people and social relations," Mr. W said.

Regionalism and Social Networks

In general, the Taiwanese Chinese have their hometown, kinship, friendship, and alumni networks in Taiwan. People in the Taiwan networks speak Mandarin and tend to socialize with each other. The globalizing activities of the Taiwanese Chinese in Silicon Valley, therefore, tend to focus on companies and countries that have connections with Taiwan. These include Singapore, Israel, and Saudi Arabia.

The mainland Chinese in Silicon Valley tend to focus on mainland China where they have *guanxi* from an alma mater, a previous workplace, or from friend and kinship links. After they have organized their companies in Silicon Valley, they immediately open up branches or travel to mainland China to market their products or talents. Companies formed in this way include RivalWatch, WebEx, and E-Commerce Technology.

The Hong Kong Chinese, such as the owners of WYSE, Central Computers, and ESS tend to have their connections in Hong Kong and Shenzhen. The fact that they can speak the Cantonese dialect, and hence similar dialects, facilitates communication and helps them establish their companies in Cantonese-speaking areas.

This tendency to interact with people who speak the same language and come from the same locality is also reflected in the Shanghainese-speaking

Chinese in Silicon Valley. When they start their globalizing activities in China, they first go back to Shanghai to network with their friends and relatives. This is called *da guanxi* (make connections). Speaking the same language and coming from the same place tends to facilitate such networking activities.

In general, these networking activities are localized by origin. The Taiwanese Chinese focus on Taiwan; the Hong Kong Chinese concentrate on Hong Kong and the Shenzhen area; the Chinese from mainland China will go back to Beijing, Shanghai, and other parts of mainland China where they are connected by kinship, friendship, and collegiate relationships. Cross-regional social networks do exist, but the formation and cultivation of most networks depend on common goals and the ability of the networkers to speak each other's dialect.

NETWORKING THROUGH MODERN TECHNOLOGY

The use of e-mail, faxes, cell phones, and the Internet to communicate and to initiate goal-seeking activities among the Chinese is quite extensive. One literately can reach the entire world through the information superhighway. The Internet is an important source of news, but among the Chinese, there is a custom of keeping in touch with the world through newspapers published in different parts of the world. Since different newspapers have different viewpoints about the world situation, many Chinese like to see how information is analyzed differently. Hence they like to read newspapers published in different locations and that support different political ideologies. Typically, a Chinese person in Silicon Valley will read the *World Journal* (pro-Taiwan) and the *Sing Tao Daily* (pro-PRC). Knowing this, several years ago Sina.com started to coordinate the Chinese media from mainland China, Taiwan, North America, Hong Kong, and Australia, and to report these media on their portal where the major news was abstracted daily. For people who were interested only in America, California, or San Francisco Bay Area, they can select for that preference on the Sina.com site.

The Chinese newspapers in America that are carried by Sina.com are: the *China Press*, the *Sing Tao Daily*, the *Zhonguo Daily*, and *China Today*. The Hong Kong newspaper carried by Sina.com is *Ming Bao*. Taiwanese papers are represented too. They are *United*, *Power News*, the *China Times*, *Digi Times*, and *Fomosa TV*. Newspapers from mainland China carried by Sina.com are *Phoenix TV*, the *Beijing Morning Post*, the *Xianmin Evening News*, the *Yangtse Evening Post*, the *Guangzhou Daily*, *Huashen*, *Cheng Du Shang Bao*, *Yang Cheng Wan Bao*, and *Life Times*. Recently, the *San Jose Mercury News* also participated in the Sina.com project. Through the media, the Chinese in Silicon Valley can undoubtedly get a more comprehensive view of world events and events in China. Additionally, the *World Journal* and the *Sing Tao*

Daily also have their own Internet editions. These last two include shopping, employment, and classified ads. Such media are not just disseminators of news. They are brokers and links between peoples and communities.

Through the websites of Chinese organizations the Chinese in Silicon Valley can conduct their daily transactions and get important business done. This is no different than what many other Americans do. On the Internet there are chat rooms, forums, and e-mail discussion groups that are organized by various professional and alumni associations. However, the transactions conducted are specifically geared to the Chinese in Silicon Valley, and their needs and interests are sometimes different from those of other groups. Critical information about visas, immigration law, and government policies on expatriates returning to work in China or Taiwan are exchanged through the internet. In one case, a Chinese woman seeking a lawyer posted a message on the SCEA's Immigration Bulletin Board. Almost immediately she got an answer from another engineer with a recommendation. Another person posted a question on how to apply for a visiting visa for a parent from China. She also got a detailed answer from the SCEA's Immigration Board. Other visitors to the board exchanged information about their personal interview experiences with the INS. Another asked for help translating Chinese to English. Some asked for information about financing. I have seen requests for traveling partners and roommates. Companies post their job openings on the bulletin boards of the various Chinese professional associations. Some people conduct surveys through the Internet and still others sell their used furniture and cars through these Chinese websites. Many websites are linked with each other, and the members of this high-tech community are extremely skillful in using their computers for networking. The high-tech Chinese use technology extensively to achieve various goal-seeking activities. However, they told me that they do not automatically trust any of these websites. Friends who have experience and are knowledgeable are consulted with regard to which sites are reliable.

E-mail also has its role in the job market. For example, The 2001 economic downturn affected many in the valley and unemployment greatly increased. According to statistics released in Santa Clara, the unemployment rate in September 2001 reached 4.5 percent, the highest since 1994. Like many others in the valley, some Chinese workers were laid off. At this time an e-mail notice about employment opportunities in China was posted. Here is what it said:

> Due to the economic downturn and the problem of war (in Afghanistan), would you like to return to China to work? China is now experiencing economic prosperity. Would you like to work in China? Currently, the U.S. has wave after wave of unemployment, are you being affected? Is your H1-B, TN or L1 work visas affected? Are you on the verge of being deported? Do you still plan to stay in the U.S.? What is your decision? If you seek answers to the above questions, you should participate in Sina.net's meeting on "How to survive from layoffs. How one does retains one's residence status and obtains employment in China." Join

our meeting on October 28, 2001 at Santa Clara's Convention Center! (Sina.com, *netizens*, e-mail, October 26, 2001)

This notice is reminiscent of notices posted by Americans in Hong Kong and Canton in 1871 to recruit Chinese people to work in the United States (B. Wong 1982, 3). However, this time there was a reversal: Chinese were being recruited to return to China to work. What is more interesting is that there was now concern among the Chinese with keeping their residence rights in the United States. Another difference was in the use of the media. In the old days, such advertising was done through newspapers or by using posters. In the modern era, and in Silicon Valley as well, it is often through the use of e-mail and the web that employers reach potential job applicants.

Of course, e-mail is used by the Chinese to keep in touch with each other in Silicon Valley as well as with family and connections in Asia. All my informants tended to be savvy internet users and could use both English and Chinese to communicate via the web. They told me that e-mail was convenient, fast, and economical. Working as high-tech personnel, they were quite busy and had no time to sit down to write letters. Hence, they used high-tech ways of sending Chinese New Year greetings and personal correspondence. It is a case of using technology to maintain social networks.

POLITICAL AND COMMUNITY ORGANIZATIONS IN SILICON VALLEY

There is much fear about the possible demise of localism as a result of globalization (Krasner 2000). There is also the concern that globalization threatens the survival of nation-state and local governmental organizations. Will globalization create ungovernability and diminish the importance of local political organizations? To the contrary, from my study I found increased social and political participation of the Chinese in Silicon Valley. "Place" has been elevated in the consciousness of the transnationals. There have been place-based struggles and more place-based networks formed in recent years to obtain civil rights, social equality, and justice. This phenomenon has also occurred in other parts of the world (Vargas-Llosa 2001; McCorquodale and Fairbrother 1996; Benhabib 1999; Escobar 2001).

In the past ten years, political activism has been on the increase among the Chinese in Silicon Valley. This can be measured by the high degree of Chinese involvement in American politics. A Silicon Valley Chinese scientist told me:

If we do not involve ourselves in politics and participate in political activities, we will have no protection. We will be treated as foreigners and have no rights. Look at Indonesia, look at other parts of Southeast Asia, the Chinese are not treated like citizens. They have been persecuted! (Informant Y, interview with author, May 15, 2001)

His sentiment was shared by all the Chinese I interviewed. Due to a high level of education and commitment, many Chinese see the need to get involved in their new country, and all realize the importance of gaining civil rights and equal treatment through participation in the politics of the mainstream society.

In the last election, many Chinese were involved. Barry Chang, a civil engineer, ran for a seat in the Cupertino Union School District. A software engineer, Ben Liao, and Julius Chang, a banker, did the same. In the Foothill/De Anza Community College District, Hsing Kung and Kathryn Ho have been involved in their school board. It is easier for the Chinese to gain entry into politics by way of a school board because of the perception that the Chinese value education and are good educators. Immigrants being elected are a new phenomenon. The fact that there are candidates, both from Taiwan and Hong Kong, running for political offices indicates their degree of commitment to this country. Currently the job of mayor of Cupertino is held by a non-Chinese, Sandra James. Her predecessor was Dr. Michael Chang, a college professor. Next in line to succeed Ms. James is a Chinese American, Patrick Kwok, who is a civil engineer. Getting involved in politics requires networking. To this end, Chinese Americans have organized many formal and informal gatherings to plan strategies and raise funds for elections. These new immigrants are fighting for a place in America for themselves and their children, and the immigrant politicians who represent then can be seen as pioneers who have made a heroic journey, opening up a new land for future generations of Chinese Americans.

There are also many civic organizations that encourage Chinese participation. The Organization of Chinese Americans (Silicon Valley Chapter and East Bay Chapter), the Asian American Public Policy Institute of San Jose, Asian Americans for Community Involvement of San Jose, the Asian Pacific American Consortium of San Jose, the Cross Cultural Community Services Center of San Jose, the Chinese American Cultural Association of Palo Alto, the Wen Ho Lee Defense Fund in Fremont, and the Silicon Valley for Democracy in China, are a few examples.

Churches

The important role of immigrant churches in immigrants' lives has been recognized by social scientists. Palinkas (1990), Guest (2003), and others have depicted the churches as agents for the social change, incorporation, and psychosocial adjustment of immigrants to a new country. With the migration of Chinese from Taiwan and Hong Kong to Silicon Valley, many immigrant priests, ministers, and pastors also came to serve them. Among the many Chinese Protestant organizations, a few that I might note are the Taiwanese Lutheran Church in Cupertino, the Taiwanese Presbyterian Church in Santa Clara, the Tri-City Chinese Baptist Church in Fremont, the Tri-Valley Chinese Bible Church in Pleasanton, the Canaan Taiwanese Christians, the Chinese Bible Baptism Church in Los Altos, the Chinese Church in Christ in Mountain View, the Christian Assembly in Cupertino, the Faith Chinese Lutheran Church in Cupertino, the First Chinese United Methodist Church in Fremont, the Freemont Chinese Alliance, the Friendship Agape Chinese Church in San Jose, the Gospel Chinese Christian Church in Campbell, the Grace Chinese Baptist Church in Cupertino, the Kwong Wah Baptist Church in Sunnyvale, and the Mountain View Chinese Christian Church. Among Cantonese churches, there are the Chinese Baptism Church of San Jose and the Crosspoint Chinese Church of Silicon Valley in Milpitas. For Chinese Catholics, they can go to the San Jose Chinese Catholic Community and St. Clare Church in Santa Clara, or St. Joseph Church in Fremont. Both of these have Cantonese, Fujianese, and Mandarin Services. The preponderance of Protestant churches can be attributed to the fact that there are more Protestants than Catholics from Taiwan. But churches are not just places for worship; they are important places for social activities and networking. Many of the engineers from Taiwan whom I interviewed told me that they do three things on the weekends: go to church, eat in Chinese restaurants, and go shopping with their families. Before or after church services, they may then network about business, getting information about who is a reliable financier, where can one rent an office cheaply, and so on. There is thus yet another networking opportunity for the Chinese who attend the church activities. Members of the church will also get together to talk about entrepreneurship opportunities in Silicon Valley and Asia.

In contrast to the Christian churches, there are Chinese temples. However, the latter are far fewer in number than the former. This is due presumably to the fact that many of the highly educated Chinese in the valley tend to be more Westernized. Many institutions of education in Taiwan and Hong Kong were influenced by Christianity and its missionaries. Among the Chinese temples in Silicon Valley, the Amituofo House of Cupertino, the Avatamasaka Buddhist Lotus Society, and the Tzu Chi Foundation have temples but not many followers. Going to church and attending religious activities brings people of the same faith and interest together. Fellow parishioners become friends who can become important in each other's lives.

CONCLUSION

Globalization has induced frequent social contact and travel between many nations. Crossing national borders to achieve global entrepreneurship has become a necessity for many Silicon Valley Chinese. In circulating through a large area, the immigrant engineers and high-tech entrepreneurs of the valley must utilize both economic and social resources, and these resources include social networks. As demonstrated in this chapter, social networks contracted within and outside formal organizations have the ability to facilitate many business transactions. Owing to their importance, such social networks are created continuously within the Silicon Valley community, not only between the Chinese community and the larger society, but also between Silicon Valley and Asia. These networks and various professional and alumni associations are in turn instrumental in economic globalization. They open up the transnational space linking the local with the global. Thus, ethnic organizations and informal social networks do not die. Rather, they thrive in the face of globalization. Contrary to the claims of Blau (1995) and McPherson, Popielarz, and Drobronic (1991), I have found that ethnic networks and social networks based on similar socioeconomic background do link individuals to the larger society. Informal social networks, it appears, help rather than hinder the process of incorporation into American society. This finding is echoed by Franklin Ng (1988), Fugita and O'Brien (1991), and Avenarius (2003). Clearly, informal social networks and traditional ethnic institutions connect the Silicon Valley Chinese with their family, relatives, former classmates, friends, and colleagues. In a way, social networks can be seen as prerequisites of the global economy because they help the transnational to navigate in the global economy. Before leaving home, a transnational must first put his or her house in order. Putting it differently, immigrants have to have a mooring in their host society before they are able to return to their ancestral lands to link up a business spanning two or more continents. By practice and by design, the Chinese transnational migrants have built their own social foundations in Silicon Valley. These are the various community organizations, professional and alumni associations, and interest and pressure groups that I have touched on, all of which were built with the goal of globalizing Silicon Valley's economy. These various local organizations, as will be demonstrated in the next chapter, have grounded the Chinese in the United States, and they have also facilitated their transnational economic pursuits. These associations and informal social networks have played an important role in helping the Chinese to adjust locally and to reach out globally. These social networks are culture brokers (Wolf 1966), mediating between Chinese and American cultures. Contrary to the assertion that globalization decreases the importance of traditional institutions and the individual's participation in local affairs (Appadurai 1998; Friedman and Ramonet 1999; Castells 2000b; King 1995), the present study finds that informal social relations and traditional institutions are the key for transnationals who want to secure a place in America.

4

Establishing Roots in America

Globalization goes hand in hand with localization. Though many scholars suggest that globalization will create a rootless society of transnationals who have severed their ties with family and nation-states (Appadurai 1996; Hannerz, 1993, 1996) and become noncommittal flexible citizens (Ong 1999; Ong and Nonini 1996; Soyal 1994; Jacobson 1996), the present chapter will argue that this expectation is far from the truth. The data obtained from this study show that the Chinese in Silicon Valley have made extraordinary efforts in grounding themselves economically and politically in their new land. As I have stated, the process of localization includes the use of cultural and economic resources to find lucrative employment at home and overseas and to develop global and local entrepreneurship. In an effort to participate in the multicultural society of Silicon Valley, these Chinese transnational migrants have utilized civil societies and social networks, and they have developed coalitions with other ethnic groups. Globalization, as will be demonstrated later in this chapter, propels citizenship making rather than rootless existence among the Chinese in Silicon Valley. Globalization intensifies their use of cultural resources and social connections to help in establishing themselves in the community. The culture of these transnational migrants, on the one hand, influences their career choices and other economic activities. On the other hand, culture is also an asset that they use to establish roots in America.

CULTURE AND ECONOMICS

It is frequently asserted in the literature on economic development that kinship ties that include a big circle of relatives (and its accompanying obligations and

constraint) is detrimental to entrepreneurial activities. This view implies a necessarily inhibiting influence of cultural institutions such as family and kinship
on economic activities. Contrary to this view, some anthropologists and soci-
ologists argue for the beneficial connection between culture and economic development. Max Weber specifically links the ethics of work to religion (1951,
1958). More recently, Alan Smart (1998), Gernot Garbher and David Stark
(1998), John Wilkinson (1997), Bernard Wong (1987, 1997), and Wong,
McReynolds, and Wong (1992) have shown that family, kinship, and culture
play a decisive role in economic development. In fact, cultural practices are often intertwined with economic practices (Yang 2004). Other studies have emphasized that ethnic and cultural resources are instrumental for the economic
success of ethnic entrepreneurs (Light 1971, 1984; Waldinger, Aldrich, and
Ward 1990; Portes 1980; B. Wong 1987, 1998a; Wong, McReynolds, and Wong
1992). Anthropologists prefer to discuss economic institutions in the context of
culture. However, ethnic resources in themselves do not necessarily guarantee
economic achievement. Successful and unsuccessful individuals exist in every
ethnic group. How ethnic and social resources are put together for the exploitation of the domestic and global economy is a crucial matter. This chapter will demonstrate how on the one hand global influences become an important guide in directing local economic activities, while on the other hand,
local grounding is a necessary foundation for meeting the challenge of the
global markets.

To become grounded economically in Silicon Valley, the transnational has
four options. The first is to be employed as a scientist or engineer in a high-
tech company; second is to be an entrepreneur; the third is for the transnational, after obtaining a green card or U.S. citizenship, to return to China or
Taiwan to start a company; and the fourth is for the transnational to return to
China or Taiwan to work, and after succeeding in China or Taiwan, to
reestablish business or retire in America. Before explaining these methods of
establishing roots in America, a discussion of why so many Chinese study
engineering in the first place is necessary here.

WHY SO MANY ENGINEERS?

Practicality and employment opportunity are important factors for many Chinese students. Likewise, going to college is an important tool for social mobility. The science and engineering fields are seen as more practical than
other fields for one's career, especially in developing countries such as China
which always have a need for engineers to build the country's infrastructure.
One informant told me that he liked chemistry more than any subject. He actually wanted to study chemistry, but his parents directed him to study something more concrete.

I came from a very poor family in Hong Kong. When I was younger, I could not even go to regular school in Hong Kong. I could only go to evening school. After graduating from high school in Hong Kong, I got a scholarship to come to the University of Illinois to get a degree in electrical engineering. I always liked chemistry. But my father said that electrical engineering is better because I can find a job and get better pay. So, I studied electrical engineering. After Illinois, I went to Cal Tech for a PhD in the same field. (Informant M, interview with author, October 19, 2001)

This statement is not uncommon among many of the Chinese from Hong Kong, China, and Taiwan. Chinese parents always encourage their children to study in a field that offers good employment opportunities. There is a saying in China, "If you are good in engineering and science you won't have any fears making a living in different parts of the world." Some parents impress on their children that engineering is a sound field for any career. Even if their children want to do something else, the parents will insist that one needs to be an engineer first. In so doing, they say, one has something solid on which to fall back on, should other things not work out.

Another informant told me that family influence and language obstacles were reasons for his choice of a field:

Why are there so many Chinese in high tech? It is easy to answer this question. First is the influence of one's family. Parents tell their children to study something that will be easy to find employment in. Second is the language. It is easier to succeed in the area of science and technology as a foreign student. It does not require a high level of sophistication in English. One can compete in equal footing with white people. Third is the pay. It is quite good. (Informant C, interview with author, September 19, 2001)

There are also cultural reasons for one's choice of career. It has been a tradition in China since 1919 to emphasize science, technology, and democracy. The May Fourth Movement (1919) was a revitalization movement to modernize and strengthen China, and it pushed the young Chinese to champion science and technology. This goal of energizing China through science was embraced by both the Chinese and Kuomintang governments. In both PRC and Taiwan, the best students from high school go on to study science. The second-best study the arts and literature. Understandably then, there is more prestige in studying science than in studying literature or law. Furthermore, the Communist Party instills in students the belief that science and technology are important for the modernization of mainland China. During the Cultural Revolution, which lasted from the 1960s to the 1970s, students learned from experience that literature and liberal arts were not practical, and could even be dangerous. Many outspoken intellectuals in the field of the liberal arts were sent to labor camps and persecuted because of their published works or political positions. It was safer to be a scientist because scientists and engineers generally do not deal with ideology. Chinese students who wanted to come to American universities also found that it was easier to do so when they were better prepared in science, especially since in these fields there was less of an emphasis on English ability. And U.S. universities accepted and continue to accept engineering and physical science students from China since many PhD programs in American universities are not able to recruit enough American students. In fact, some American PhD programs have students only from foreign countries. Those foreign students graduating with PhDs in America can easily find jobs, and therefore they have an opportunity to stay in the United States permanently. Thus, there are historical, cultural, and political factors in a Chinese student's selection of his or her course of study and occupation.

TO BE AN ENGINEER OR TO BE AN ENTREPRENEUR?

Most of the Chinese in Silicon Valley are high-tech workers or professionals. Only a minority are entrepreneurs. There is a great deal of confusion about the term *entrepreneur*. Some use it loosely and refer to all high-tech engineers as *entrepreneurs* (Saxenian 1999), while others use the term to refer only to employers and business administrators. But the entrepreneur is a risk-taker and an initiator of profit-making activities (Schumpeter 1961), not merely a business administrator who does business accounting and paperwork. Not every Chinese engineer is an entrepreneur and to call them such is a misnomer.

From my research, I found that 90 percent of the high-tech Chinese in Silicon Valley are not entrepreneurs at all. In generational terms, the first generation has more interest in entrepreneurship. The second- and third-generation Chinese American is not anxious to start a business. According to my informants, the American-born Chinese have seen from their parents' experience how difficult it was to start and maintain a business. The second- and third-generation Chinese Americans also start from a different economic platform and can obtain better employment than their parents. Even though their parents are entrepreneurs, second- and third-generation Chinese Americans may not want to take over the family business. This has always been a problem for Chinese ethnic entrepreneurship (Wong, McReynolds, and Wong 1992; B. Wong 1998a, 1998b). Despite this generational trend, many first-generation Chinese told me that they, in fact, have no interest in starting their own businesses. This should not be confused with a lack of initiative to get ahead. In fact, all of them seek economic and social mobility. They are interested in improving their working conditions and in increasing their financial reward. In order to do so, they may move from firm to firm, testing out new territories and new opportunities. They consider issues like salary, benefits, stock options, and favorable working conditions that involve schedule, holidays, and corporate culture. I asked one hundred engineers, *Ni shi chuang ye jia ma?* (Are you an entrepreneur?). Ninety percent of them said, No. When asked if they wanted to be entrepreneurs, the majority of them (75 percent) again said, No. The remaining 25 percent said they are thinking about being entrepreneurs, and of these, 25 percent said they would like to be entrepreneurs if there were opportunities.

Although most start-up Chinese companies are run by the Chinese from Taiwan, there are more Chinese from mainland China who are interested in starting up companies. At the time of this study, these mainland Chinese engineers had not yet started businesses, but according to my informants, many of them would start their companies in the future. One informant said:

> The mainland Chinese engineers are still new to this country. As they accumulate more savings, they will do the same as the Taiwanese engineers. They will be entrepreneurs. Essentially, their career path is the same as the Taiwanese engineers: First, find employment [*da gong*]. They will be entrepreneurs and investors later. In recent years, there are more mainland Chinese engineers than Taiwanese engineers in Silicon Valley. So, proportionally, there will be more mainland Chinese entrepreneurs from this pool. They want to get rich [*da men ye you zhuang qing*—the house also has rich youth]. (Informant DL, interview with author, February 7, 2002)

Another informant qualified the above statement by saying that mainland Chinese who are younger than forty-five are more entrepreneurial than older ones.

> People who are born after 1980 were influenced more by the recent economic reform in China. "To get rich is glorious" [*fa cai guang rong*] is an ideology among the young Chinese. Besides, many Chinese are rich now. They can get investors easily. The Chinese engineers in Silicon Valley can go back to China to raise money. If they have an innovative idea and figure out the market needs, they will try to be entrepreneurs. They need time to figure out what they can do. You will see in the next several years that the mainland Chinese entrepreneurs will outnumber those from Taiwan. (Informant L, interview with author, February 7, 2002)

According to this informant, the number of Taiwanese Chinese engineers in the United States has reached saturation. Those who are qualified and want to come to the United States have already. They started migrating to the United States in the 1960s and their pool was smaller. Whereas mainland China has been producing many engineers, who only started to come to the United States after the 1980s. Furthermore, many companies in Silicon Valley target mainland Chinese as potential candidates because they are less expensive to hire. Chinese universities have turned out a large number of excellent computer specialists in recent years.

WHY START A BUSINESS IN SILICON VALLEY?

Starting a company in Silicon Valley requires money, time, and commitment. It is done not just for financial gain; it is also an indication that one wants to settle in the community permanently. This is particularly so among new immigrants. After they have been in Silicon Valley for awhile, and if they plan to stay in the United States, they will take certain decisive steps like purchasing a house, establishing a business, or continuing their employment in the United States. There is even a Chinese saying, "It is human nature to live comfortably in a house and happily establish an enterprise" (*an ju le ye*). One informant told me that to be successful and to be respected in America one must own a business:

> I worked for a number of years for a big company after I got my PhD. From working and living in America, I learned that I could teach in a university and publish a number of books. It would be a comfortable life for me. But this will not earn me much respect in society. I would be known among my colleagues and in the university circle. I will not be respected by my fellow men and American society. I notice that if you are a Ford, a Rockefeller or a successful entrepreneur, and if you have a business and contribute employment to the community, you will be somebody. Since I left China, I wanted to be successful in the United States, I decided that I need to start a company. After I have a successful business and contributed to society by producing a useful product, hiring employees and giving much to charity, I would be respected by the community. (Informant Y, interview with author, March 27, 2001)

Another Chinese CEO echoed this sentiment. He said that having a successful company that provided others with employment would earn him respect in American society. He said he started first as an engineer, and then later became an entrepreneur. With his financial success, he was able to contribute much to the community. Now he is an important member of the board of regents of the University of California system. Thus, entrepreneurship has helped him to establish a position in the community. He is totally rooted in America. For immigrants, one's business is thus a means to establish roots.

David Lam of Lam Research told me that there are more first-generation Chinese than American-born Chinese interested in becoming entrepreneurs:

> There are three groups of Chinese: Hong Kong, Taiwan and mainland Chinese. Among those who run start-up companies, the foreign-born Chinese are more numerous than the local-born Chinese. Entrepreneurship requires risk-taking. Immigrants work hard and are willing to take more risk. Chinese immigrants also want to achieve social mobility through the accumulation of wealth by establishing businesses. (Dr. David Lam, interview with author, September 19, 2001)

Another reason for starting a firm is to fight the glass ceiling. Many of my informants as well as other researchers insist that the glass ceiling exists because

Chinese immigrant engineers are often bypassed for promotion. Discrimination also exists in another form: receiving less pay for doing the same job. Ana Lee Saxenian (1999) has found similar practices. But the glass ceiling phenomenon was more prevalent in the 1990s than it is in the 2000s. This is due presumably to a better understanding of the Chinese as well as to the recognition that it is not good business practice to discriminate against people on the basis of race or ethnicity. This is particularly the case in Silicon Valley where a performance meritocracy has now become the norm. By doing otherwise, a good company may lose its most talented workers. Mr. Chun Xia is an example.

> After I graduated from the University of Illinois, I started to work for a company. The salary was quite good. However, as a foreign-born, you always feel the glass ceiling. After working for a while, I thought about opening my own company. (Zhang 2000, 137)

When people become their own boss, they feel that they do not have to put up with prejudice. One informant told me that it made no sense to him when he had to train someone who was inferior to him and who would be promoted above him. Such practices create a serious morale problem. Furthermore, in Silicon Valley it is difficult to obtain and keep the best talent. And it is costly for a company to hire headhunters to replace continuously departing workers. The point here is clear: discrimination and a glass ceiling forced some of the Chinese in Silicon Valley to resort to starting their own businesses or look for another job.

Some of my informants attributed their entrepreneurial undertakings to the valley itself because it already has many entrepreneurs and so it encourages entrepreneurship. Take Ms. Liu for example. She came from Taiwan to study at the State University of New York, Stony Brook. After graduation, she got a job with NYNEX Corporation and later worked for MARCORP. When she arrived in Silicon Valley, she said she was so inspired by the environment that she thought about creating a start-up company of her own:

> When I worked for large corporations elsewhere, I never thought about starting up any company. Only after I came to Silicon Valley, and influenced by the environment, I changed my mind. I told myself, "Chinese can start businesses too." (*Sing Tao Daily* September 28, 2001, p. 7)

According to Ms. Liu, entrepreneurship fits a certain personality. For people who want flexibility, mobility, and to be their own bosses, start-up companies are good for them. In a similar vein, the founder of WebEx, a company that specializes in Internet conferences, had this to say:

> Entrepreneurship needs a special personality. I worked for a number of good companies and made quite a bit of money. But I was restless and not satisfied.

I did not want to teach at the university or to work quietly as a researcher. (Zhang 2000, 137)

The CEO of RivalWatch, a provider of business information, made a similar comment:

> To found a company is hard. I think an entrepreneur likes the stimulation of founding a business and making money. You need to have a certain risk-taking personality. Working as an engineer brings in money too. From a certain vantage point, entrepreneurs enjoy more material success. But they work for it. As for me, I have to work from day to night. I finish my work at 11 pm every night. If I return early at 8 pm, my wife would ask me, "Are you feeling sick today?" (Zhang 2000, 137)

Some of these entrepreneurs are motivated by the financial success of starting their own business. Wu Fu Chen, founder of more than fourteen high-tech companies is currently a partner of Acorn Campus, a venture capital corporation in Cupertino. He is from Taiwan, and studied electrical engineering at the University of Florida and the University of California, Berkeley. In 1976 he got a position as a technical support engineer in a high-tech company on Market Street in San Francisco. When he worked there, he noticed that the boss came to work late everyday. Wu Fu Chen's boss would come in at ten and would principally pick up messages and return phone calls. After one, his boss would leave, and only return to the office at about three. Again, he would pick up messages and return phone calls. That was more or less the life of Mr. Chen's boss. Wu Fu Chen also noticed that all the well-dressed salespeople made a lot of money but seldom stayed in the office. From these observations, he got an idea:

> The "closer you are to the money, the more opportunity there is for you to make money." From that moment on, I decided that I needed to learn how to become the head and move to the front office. All these people were not working as hard as I was, yet they made a lot of money from commissions. This is the same with my boss. I should be my own boss! (Wu Fu Chen, interview with author, Nov 6, 2001)

Mr. Chester Wang, also of Acorn Campus, told me that talented Taiwanese engineers and scientists wanted to achieve financial success. These highly educated individuals wanted to show their fellow countrymen that they could succeed. A saying popular among the Taiwanese Chinese engineers is *ning wei ji tao bu wei niu hou* (I'd rather be the beak of the chicken than the behind of a cow). To translate loosely, it means the importance of being at the top of a small business rather than at the bottom of a large one.

One reason why some Chinese engineers in Silicon Valley want to start their own business is the lack of stability in their employment. Economic cycles and the vicissitudes of a company's fortunes may cause the layoff of employees. Informants told me that they had had to learn this the hard way. For instance, Mr. Lee was trained as an engineer, but now he is the CEO of three companies. One of his companies deals with the export of a high-tech component for X-ray machines, one is a restaurant, and the third is a lighting company. When I asked him what motivated him to change from an engineer to an entrepreneur, he said:

> I graduated from Beijing University. I came to the U.S. in the '80s and got my advanced training in engineering in Boston. After graduation, I worked as an engineer for a number of years. I was laid off three times. Now I am a CEO of three companies doing business not related to my training at all. Why did I change my job? I was forced to do so. I did not plan it that way. After getting laid off three times I decided that I needed to control my destiny and use my abilities to do something else. (Mr. Lee, interview with author, September 29, 2001)

Opportunity is another reason why an entrepreneur starts a firm. Another of my informants (Mr. B) told me that he just could not resist the opportunity to start his own business. He started an export trade company because he had an old friend in China who was trading. His friend told him, "When you start your export company, I will join you. I have all the connections and I will be your distributor." With that promise, Mr. B started his firm. He told me that it was a business deal depending entirely on *xin yong* (trust). There was only a verbal agreement. No written contract was made, and at the time of our interview they have been doing business for five years. Using the money made from this business, he started another business in Silicon Valley. When I asked him why he started another business, he told me it was the American way of life. He said that after one has made a lot of money, one has to look for business deductions. Looking for tax advantages, he started his second business. Mr. B's experience is unique in a sense. However, opportunity can surely be a factor in the launching of a new business.

Working for someone requires putting up with inconveniences, and with regard to the glass ceiling effect, some Chinese engineers feel that the only way out of discriminatory treatment is to start a firm of their own. It should not be surprising then that some Chinese engineers constantly talk about starting up their own business. And with good reason. In 1999 there were 2,008 companies run by Chinese CEOs (*San Jose Mercury News* October 18, 1999). And in the year 2000, more such firms were established. Informants have told me that some of these firms went out of business but others continued. According to AnaLee Saxenian, the Chinese owned and controlled 2,472 companies in 2002 (personal communication, March 15, 2002), and as of this writing (2005), my informants estimate that the number of high-tech firms run by the Chinese is between 2,500 and 3,000. But as previously stated, a common denominator among all the entrepreneurs whom I interviewed was that they wanted to create a sound economic foundation so that they and their families could settle in America permanently and comfortably. Furthermore, founding a company earned these founders prestige in and the recognition of their local communities.

Starting Up—Capital Formation

Where do they get the initial capital to start a business? There are several avenues for obtaining financing. One is through personal or family savings. If a husband and a wife work, they may be able to accumulate enough money, especially those who have stock options, since they can sell their stock when they leave their jobs. In the past five years, many husband and wife teams have accumulated resources in this manner. Others pool their resources among relatives. From their immediate family, extended family, in-laws, and kin, entrepreneurs may get enough to start a mom-and-pop business in software or computer products. However, this kind of business is quite rare. It is also small in size. In the high-tech business, most firms require a huge amount of start-up capital, which is beyond the means of a single family.

It is possible, however, to have friends and family who contribute the needed start-up seed money. David Lam of Lam Research is an example. After working for a number of companies in Silicon Valley, he decided to start one of his own. During the first year of his company's operation, he had fifteen people working for him. In the second year, he had fifteen to twenty people. Now, twenty years later, the company has about seven thousand employees. It started out as a private company in 1980, went public in 1984, and now is a global company. But when he first started he raised the needed capital only from personal savings and his family.

> When I started my company, my mother was the investor. She just trusted me. She did not know what I was doing but she did not care either. My savings together with her money was the only seed money. High-tech business differs from other Chinese ethnic businesses such as restaurants and gift shops. You need a large sum of money. You need to have a sound business plan, then go to raise money from venture capitalists. In my time, there were not many venture capital companies in Silicon Valley. I had to go to San Francisco to make business presentation to venture capitalists and they eventually funded my factory. (Dr. David Lam, interview with author, September 19, 2001)

When Wu Fu Chen started his first company, Communication Equipment Corporation, in 1986, he pooled seed money from his savings and the savings of his partners. He said:

> When I first started my company I had little money. The seed money came from savings. Each of the four engineers worked for free, without salary for a year.

We lived on money saved previously. Each had about forty thousand dollars. That was it! A year later, I went to venture capitalists. They saw my work and my products and were happy to loan us the money to expand. We sold the company later for seven million dollars. (Wu Fu Chen, interview with author, November 6, 2002)

Though at an initial stage seed money may come from classmates, friends, and kinsmen, a business eventually needs the support of venture capitalists. Unlike Chinese entrepreneurs in enclave businesses where most of the financing comes from their families, the Silicon Valley Chinese often get their financing from outside sources. The most important way of obtaining such financing is from venture capitalists. (There are both Chinese and American venture capitalists, and many of them are important financiers.) Some entrepreneurs go to Taiwan to raise money from their friends and relatives or to raise money from Taiwanese venture capitalists. Others go to Hong Kong and mainland China to raise money. In the past, many entrepreneurs in Silicon Valley went to Sand Hill Road of Palo Alto where most of the venture capital companies in the valley were located. Recently, venture capitalist firms have migrated to Menlo Park, San Jose, Cupertino, and San Francisco. When approaching venture capitalists the entrepreneur needs a workable business plan and connections. Again, previous friendship and business connections help.

When the company is doing well, it can then go public. Transforming from a private firm to a public firm often indicates success. With public investors on board, the company may grow rapidly; it may even be purchased and merged with another company. When that occurs, the original owner may choose to retain or liquidate his shares, and the money made from selling these shares can be used to start another company. That explains why successful Chinese entrepreneurs often establish a series of firms. In so doing, they expand their fortunes and maximize their returns quickly. This is in fact a recent phenomenon among some start-up companies. One Chinese entrepreneur told me that the best thing for the owners of a start-up firm to do is to find a buyer and sell their firm. When I asked why such a strategy was pursued, he answered:

After you have started a successful company, you should find a buyer and sell it. After you sell it you start another one. There are several advantages of doing so. One is to minimize risk. When the company is growing, there is a certain amount of risk. Selling it neutralizes your personal risk. Second, when the company is growing, you can sell it with profit. Third is the cash liquidity. After you sell it, you have cash again to start a new one. For the above three reasons, I have been advocating this strategy: after your company becomes successful, find a buyer and sell it. I have been giving talks on this topic in different professional associations in Silicon Valley. (Informant L, interview with author, September 19, 2001)

Taiwanese venture capitalists have supported several Chinese firms in Silicon Valley. Likewise, there are American venture capitalists supporting Taiwan companies. And now other venture capitalists from China and Southeast Asian support some of the valley's start-up companies. Instrumental in the activities of these venture capitalists are Chinese entrepreneurs in the financial field. These Chinese financiers are bilingual and bicultural Chinese who are familiar with both Chinese and American culture. Thus, paradoxically, the globalization of American business sometimes requires a certain degree of knowledge of the Chinese culture and language.

TYPES OF FIRMS

Family Firms

Family firms are uncommon in Silicon Valley. These are most often small computer supply companies, software facilities, and other retail or wholesale businesses. Such family firms represent an early stage of development and many end up as public corporations. In Silicon Valley many of these small firms were started as husband-and-wife companies. For example, Eva Chen was originally a student in Taiwan's Cheng Chi University where she studied international management. When Ms. Chen was a student, she was a teacher's assistant in the computer center because she was a computer expert. Later she decided to study management information systems. She met her husband in the university and after marrying, she and her husband, Daniel Chiang, came to the United States together to study at the University of Texas in Dallas. Her husband got a master's degree in political economy while she got a master's degree in both international management and management information systems (Teng 1998).

After graduation, both Eva and Daniel returned to Taiwan. Daniel got a job with the government in the Department of Economics and Eva worked for Acer. Later, she left Acer and worked with her sisters-in-law at their company that was called Trend Micro Devices. In 1991, Daniel decided to join the company, making it a family business. The initial investors in this company were relatives and family members. Eva remarked, "Nobody believed in the antivirus software business except my own family who had confidence in me." Her family not only provided money, technical resources, and labor, it also provided emotional support (Teng 1998, 359).

In order to be close to the market, this husband-and-wife team decided to immigrate to the United States. Eva and Daniel settled in Silicon Valley in 1995, and their antivirus products have been quite successful, being produced in eighteen different languages. The company has continued to be successful (Teng 1998, 359).

In 1987 in Fremont, California, to take another example, Marcel Liang and Christine Liang started Asia Source, a wholesaler of computer products. (Marcel got his MBA from U.W. Emphoria State University. Christine got an accounting degree from Der Min Commercial College in Taiwan.) Marcel and Christine entered the computer business mainly due to the fact that Christine's brother had already founded ViewSonic, a company specializing in surveillance systems. At the beginning, their company sold ViewSonic products and Christine's brother helped them find resources, thus benefiting both companies (Teng 1998, 414).

A family business can also be the foundation for a large enterprise, such an enterprise as Central Computer Systems. This company started in 1986 as a family business, but had its beginning in a garage where Mr. Saul Yeung, the company's founder, fixed computers for his friends as a hobby. Mr. Yeung had been a political science major working toward his PhD at the University of California, Berkeley. He never finished his degree, becoming an entrepreneur instead, by importing computer hardware from Taiwan and distributing it across the Untied States. In 1990, this business was incorporated under the name Central Computer Systems, with both wholesale and retail operations. The company currently has three locations: a headquarters in Santa Clara, and branches in San Francisco and Newark, California. The company continues to import computer hardware from Taiwan, but it is no longer just a family business.

Partnerships with Friends and Colleagues

After the publication of Eric Wolf's article "Kinship, Friendship and Patron-Client Relations in Complex Societies" (1966), the study of friendship in complex societies gained momentum In contemporary societies, many immigrants have to depend on friendship rather than their extended families due to the fact that they cannot migrate to a new country with their whole family. These immigrants will then depend on friends and colleagues, people they've met at school or worked and socialized with, in order to form close personal social networks. As mentioned above, in the high-tech world in Silicon Valley it is quite common for people who work in the same firm to have also graduated from the same alma mater in the United States, Taiwan, or China. Often employers prefer to save money by hiring through these social networks rather than paying recruiters (headhunters). Not only are headhunters are expensive (it is not uncommon for an employer to pay twenty thousand dollars in fees to these recruiters for a single new employee), but sometimes network hiring will ensure the quality of a new employee. With network hiring and the personal knowledge thereby gained of an individual, according to some entrepreneurs, there is a good likelihood that the employer will find a suitable individual. This is not unique among the Chinese in Silicon Valley. Many American firms do the same. However, from interviewing informants in Silicon Valley I have learned that network hiring has its defects. First, it may discourage productivity of the work force because existing workers may think that their talents and contributions are not being recognized. Second, when someone has been hired in this way it is difficult to get rid of them if they cannot do their job, especially when they are related by friendship or other personal relationships to other employees of the company.

In many larger firms, increasingly, there is a tendency to hire employees through an in-house professional staff. However in smaller firms, due to the exorbitant expense this may incur, and due also to the risk of not getting the right person, network hiring is preferred. As I have mentioned, employees are sometimes given bonuses if they can refer new workers to their companies. "If you know someone who can meet the needs of the company and can work with our people, let us know." This is a common instruction given to employees. Network hiring is particularly a necessity when the labor market is tight during peak employment. During the year 2000, for example, it was extremely difficult for many companies to get qualified professionals. There was even a bidding war going on in order to get the right individuals. At such times an employer may then have to use friendship to persuade former friends and colleagues to come on board.

In Silicon Valley there is another interesting phenomenon. Friendship often becomes the basis of many start-up companies, and former friends then become business partners. The firms they create may be registered as corporations, but they are often staffed and run like partnerships. Such partnership firms often turn out to be important in this era of economic globalization. Instead of using one set of social networks for economic globalization, these firms already have several sets of personal social networks to use in linking up resources in different parts of the world. The following examples show how friendships can play a pivotal role in the economic globalization of Silicon Valley.

In the 1980s a husband-and-wife team, Tse and Yang, and their colleague Ga Wing Wu started WYSE (its name was taken from their three family names). The company made PC terminals, and it grew rapidly and was acquired by a Taiwan conglomerate in the 1990s. Tse and Wu are from Hong Kong, and so they had (and have) Hong Kong and China connections. Yang is from Taiwan, and he has connections in Taiwan. In the 1990s the company had three thousand employees in Taiwan producing terminals and other computer equipment like surveillance systems. WYSE today is a global company with headquarters in San Jose, California, and Hsin-chu, Taiwan, and it is publicly traded on the over-the-counter market in Taiwan. This husband and wife team also founded other businesses in Hong Kong and mainland China (Teng 1998, 209).

Paul Huang and his colleagues founded two companies, ECAD and PiE, among a number of others. Paul received his BS in physics and an MS in electronics from Jiaotong University, Taiwan. Later he obtained his PhD in computer science from Santa Clara University. Paul was one of the first entrepreneurs in the electronic design automation business. PiE was acquired by NewSoft of Taiwan in the late 1990s.

Epic is rated one of the top fifty fastest growing companies in Silicon Valley. In 1995, it was rated eleventh, with business revenue reaching $50 million. It is a company specializing in Electronic Design Automation (EDA), and its founder, from Taiwan, is Sang Wang, a graduate in electrical engineering from Taiwan University. He also has an MS in physics from Ohio State University and a PhD in electrical engineering from Stanford University. He founded Epic with the help of a colleague (Teng 1998, 194).

David Tsang is another Taiwanese Chinese who, with the help of friends, founded Oak Technology. He attended high school in Japan and came to the United States in 1962 where he received a BS in electrical engineering from Brigham Young University. He also received an MS in the same field from Santa Clara University. His connections in Japan and Taiwan have helped him globalize his business in both countries. Oak Technology manufactures VGAs, DVDs, and CD-ROMs, and has a revenue of more than $248 million (Teng 1998).

Jerry Shaw-Yau Chang founded Clarent Corporation, also with the help of friends. Clarent specializes in voice and message systems, and its products are used by AT&T, NTT, and China Telecom. It is a company that has business connections worldwide. Chang was born in 1959 and studied science in Jiaotung University, Taiwan. After college he was exempted from military service because he was overweight by 2.5 kilograms. He came to Pennsylvania State University with a teaching assistantship. After graduating from Pennsylvania State with a PhD in 1984, he had only twenty dollars in his pocket, and he was desperate to find a job. He first worked for a company in Los Angeles, but his girlfriend did not like it. He then called up his Taiwanese classmates working in Silicon Valley. Through them, he got his first job working for Intel. Later, he branched out into voice technology, eventually founding Clarent in 1996. The company is headquartered in Redwood City and has offices in Asia, Europe, Latin America, and North America. It was through the introduction of his Taiwanese friends that Jerry Chang met the partners of Acorn campus, where he is now himself an investor assisting other entrepreneurs in Silicon Valley. He is one of those entrepreneurs who simultaneously think globally and act locally (Teng 1998).

Interethnic Business Cooperation

Jackson Hu graduated in 1971 with a BS in electrical engineering from Taiwan University. He got his MS and PhD from the University of Illinois,

Urbana-Champaign. He also received a MBA from Santa Clara University. Hu is competent in business and technology, and he has gone beyond his coethnic ties by cooperating with non-Chinese friends. With former colleagues from Zilog, Hu started a company called Verticom in 1983. It was a company producing graphic terminals. The company was later sold to Western Digital in 1989. In the same year, Hu teamed up with a Filipino friend, Dado Banatao (an engineer), and a Japanese friend, Ron Yara (a sales specialist), to start S3. This international team sold semiconductor products to Taiwan and Japan and was financed by venture capitalists from both countries. Becoming highly successful in 1995 (Teng 1998, 219), SE went public in 1997 (www.sc.uiuc.edu/whatsnew/newsletter/winter99).

In 1996 Hu left S3 to join former S3 colleagues who had founded SiRF (Si for silicon and RF for radio frequency), later becoming the company's president and CEO. SiRF specializes in the application of GPS (Global Positioning System) technology, a field with a high potential in consumer applications and the global market. Through his informal social networks, Jackson Hu has participated in both the social and economic activities Silicon Valley. Hu and his wife are also active in the Asian American Parent Association, which addresses educational issues in Silicon Valley's Asian American Community.

Finally, Gerry Yang and David Filo, two classmates from Stanford, founded Yahoo! Here again, friendship and a common interest led to economic success. The business began as a hobby and then developed into the globally branded online media company we all know and use. Gerry Yang came from Taiwan with his family at the age of ten, and he attended high school and university in the United States. He has BS and MS degrees in electrical engineering from Stanford. Both Yang and Filo were PhD students in electrical engineering when, in 1994, they received funding from the venture capital company, Sequoia. Their company, Yahoo!, went public in 1996, and by 2000 it had become a global network spanning twenty-four countries and available in twelve languages. The company's expected revenue for 2001, was $708 million dollars (http://docs.Yahoo!.com/info/investor/outlook.html).

Family, kin, colleagues, classmates, and friends are important for Chinese entrepreneurship. Among these, former classmates and colleagues have become indispensable. My informants make a special distinction between *tong xue* (classmates) and *tong shi* (colleagues and friends). Classmates and colleagues are friends or potential friends, and therefore they have some kinship quality. However, friends are not necessarily classmates or colleagues. Rarely would a Chinese businessperson start a business with someone with whom he or she didn't have a trusting relationship. This should not be interpreted to mean that non-Chinese are excluded from such partnerships. In fact, there are many interethnic firms that have been started by Chinese and their non-Chinese colleagues, companies such as Viador, established by Stan Wang from mainland China, that has been providing its customers with portal solutions since 1995 and has had more than 350 of the world's leading corporations and governments as its clients. Another example of interethnic cooperation is WebEx Interactive Global Network, which supports businesses with integrated data and voice and video conferencing, and was founded by Min Zhu, a Chinese entrepreneur, and Subra S. Iyar, an Indian engineer. WebEx has clients all over the world that use it to lower their travel costs through on-line meetings, seminars, and events.

In the social networks of the Chinese of Silicon Valley, foreigners can be insiders and partners. In fact, the social networks of the Chinese in Silicon Valley include Indians, white-Americans, Filipinos, Japanese, and others. This should dispel the myth that the Chinese accept only coethnic partners. It is a kind of interethnic cooperation that differs significantly from that in enclave Chinese businesses, where interethnic joint ventures are not common.

OTHER ADAPTIVE STRATEGIES

What of the other 90 percent of the Chinese engineers in Silicon Valley? Are they happy with their jobs? Some still keep changing their jobs with the hope they can reap a greater financial reward, but this is not always a successful strategy. For instance, there is the case of an engineer who is known to have changed jobs ten times in six years. As it turned out, however, his last job was not as good as his first job in terms of working conditions. He found out that the corporate culture of his latest company was impersonal, and that his coworkers were extremely individualistic and competitive. He then tried very hard to return to one of his previous jobs. His story is not unique: other Chinese engineers in Silicon Valley constantly try to improve their destiny and shape their own world.

Another high-tech engineer became a headhunter for computer companies. He had accumulated plenty of experience by working for many high-tech companies, and with his knowledge of the field of engineering, he was well-versed in the complexity and diversity of engineering technology. He knew exactly what kinds of engineers and what kinds of technical work were in demand. He was very successful in his talent search company until the economic downtown, when he joked that, in such a poor economy, a headhunter can't even find himself a job.

Some engineers become realtors. Recognizing the shortage of housing in Silicon Valley in the past ten years, these engineers have decided that there is more money to be made in real estate rather than in computers. In real estate they also don't have to deal with a glass-ceiling, long working hours, and the other complicated technical and personnel issues of the high-tech industry.

TWO KINDS OF ENTREPRENEURSHIP: CHINESE AND AMERICAN

The difference in the entrepreneurial styles of the Chinese and American cultures is reflected in the high-tech industry. Culture affects economic activities in general and high-tech entrepreneurship in particular. Chinese entrepreneurial pursuits can be characterized by (1) an emphasis on technology; (2) an emphasis on personalism, (or *renqing wei*—literally, human feeling); (3) hard work; (4) group orientation; (5) the use of *guanxi*; and (6) hierarchy. These traits have both positive and negative effects. I must also emphasize that there are Chinese entrepreneurial pursuits that may not have any of the above characteristics. In every culture, there is individual variation. In a general way, however, Chinese high-tech companies are likely to have the above six characteristics.

All the entrepreneurs that I interviewed said that they wanted to hire the employee who was the best in his or her field. They wanted to get the latest technology from the most competent candidates. Excellence in "domain knowledge" is important in technological competition. However, domain knowledge in itself is not sufficient. Potential employees may be geniuses in technology but socially idiosyncratic. Many Chinese high-tech companies realize that an individualistic and idiosyncratic person may not work well in a team. Here is a typical statement from a Chinese entrepreneur:

> Every time when I emphasized only technology and resume, I inevitably made a mistake. It happened every time. Now I learned how to identify people who can work as a team. Technology is not the only thing. I would like to have a combination of desirable traits in which technology is a component. (Informant L, interview with author, September 19, 2001)

Many Chinese look for the attribute of *renqing wei* (personalism). Chinese engineers as well as employers emphasize this value. To be humane, in the context of the Chinese, means to have *renqing wei* and flexibility. The value of *renqing wei* implies that its possessor is considerate about the feeling of other human beings and that they are, in Chinese terms, reasonable. The downside of this is what is called blind-siding. When the virtue of *renqing wei* is overemphasized, performance may not be recognized.

The hardworking habits of the Chinese are recognized in Silicon Valley. All the Chinese CEOs told me that the good thing about hiring Chinese is that they will work hard, day and night, putting in easily a twelve-hour day. The problem is burnout. Once overworked, the Chinese worker, like any other, becomes ineffective. Competent managers need to recognize the symptoms of burnout. Some CEOs told me that the trick is to prevent burnout by telling an overworked engineer to take a vacation or to stay home for a number of days.

Although the use of social networks for business is also a characteristic of American culture, the difference in its use in Chinese culture lies in degree and intensity. It is almost impossible, for instance, to conduct business deals with companies in China without *guanxi*. The use of *guanxi* is extremely common in employment, globalization, business expansion, and product distribution. Without *guanxi*, a company may not be able to get financing or contracts, or it may not be able to get its computers or cell phones distributed in the Chinese market. However, *guanxi* is not totally exclusive. It must be cultivated, developed, expanded, and maintained. As mentioned earlier, Chinese social networks are open to outsiders. A non-Chinese American can develop *guanxi* with a Chinese businessperson through their mutual friends or classmates. Sometimes a non-Chinese person and a Chinese colleague will get along well and become friends. The two may then enlarge their friendship circles to include other individuals who have common tastes and common interests. Suffice it to say that the Chinese like to interact with people who have *guanxi* with them. This kind of informal social relationship survives in the modern world, with the result that *guanxi* is pivotal for business globalization in Asia.

Guanxi has its downside as well. While it is good to have the *guanxi* needed to get things done, this may encourage corrupt business practices. Some companies may use bribery to establish *guanxi*. And bribery can lead to other forms of business corruption: nepotism, favoritism, monopoly, price-fixing, exclusion of competition, lawlessness, or loss of morale.

Chinese companies tend to be hierarchical, and one must function within this system. Sometimes an individual opinion is not valued, and orders from superiors need to be carried out. As a result, the employees of a Chinese company do not openly express themselves. By comparison, white American companies are more institutionalized in hiring and in business operations. Working hours are more democratic. The company is more open, and it is governed by clear business procedures. In business meetings, employees are encouraged to speak out. Some Chinese engineers feel that working in an American company is a lot easier because of these clear rules; the expectations of both the employer and the employees are spelled out. However, others see in this type of company a lack of personalism and cultural sensitivity.

PROBLEMS OF AND BARRIERS TO
CHINESE ENTREPRENEURSHIP IN AMERICA

To start a company, even with high motivation and financial support, is no easy task. Many Chinese engineers and scientists in Silicon Valley have been trained as academics. A lack of experience in working in the American environment and unfamiliarity with American business practices makes it difficult for them to function effectively as entrepreneurs. These and other common

problems, including funding, management, transition, and teamwork problems are discussed in the following sections.

The Transition from Engineer to Entrepreneur

The first problem encountered by those who want to be entrepreneurs is
transition. Many of these Chinese engineers have worked as designers or
technical support or research scientists, and they are specialists in their own
field. But because of this, many have no experience in business management,
financing, and human resources. Some have never taken a course in marketing, accounting, or economics. They may be excellent in technology, but it is
not in business management. Those who succeed in being entrepreneurs are
aware of the problems that may be encountered. Several informants told me
that some engineers place too much emphasis on technology and ignore the
business side of their operation. They may, for example, encounter cash flow
problems because they neglect to pay attention to the issue of cash conser-
vation and sales. Others say that Chinese engineers have no idea about human resources, because many of them are not used to the American way of
social interaction. They do not know how to develop morale and solidarity
among employees. They do not know how to motivate engineers to work as
a team. Realizing these problems, entrepreneurs may take courses at a community college or they may return to school to get an MBA. Some learn from
colleagues and other business organizations or in special programs for business executives. Dr. David Lam told me that he went to a community college
in the South Bay to take courses like Economics 101 and Introduction to Business Management and Accounting. He also took courses organized by banks.
Dr. Milton Chang said that he learned a lot in a course organized for non-
MBAs by the Harvard Business School. He also learned a great deal from
hearing about the experiences of his classmates and peers. Mr. Wu Fu Chen,
the entrepreneur who started fourteen companies, told me that he went back
to graduate school to take courses toward an MBA. Dr. Chester Wang, a physi-
cist, told me that he went to San Jose State University to get an MBA.

Coordinating with Other Highly Trained People

Many Chinese entrepreneurs told me that while Chinese engineers are often highly trained and well-educated in their own field, it is not easy for them
to cooperate with other engineers who are also highly individualistic and
highly specialized. A good working relationship has to be cultivated. One informant said:

> I have to pay attention to my engineers. When they are trying to avoid me, I
> know there are some problems. You have to get them to talk. Every time upon

my return from my overseas tour of duty, I had to make the rounds to say hello to all my engineers to make small talk and tell them about my trip. It is important to keep communication channels open. (Informant WY, interview with author, September 26, 2001)

Education has a part to play in this, because American universities tend to encourage individualism. Professors want their students to excel in their fields. Many scientists and engineers are therefore expected to have special achievements, and each student in graduate school is trained to be a "hero" in a certain area. Students are not trained to cooperate with each other, nor are the aspects of teamwork emphasized. All of my informants said that teamwork is one of the most difficult issues in business. They said that in the high-tech business technology is of course important, but it is not enough. These entrepreneurs told me that business is about more than just technology. It is about people.

Organizing and developing a dedicated team is a challenge, but when culture enters the equation, it becomes even more complicated (Serrie 1996). How not to offend someone's ego when making a necessary correction is not easy. What the Chinese call *mianzi* (face) is a very important value in Chinese culture. It is essential to not cause someone the "loss of face." One has to give face to others by not openly embarrassing someone else in public. One informant told me that in the Chinese companies that he coached, he emphasized the following distinction:

> When I gave training courses to my Chinese business managers and entrepreneurs, I always told them to separate the issue of business from people. When we deal with issues related to business, we need to treat them in a business-like manner. When we attack certain business issues, we are not attacking the person. Business practices and procedures should not be confused with friendship issues. How to separate the issue of face from business procedure is difficult sometimes. But we need to separate them. *Dui shi bu dui ren* [things and people] need to be differentiated. (Informant CW, interview with author, October 24, 2001)

Communication Problems

Many Chinese companies hire non-Chinese Americans or American-born Chinese to staff their middle management positions. Since these employees are native speakers of English, it is believed that they are more suitable to staff positions in PR and to head sales departments. They are also made presidents of external affairs and are assigned to positions that require communication skills. Informants told me that often Chinese engineers from mainland China or Taiwan require more training in their English skills and a greater knowledge of American culture. They told me that there is one difference between Chinese and Indian engineers: English. Indian engineers go to English-speaking schools from childhood, whereas the Chinese do not learn to speak English until they come to America for graduate training. One solution to this problem is more training. CEOs or company heads have realized the importance of this, and they have begun sending their Chinese engineers to English schools. Some Chinese companies in fact have English tutorial programs for their employees. Others pay their employees to attend English classes on company premises. In addition to the language barrier, there is also a difference in *biao da fang fa bu yi yang* (communication style). Chinese informants told me that Americans are more direct and frank; the Chinese more indirect and subtle. Some Chinese immigrants have learned how to deal with these differences. But newcomers may not be able to do so initially. Given enough time, both parties will learn and come to understand each other. Both Chinese and American colleagues have room to learn. Multiculturalism is thus a necessity in the multiethnic workplace.

Name Recognition

When a start-up company comes into existence, its name may not be well recognized. This lack of name recognition may make it difficult for the company to attract talented Chinese engineers, who often prefer to work for an established company whose name is well recognized like HP, IBM, Applied Materials, Intel, or Fairchild. Many Chinese start-up companies are small and without an established reputation, and may not be able to attract the most talented Chinese engineers in the United States. Therefore, some Chinese entrepreneurs will go to mainland China to recruit the talent they need.

Maintenance of a Stable Workforce

The maintenance of a stable workforce is a common problem for many companies, especially during peak hiring seasons when every company is looking for good people. And when jobs become plentiful during downturns in the economic cycle, many Chinese start-up companies again find it difficult to maintain their workforce. During peak hiring seasons, employees are enticed by headhunters who offer them attractive salaries and benefits. Also, many Chinese companies do not have stock options. As a consequence, these companies may lose employees to the companies that do offer stock options. Other Chinese companies do not have the resources needed to fix their employees' complicated visa problems. Of course, not all companies have problems of employee retention. Some employees told me that they preferred to work for Chinese companies because of the ease of communication and because of their familiarity with the Chinese mode of operation. They felt that Chinese companies were more personable and flexible. Chinese companies allowed their employers to go home for special Chinese celebrations like the Chinese New Year, and they did not fire people easily; some bosses in fact would make overworked employees go on vacation with pay.

Flexibility is an important consideration for many employees. Some work until three then go home to take care of their children. This is particularly the case for the female engineers. Some are allowed to have a sliding schedule. When one starts at seven, he or she can go home at four. Other employees start at four and finish at eleven. It is interesting to see that even in this field, people desire flexibility at work. This preference resembles the values of "low-tech" garment factory workers in New York City (B. Wong 1986).

There is also the element of trust. Employees are trusted with their own schedule. Some engineers told me that sometimes they work twelve hours a day and sometimes four hours a day. It all depended on their projects. Employers do not count how they spent each minute. Having confidence and trust in employees also encourages commitment and loyalty on the part of the engineers, who feel that they are being treated as mature and responsible people. Many Chinese engineers like this aspect of the personal trust displayed by most Chinese employers.

There is another advantage for Chinese employers who have Chinese employees. All of the entrepreneurs that I interviewed told me that their Chinese employees always work hard. They always give themselves 100 percent and work long hours. However, these employees also want to be appreciated. If they feel that their hard work is not appreciated, they leave. The values of *kan chin* or *ganqing* (sentiment) and *yee chi* or *yiqi* (righteousness) are sometimes verbalized. Employers who do not show appreciation for their employees are said to be lacking *ren qing*. This term is most often used by Cantonese speakers. Thus, the influence of Chinese culture in the Chinese high-tech companies is palpable. Traditions, cultural values, and customs still exist in the modern high-tech industry.

I should note here that one of the extraordinary advantages of having Chinese employees is in the area of globalization. Chinese engineers, scientists, or business managers who are bilingual and who have intimate local knowledge and *guanxi* in China, Hong Kong, or Taiwan are extremely valuable as players in any company's globalization projects in Asia. They can be sent to China or Asia as troubleshooters of technological or personnel problems. Knowing a culture and language can help an employee perform certain tasks more efficiently, thus saving time and money for the company.

RETURN MIGRATION

Since 1978, more than 320,000 mainland Chinese have gone abroad to study in more than 103 countries (*Zhongguo Daily–China Press* May 14, 2000), the majority going to the United States. In the past, less than half of these immigrants returned to China, but recently (from 1998 to 2001), many of them began returning to China. According to the *Xinhua* News Agency, the number of students who have returned to China has increased by 13 percent annually (*Zhongguo Daily* May 14, 2000). In 1999 alone, mainland Chinese students from different parts of the world returned to China to set up more than three thousand scientific and high-tech companies (*San Francisco Chronicle* January 2, 2002).

Why do these Chinese return to work in Asia? One of the reasons is that globalization has created employment opportunities for Chinese Americans. Another reason was the slow job market during the recent recessions in the United States. A third reason is the glass ceiling of U.S. corporations that prohibits the upward mobility of the Chinese in Silicon Valley (*Wall Street Journal* March 7, 2003). The movement of these former immigrants does not follow the direction prescribed by globalization theorists like Andre Frank (1967) and Immanuel Wallerstein (1989). People and goods, as indicated in this chapter, flow in a bidirectional or circular way (Rouse 1996).

GLOBALIZATION AND NEW ECONOMIC OPPORTUNITIES

When economic spheres extend beyond traditional national boundaries, economic opportunities become enlarged as well. Not only do Chinese engineers of Silicon Valley return to the other side of the Pacific, but an excess of talent in China will come to fill market gaps or shortage areas in Silicon Valley. Globalization can assist employment in both the United States and China, enlarging investment opportunities

The success stories of Silicon Valley have created envy among many nations. Both European and Asian nations would like to have their own Silicon Valleys. Many of them would like to recruit the valley's talented engineers. Malaysia's Multimedia Super Corridor, Hong Kong's Cyberport, and Beijing's Zhong Guan Chuan are just a few examples of would-be Silicon Valleys. India, South Korea, Taiwan, Ireland, the Netherlands, and others are trying to build the same sort of high-tech regions that will be able to jump-start their national economies.

Taiwan's Hsinchu Industrial Park has come closest to California's Silicon Valley, and India is fast setting up alliances with U.S. partners. China is also anxious to set up Internet companies. It is estimated that the number of Internet users in Asia, outside of Japan, grew from 8 million in 1997 to 79 million in 2003. This represents nearly tenfold growth (*San Francisco Examiner* November 19, 2000, B1).

When the U.S. economic downturn was hitting hard in 2001, many cities and provinces in mainland China attempted to seize the advantage and lure high-tech professionals from Silicon Valley. On November 28, 2001, at a job fair in Silicon Valley, more than one hundred representatives from seventeen provinces and the national government of China sought candidates for eight hundred positions (*Sing Tao Daily* November 30, 2001, C12). Because China had just been admitted to the WTO and was positioned to develop a global economy, employers wanted to meet potential employees and vice versa. The occasion was festive and attendance was good. Despite poor weather, thousands of job seekers participated.

China needs not only well-trained engineers from America, but also management talent. For this reason, bilingual and bicultural Chinese Americans are perfect targets. Other American companies have also realized the potential of the Chinese market. Cisco increased its presence in China from one hundred employees in 1997 to six hundred in 2000 (*San Francisco Examiner* November 19, 2000). Other American companies are similarly expanding their workforces. Again, Chinese-speaking engineers are often recruited by these companies to work in China. In Shanghai more than thirty thousand Chinese returned there to work in 2003. According to an estimate by the Shanghai authorities (*Wall Street Journal* March 7, 2003, A6), the number of these returnees will grow to 120,000 by 2010. In fact, Shanghai has established a Shanghai Pudong Service Center for Returned Overseas Students to assist returnees through the bureaucracy. One official said, "China needs these top-level students who not only understand China, but also embrace advanced foreign concepts and technologies."

Silicon Valley Chinese who have *guanxi* in China have an added advantage when launching new businesses in China. Mr. Wing Luo is one example (*Wall Street Journal* March 7, 2003). He left China in 1986 to study in the United States. After receiving his PhD in biomedical science he worked at several California pharmaceutical companies. He married, became a U.S. citizen, and made his home in Silicon Valley. His salary in 2000 exceeded $100,000 a year. However, Mr. Luo knew that he would never make more than $150,000 to $200,000 a year in the United States because of the glass ceiling. As it turned out, a businessman approached him when he attended a conference in China. This businessman said to Mr. Luo, "I want to invest in your company. I'll give you a $1 million a year." After some deliberation and with the help of a colleague whose mother was the vice mayor of technology in Shanghai, Mr. Luo accepted the offer to set up shop in China. Thanks to good connections (*guanxi*), Mr. Luo was able to raise $3.4 million from Chinese government venture capitalists. His colleague's mother from Shanghai quickly used her own *guanxi* to arrange meetings with more than twenty government-backed agencies to sort through paperwork and financial details. In early 2001, Mr. Luo left his company, Rigel, in South San Francisco, and began commuting to Shanghai. Mr. Luo returns to the United States every other month to visit his wife, two sons, and his parents in Silicon Valley.

In 2001 when the unemployment rate in Silicon Valley reached its highest levels, quite a few high-tech engineers were laid off. On October 12, the unemployment rate in Santa Clara, which is the heart of Silicon Valley, rose to 5.9 percent (*Sing Tao Daily* October 14, 2001). This translates into about forty thousand unemployed workers, many of whom were Chinese high-tech professionals. Here is a typical expression of the feeling at the time:

> Everyone is hurting, whether you are in venture capital, high-tech, travel or restaurants. In the case of the Chinese in high-tech, they are hurting too, except that they tend to save their earnings. They have more money in their savings account. As for the engineers, they could go to China to look for employment. The economy in China is still growing and they are trying to get good people from America. (Informant SC, interview with author, September 29, 2001)

Several informants told me that young Taiwanese engineers who had recently finished their graduate degrees in the United States were no longer interested in seeking employment in Silicon Valley. They were going straight to China instead, and Taiwanese high-tech companies were interested in hiring these Taiwanese graduates from the United States. In this instance, globalization did not necessarily mean the loss of employment. It created employment and the circulation of talent among Chinese Americans.

However, not all Chinese are interested in going to China or other overseas locations. Some told me that they had received excellent offers from foreign companies, but they declined.

> I could have accepted the job offer from Taiwan. I could live very comfortably there. But it is hard for my family. My roots are in America. My children go to school in Santa Clara and my wife has a job in America. My parents and my parents-in-law are now in the U.S. It does not make sense for me to accept a lucrative offer overseas but leave my family behind. Certain people would do it but I would not. Certain people want to be entrepreneurs but I do not have entrepreneurial qualities. I would rather work as an employee. If I am laid off, I will look for another job. I think I will be able to find another job. (Informant W, interview with author, October 24, 2001)

It seems that the engineers who are willing to go to Asia are often younger. They have U.S. citizenship, green cards, or permanent residency in the United States. If they have not yet acquired these, however, they prefer to wait until they have obtained them before they seek employment in Asia. This is just another indication that they are interested in returning to America.

Some complained about isolation due the lack of friends and family. Their working hours and their language skills were thought to inhibit them from having closer contact with the larger society, and the glass ceiling was cited as an important factor for why they wanted to work in Asia. This was especially the case among men who had been bypassed for promotion. Many

Chinese engineers from mainland China also complained about their narrow and limited circle of friends (*hang xiao de sheng huo quanzi*).

From my research, I found that the majority of those Chinese who return to Asia from Silicon Valley are those who have secured their permanent residency in the United States. Their base is still the United States and Asia is only a place in which to find work or to start a company. This differs from the Chinese immigrants of the nineteenth century who came to the United States to make money and who planned to return home to lead a life of elegant retirement. Some Silicon Valley Chinese professionals feel that because of the level of prejudice in the United States, their opportunities for promotion will be limited if they work in companies run by non-Chinese Americans. Some feel that there is and will always be a glass ceiling. However, I use the word *some*, because not *all* the Chinese feel that way. To avoid this predicament, there are several adaptive strategies. One is for a Chinese engineer to start his or her own business (as discussed earlier in this chapter). Another is to find other job opportunities in China, Taiwan, and Hong Kong. This is what causes return migration. But I must qualify the use of this phrase for it often is not necessarily a return since it is not permanent. These workers return temporarily to work or to be entrepreneurs in Asia, always with the notion of one day returning to America permanently.

Commonly the husband returns to Asia but the wife stays in America. This is also a reversal of nineteenth-century Chinese immigration patterns in which the men left for the United States and their women stayed in China. Modern-day Chinese returnees still believe that their children will have a better chance of getting into universities in the United States, and they themselves prefer the physical environment of the United States. There is also a concern about political stability in Taiwan, Hong Kong, and China. This practice of temporarily returning to the land of one's origins or to another overseas location in order to seek employment and other economic opportunities was quite common in the U.S. recessions of the early 1990s, and the return migration phenomenon was not unnoticed by the U.S. media (*New York Times* February 21, 1995; *Time Magazine* November 21, 1994). The *San Jose Mercury News* (August 1, 1993) estimated that 30 percent of the Taiwanese immigrant engineers who formerly worked in Silicon Valley had returned to Taiwan in search of better opportunities. My informants estimated that during this time at least a fourth of the valley's Hong Kong immigrant professionals returned to their land of origin as well. Census data taken from the San Francisco Bay Area in 1990 indicate that Chinese immigrants did tend to receive lower salaries when compared to the white population, and these data have been confirmed by the research of AnaLee Saxenian (1999). Those engineers who felt that they were being discriminated against were not hesitant to leave their jobs in the United States to return to Asia. Returning to Asia was an adaptive strategy that Chinese engineers used to fight discrimination.

There were additional factors that motivated the temporary return of high-tech Chinese personnel to Asia. During the early 1990s, the Taiwanese government made deliberate efforts to recruit Chinese high-tech engineers and companies and to secure their return to Taiwan. A counterpart to Silicon Valley, the Hsinchu Scientific Campus, was set up in Taiwan with subsidies from the government. On the Hsinchu Scientific Campus near Taipei there are research facilities, condominiums for families and bachelors, restaurants, business and factory sites, and tennis courts and other recreation facilities, all created with funding from the government. Accordingly, some Taiwanese engineers returned and became vice presidents or presidents of new companies. Others arrived on the new campus to work in research and development offices sponsored by the government. By early 2000 the tide had changed, and ever more Chinese were returning or going to China to assume employment or to start new businesses. As implied above, two factors fueled this exodus: (1) the recession of 2001, and (2) the preferential treatment given these returning workers by the government of China. Taxes, for example, were low, and the workers were given such benefits as housing subsidies and transportation assistance. Not least of these perks was the respect accorded to the returned Chinese engineers. Scientist and engineers are highly respected in China, and those who have higher degrees from overseas are particularly valued: they are said to be "gold-plated." Many informants told me that when they worked in U.S. high-tech companies, they were considered as nothing more than run-of-the-mill employees or *gao ji hua gong* (high-class laborers). But when they returned to China, they were treated as special and valuable talent, or *gao ji zhi shi fan zhi* (high-class intellectuals). They told me that in China they have higher positions and enjoy more prestige from when doing the same job in the United States.

Most of these workers go to China with the intent of only working there for a few years. After they have accumulated enough savings, they intend to return to the United States. With their savings and connections, some are then able to start global businesses with branches in the United States and in China. This is called *liang di tou zi* (investment in two places). Or they might organize a research and development office in the United States, but have their sales and production facilities in China. Having interviewed one hundred engineers, I can safely say that these returnees want eventually to settle in America permanently. They may use their connections, bilingual abilities, and bicultural backgrounds to conduct a transnational business, but they intend to stay in the United States. Thus, there is no divided loyalty. They are committed to America. It's only out of practicality and for the sake of their economic survival that they may have to go back to China or Taiwan. Chinese American engineers can be adamant about the fact that mainstream American society often suspects the Chinese of divided loyalties. One Chinese engineer told me the following story:

My friend is a German American. He lived and worked in Germany for seven years for an American company. He speaks German and his family even moved there living in a huge mansion. No one called him unpatriotic. But when a Chinese American returns to do the same, he will mostly be suspected by the immigration official as unpatriotic. My friends who have to travel back and forth between Taiwan and the United States, were often questioned by immigration officials for spending too much time overseas. This is unfair! Some people have to travel overseas to do business. They have to make a living! (Informant L, interview with author, September 19, 2001)

GLOBALIZATION AND INVESTMENT

Favorite places for American investment are Taiwan, Singapore, and, more recently Beijing, Shanghai, Suzhou, and Shenzhen. On November 29, 2001, representatives from Jiangsu Province in China organized an investment conference in Santa Clara for high-tech professionals in Silicon Valley. These representatives described the working and business environment in Nanjing, Suzhou, and surrounding cities with the goal of attracting investment to these places. Apparently, many American and foreign investors have sought out Jiang Jiangsu Province. Suzhou City alone has more than 250 foreign companies that have invested billions of dollars in the industrial park of Suzhou. More than 1,200 foreign companies from 40 countries have been established there (*Sing Tao Daily* November 29, 2001). These companies employ both locals and foreigners, some of them from Silicon Valley. This is just another example of how foreign countries can be sources of employment or investment for the Chinese of Silicon Valley. In fact, many companies, both Chinese or American, believe that Silicon Valley is a place for the outsourcing of products, talent, and investment. Trade delegates from different parts of China regularly visit Silicon Valley in order to encourage Chinese entrepreneurs to return to China and to invest in China's manufacturing facilities and high-tech enterprises. The Chinese American engineers and entrepreneurs of Silicon Valley have become magnets that draw recruiters, investment hunters, and technology searchers from different parts of the world— so much so that Chinese professional associations in Silicon Valley hold organized seminars on investment opportunities in China almost monthly.

GLOBALIZATION AND ECONOMIC BRAIN-DRAIN

When social scientists decry an economic brain-drain as the result of immigration, they are in fact making the assumption that when migrants leave their home country for a new country, they will never return home, and that their movement is nonreversible and permanent. When migrants move permanently to a new country, their departure implies, according to these social scientists, a loss of talent for the country of origin. Hence the concept of what is known as brain-drain. In the case of Chinese engineers moving to the United States, their movement implies a brain-drain in China. Similarly, when Chinese Americans engineers from Silicon Valley move back to Asia, some will assume that this is a loss of talent for America. In reality, the departure of an oversupply of man-power can be a blessing in disguise. A glut of engineers can depress wages and profits for certain industries. Several engineers recently arrived from China have told me that there are many unemployed software engineers in China looking for opportunities to go overseas. The fact that certain talent leaves one place to go to another should not be seen as a permanent or a one-way process. From my research I found this assumption to be invalid. As actors and decision mak-ers, human beings can redirect or modify the direction of their migratory move-ment. I have seen engineers who pursue a circular migration route, sometimes working here in Silicon Valley and sometimes in Singapore or China before re-turning to the United States again. In this modern world, traversing national borders is a new mode of human existence. The modern employee or entre-preneur often needs to travel to make a living. They have to make their rounds in order to be successful. It is not appropriate therefore to use the term *brain-drain*. Rather, we should consider it a circulation of brainpower or a globaliza-tion of brainpower. Synergy of talent around the globe is now a reality.

The global itinerants who take part in this circulation of brainpower may be divided into four groups. The first group is made up of the owner/entre-preneurs of transnational corporations. As we have seen, a company can be localized and globalized simultaneously. One entrepreneur, Wang Zhidong, has in fact used the concept "glocal"—an abbreviation for global and local to describe his company, Sina.com. This internet company serves Chinese com-munities worldwide by offering e-commerce and community services in the Chinese language to four localized websites targeting China, Hong Kong, Taiwan, and overseas Chinese in North America.

> Sina.com is an information site for the Chinese around the world. It is global-ized. We have to adjust our coverage locally. We have to adjust the angles, take into consideration the four places: Hong Kong, China, Taiwan and the U.S. The corporate culture of Sina.com is "Glocal"—global and local. (Zhang 2000)

As CEO of this global company, Zhidong has to commute by plane periodi-cally to visit all these locations. He is sharing brainpower with his companies in Beijing, Hong Kong, Sunnyvale, Taipei, and Shanghai. Sina.com provides comprehensive up-to-the-minute news. It also offers chat rooms, community platforms, financial information, online shopping platforms, search func-tions, and e-mail services across its four main platforms. The company's main income is derived from advertising (85 percent). The rest of its income is from sales of software (14 percent) and e-commerce (1–2 percent). Its e-commerce platform is similar to that of Yahoo!'s shopping mall.

Sina.com is registered in Hong Kong but is traded on NASDAQ. Its legal and financial departments are in Silicon Valley. There are also offices in Taiwan, Hong Kong, and Beijing. Zhidong exemplifies the concept of a "circulatory migrant" or "transnational migrant," making the rounds to all posts. He said that he comes to Silicon Valley once a month for about a week. He goes to Taipei once in a quarter and then goes to Hong Kong and Beijing. He is truly a frequent flyer. The company is localized and globalized at the same time and this operation requires what I have called brain circulation. It is not a brain-drain but the sharing of brains globally. Some have used the term *cosmopolitan personality* to describe an individual like Wang Zhidong.

The second group of high-tech migrants who travel frequently between continents spreading brainpower is made up of company-sent people assigned to places like China, Singapore, London, Hong Kong, or Taiwan. This included Americans working for American companies who have been assigned to a foreign country for a number of years and then return to America.

Problem-solvers or troubleshooters, who are truly traveling brainpower, define the third group. These technicians are on assignment to deal with certain issues or technical problems of a company in different parts of the world. They are individuals who travel with a special agenda and on a prearranged schedule. Some Chinese engineers have told me that after they arrive in a foreign country, they are immediately wined and dined and then driven to their living quarters or hotel. They are then told about their schedules and specific responsibilities. After receiving their instructions, they set to work right away on the tasks assigned to them. There is not much free time or rearranged itinerary. Their life is quite regimented. Upon finishing their assigned tasks, they return to their headquarters, which is often in Silicon Valley.

The fourth kind of brain-circulation group is made up of the so-called return-migration workers which I have discussed already, that is, those Chinese high-tech talents returning to Asia to establish companies or to work. We have seen how return migrations took place during the U.S. recessions of the early 1990s and more recently in 2001 when quite a few Chinese returned to Taiwan, mainland China, or Southeast Asia for employment. In the 1990s recession, there were more Taiwanese returning to Taiwan to work, but during the 2001 recession there were more mainland Chinese returning to China for employment. This was due to the need for high-tech personnel in those localities. In the 1990s most of the Chinese high-tech engineers in Silicon Valley were from Taiwan. There were few mainland Chinese then. Then as today, all of these returnees are either American citizens or permanent residents of the United States. In fact, they are the people who can afford to return to China or Taiwan. Then if anything happens, they have a place to return to. For whatever reason (economic, political, educational), many of these high-tech Chinese made their decision a long time ago to stay in the United States permanently. After they have made a fortune or after the U.S. economy has revived, they will return to the United States. Thus, they cross national borders back and forth to make a living. This circulatory movement of contemporary migrants differs from those in the past. Oscar Handlin (1972), Milton Gordon (1964), Herbert Gans (1963), and other immigration scholars have not studied this kind of immigration movement. This is presumably due to the fact that today's economy is globalized. Achieving the American Dream sometimes requires multiple departures from America and work overseas.

The departure of the educated Chinese from Silicon Valley does not therefore indicate brain-drain. As a circulatory migration movement, it is a "global sharing of brain power." To what extent this is the case universally still awaits verification from further research. But among the Chinese in Silicon Valley, I found that this departure is often temporary. There are numerous facts to support my contention. First, the family of the itinerant wage earner always stays behind in the United States when the wage earner goes overseas. This indicates the preference of the wage earner and the family for a permanent home in Silicon Valley. Second, if the entire family does go overseas with the wage earner on a work assignment, I found that the family normally does not liquidate its properties in Silicon Valley. From talking to realtors, I learned that when Taiwanese Chinese families go back to Taiwan, they always hire property managers to rent out their homes. In the early 1990s, one saw many departures. These departing families eventually returned to the United States, and their formerly rented homes are now occupied by the original owners.

Only a minority of mainland Chinese will stay in China. Most of them, according to my informants, plan to return and settle in the United States permanently. One point needs to be emphasized, however: some mainland Chinese feel that they will never be part of mainstream American society. They want to return to China and to see what it has to offer, but at the same time they want to keep their residency in the United States. Mr. Liu, a brilliant integrated circuits (IC) engineer sums up the reasons why some mainlanders want to return to China, at least for a couple of years:

> There are several reasons why they want to return to China after they get their green card. First, the pay in China is quite good. In comparing the real purchase power, the income here and there does not make much difference. In the U.S. a beginning engineer may make five thousand dollars a month but in China the pay is seven hundred dollars. In spending power it is about the same because the taxes are high in the U.S. The clothing is five times more and food is five times more in Silicon Valley. Housing is a lot more expensive. Transportation is expensive because you do not need cars in China. Second, you could save more money there because you don't have to pay a lot of taxes and spend a lot of money. Third, you don't need to buy houses or cars. Public transport is good.

Taxis are cheap. Fourth, you are respected and considered to be important by society. Fifth, you have your fiends and acquaintances. (Mr. Liu, interview with author, February 7, 2002)

Mr. Daniel Xu added the following:

> When you work as an engineer in China you get more respect. This is particularly the case for those Chinese who graduated from famous universities and have studied and worked in the U.S. You have more prestige when you return to work in China. There is more stability working in China because people like engineers do not get laid off and China gives special treatment to those who were born in the 60s and educated in the universities in the 80s. (Mr. Daniel Xu, interview with author, October 6, 2001)

This return to China is thus a rational decision. According to a report in the *China Press*, 21 percent of Chinese students plan to return to China in the next five years; 37 percent plan to return to China in the next five to ten years; and 23 percent plan to return to China after ten years. But 19 percent do not plan to return to China at all. Those who plan to return to China are mostly in the thirty-to-forty-year-old age-group. When they return to China, they plan to operate a start-up company in Beijing, Shanghai, or Tienjin (*China Press* May 14, 2000). Since this survey focuses mainly on Chinese students in the United States, it is difficult to apply the findings to Silicon Valley. But it does indicate that some Chinese indeed want to return to China. In the case of Silicon Valley, after interviewing many of these Chinese students, it is safe for me to say that some plan to return to China after they have gained their permanent residency.

Some want to take advantage of the booming economy in China. People told me that *now* is the time to do business in China because China's recent entry into the WTO is thought to be advantageous for entrepreneurs in the high-tech businesses. These people believe that there is a huge Chinese market waiting for American goods such as computers and other high-tech products. They also believe that the tariffs for American products in China will be lower because of China's admission into the WTO. Many mainland Chinese are anxious to seize this opportunity to open up a firm and to return to China to participate in the new economic era. Again, this group of entrepreneurs has no intention of returning to China permanently. The globalization in this case is for the sake of localization!

How about the loss of talent in developing China when engineers leave the country to join companies in Silicon Valley? Since 1989 many engineers from mainland China have left, but certainly not all. Some have been sent by headquarters in China to branch offices in Silicon Valley, and still others have been recruited by Silicon Valley companies through branch offices in different parts of the world. China, in fact, lets people leave the country easily, as long as they are accepted by the United States. Therefore, does China worry about a brain-drain? After interviewing many informants, I have come to the conclusion that China actually benefits from the departure of these workers due to a talent glut. China also believes that it is a good way for them to develop additional knowledge and skills. In certain areas of specialization, some high-tech engineers are not employable in China due to a lack of jobs. Wayne Liu, a recent migrant from China and an IC design manager of a new start-up company had this to say:

> There is no fear about a brain-drain in China. It has too many talented workers! It is good that some leave so that they do not depress the job market and their high-tech industry. There is a glut of engineers. It helps China if some people leave. The country just produces too many every year. They have overproduced in the area of biotechnology fiber optics. Some people could not find jobs in these fields. My wife is in biotechnology but she had to come here with me to find a job in Silicon Valley. (Wayne Liu, interview with author, February 7, 2002)

MULTICULTURALISM IN SILICON VALLEY

Amidst the glass ceiling phenomenon and discriminatory practices, paradoxically, every informant of my project pointed out that diversity is an important asset of Silicon Valley. Occupational diversity and cultural and ethnic diversity are important elements of a "Silicon Soup" that is made up of many ingredients. This soup, as one of my informants put it, is unique here and cannot be duplicated in any other part of the world. When asked to define the uniqueness of Silicon Valley, many of my informants agreed that the valley's climate, location, availability of space, transportation system, availability of capital, acceptance of risk, support system in the presence of a major university and research institutions, and its diversity of skills, talent, and people make the valley what it is. Most important in this soup are the valley people who come from different parts of the world with special talents.

When I asked Dr. David Lam of Lam Research about diversity, he made this observation of Silicon Valley:

> In this region, there is a culture. I call it the Silicon Valley culture. Here are the characteristics: (1) diversity with a high percentage of Asians, (2) a merit-based culture, (3) a sense of egalitarianism, (4) risk taking, (5) acceptance of failure, and (6) a multicultural society. (Dr. David Lam, interview with author, September 19, 2001)

He said that different ethnic groups in the valley work together quite well and are integrated in the workplace. On the other hand, socially, each group can have its own cultural practices.

Among the high-tech companies and business establishments that I visited, I noticed one common characteristic: the existence of ethnic and cultural diversity. There are the Chinese and Indians who work in the integrated circuits department, and in any given company, one can see Mexican Americans, Asian Americans, and white Americans all working together.

Marc Nehmakin and David Liu of a venture capital company in San Jose had a similar observation about Silicon Valley. This is what Marc told me:

> Silicon Valley cannot be duplicated. There are many elements interwoven and mixed to make this place work. It has talent, diversity, brilliance, people, weather, money . . . All these work together to produce the Silicon Soup. It has the sustainable power and it is a construct that cannot be duplicated. (Marc Nehmakin, interview with author, October 2, 2001)

The above statements were echoed by all my informants. All agree that diversity is a strength, and that the talent and contributions of different ethnic groups were recognized in the valley.

Aside from engineering, there are talented workers in business management, accounting, banking, and financing in the valley. The bicultural background of these professionals is an important asset for economic globalization. Many informants cite diversity as one reason why Silicon Valley succeeded and Route 128, a high-tech area near Boston, failed. But one thing is clear: the Chinese have made a vital contribution to the success of high-tech businesses in Silicon Valley. Silicon Valley sees itself as a meritocracy and a place full diversity in the workplace. At the same time, after further analysis, in certain areas one can see pockets of ethnic segregation. Of the top 150 public companies in Silicon Valley, 89 percent of the chairmen and CEOs are white, 10 percent are Asian, and 0.6 percent are black. Of the white-collar workforce, 60 percent are white and 31 percent are Asian. And among blue-collar workers and technicians, 57 percent are Asian, 21 percent are white, 18 percent are Latino, and 4 percent black (*San Jose Mercury News* April 16, 1999). Thus, whites and Asians tend to dominate the workplace in Silicon Valley. African Americans seem to be underrepresented. Studies have found that companies have not done enough to diversify the blue-collar workforce (English-Lueck 2002; Hossfeld 1988). Other sources suggest that companies actually prefer to hire people from the same ethnic group for communication and productivity reasons (*San Jose Mercury News* April 16, 1999). It is also useful to remember that in the high-tech business, informal hiring is quite common. Cris Benner of Working Partnerships U.S.A. says that Silicon Valley's contract manufacturing companies tend to rely on informal recruiting practices much more than other industries do. Hiring is often done by word of mouth, and workers are encouraged to refer their friends or relatives from their ethnic communities. As a result, certain ethnic groups dominate certain sectors of employment. From my fieldwork, I have found other factors at work. Stereotypes continue to influence hiring decisions. Some people think that the Chinese are good in technology and engineering but lack verbal skills and aggressiveness. The Chinese are thought likely to work for less money because they are immigrants. Companies may also prefer to hire Asians to be packers and assembly line workers because Asians are perceived to be hard-working and willing to accept less pay.

Whatever the reason, ethnic segregation or division does exist in Silicon Valley. Still, the engineers I interviewed said that they feel they are more appreciated in Silicon Valley than in other places in America, and this was one of the reasons they came here. One optical engineer with a PhD who had worked on the East Coast for a number of years before migrating to Silicon Valley had this to say:

> Silicon Valley is, relatively speaking, the best place for Chinese immigrants. They can utilize their potential fully. The environment is conducive. People accept Chinese culture and the Chinese people. The area recognizes that the Chinese high-tech people are good. They are hardworking and well-educated. They trust the Chinese talent and are sometimes looking for Chinese engineers, especially in fiber optics and electronics. People on the West Coast are more familiar with the contribution of the Chinese who came here to build the West, the railroads, the bridges. They worked in the gold country and the western frontier. In comparison to the East Coast, the West Coast seems to accept and appreciate the Chinese more. (Informant WW, interview with author, September 26, 2002)

HURDLES TO OVERCOME

The debate on racism goes on in Silicon Valley. David Lee was one of the Chinese engineer pioneers in Silicon Valley. Educated in China, Taiwan, Argentina, and the United States, he graduated from Montana State University in mechanical engineering and received his master's in the same field from North Dakota State University. After graduation he worked as an engineer for NCR and later became a manager for Printer Engineering of Diablo Systems. He developed the daisy wheel printer. Between 1973 and 1998, David Lee founded nine companies in Silicon Valley. He was nominated and appointed as a regent of the University of California System in 1996. But he himself had some bad experiences. As an engineer in a non-Chinese company he was once bypassed for promotion by someone his junior and whom he had actually trained! This was one of the reasons why he left that company and founded his own start-up company in 1980.

Lee noted that there is a tendency for many white Americans to use "communication problems" as an excuse for not promoting Chinese workers:

I have invested in many companies. Few people are willing to support the Chinese. I always want Chinese in the companies. A lot of companies don't want to promote Chinese—they just want to use them. It's so easy for people to say, "You have a communication problem." Sometimes it may be true, but sometimes it's an excuse, and the person has real ability. (Yu 1986, 86)

David Lam also felt that much needs to be done to correct the attitude of many white employers. He told me that white engineers who were less capable were often promoted above more capable Chinese engineers. The excuse was communication problems. In a speech given to AT&T, Mr. Lam advocated the immediate correction of this attitude. He also said that companies will sustain great losses if this is allowed to continue (Dr. David Lam, interview with author, September 19, 2001).

However, when I talked to Dr. Lam recently, he told me that the glass ceiling practice was more prevalent in the 1980s and 1990s than it is today. He said that prejudice against the Chinese still exists but he attributed it to ignorance. Many white employers erroneously assumed that the Chinese were less capable in dealing with personnel matters because of a lack of English. He also told me that even in this case, it could be corrected. He said when he finds an engineer who is highly capable but has an English language problem, he sends him to English classes or finds a tutor for him. He said, "It is too bad to lose an exceptional engineering talent!" (Dr. David Lam, interview with author, September 19, 2001).

From my research, I noticed that certainly some of the Chinese have problems with English, but not all. Many Chinese from Hong Kong and mainland China have an excellent command of English, and some Chinese engineers were educated in England or Canada before they came to the United States for further education. Some of these engineers in fact lead the fight against racism. Whenever they can, they speak out on issues of racism. Gerry Yang, David Lee, David Lam, and others have openly spoken out against the harms of racism in the high-tech business.

Gender dominance is another issue. Entrepreneur Pauline Lo Alker remarked that the high-tech industry is dominated by men. In her case, as a Chinese American woman, she experienced discrimination. Sometimes, she was mistaken as a secretary. However, she was able to rise to the occasion and become a successful entrepreneur despite this racism and sexism. She has been active in the computer business for more than thirty years. She founded Counter-Point Computers and was the CEO of Network Peripherals (Liu 1995, 183).

Frank Lin, CEO of Trident Microsystems, also felt the need to correct the stereotype that the "Chinese can create but cannot do well in management" (Teng 1998, 225). Lin, a BS graduate in electric engineering from Jiatong University and with a master's in electric engineering from the University of

Iowa, wanted to correct this stereotype. In 1987 he founded Trident, and from 1994 to 1995 Trident's stock went up from $5.00 per share to $25.00 per share. His company can now rival other companies like S3 and Cirrus Logic. It receives numerous original equipment manufacture (OEM) orders from American clients.

Lin said that it is not easy for the Chinese to compete in white society. Skin color, accent, and social background are a perceived disadvantage and a source of discrimination in U.S. society. However, if one persists, working hard with their skills, they can still succeed (Teng 1998, 226).

Some of my informants suggested that American society is not a color-blind society. They said that one needs to know the differences between one's ethnic group and the larger society, and between the values of one's ethnic group and how differences can affect its interaction with the larger society. The following statement from one of my informants is shared by many:

> In the Asian American heritage, we often listen and take orders without question from those in authority. But in American society, this kind of behavior is misinterpreted as being quiet and uninterested or aloof or even negative. We need to be aware of this misinterpretation and correct it accordingly. We need to assert ourselves more and learn how American society operates. (Informant Z, interview with author, September 12, 2001)

George Koo, in his speech to the 2001 annual meeting of the SCEA, suggested that the bicultural heritage of Chinese Americans should be recognized by all Americans. It is an asset rather than a liability, and Americans were wrong to blindly assume that Chinese Americans are unpatriotic because they embrace two cultures. He commented:

> If you are an American citizen, your loyalty is with this country. Operating from this basis, your knowledge of the American and Chinese cultures will help rather than hinder your work in globalization and in any intercultural transaction. The Chinese should recognize this positive contribution that they can make. (Koo 2001)

David Lee, in exhorting Chinese Americans, said, "If we don't blow our own horn, who will?" (Yu 1986). For some Chinese, this avoidance of recognition lies partly with themselves. They should change the attitude of the larger society through formal and informal education. A local Chinese newspaper reported a similar remark: The Chinese should learn how the mainstream society functions and use their rules to "beat them at their own games" (*Sing Tao Daily* November 12, 2001).

Racism and prejudice in the workplace do exist, although much less in Silicon Valley than elsewhere. Even so, many of the Chinese I interviewed told me that you have to be a superstar to escape discrimination.

If you are Jerry Yang of Yahoo!, you probably do not encounter discrimination. If you are just an engineer, you are treated like a high-class laborer. You are expected to work hard and get your regular paycheck. If you are better than your fellow engineers by 20 percent, you are still treated the same. Even if you have a PhD and your white peer has only a BS, you are still paid the same. Only if you work very hard and excel over all the other engineers in your department and become a superstar, only then will you be treated better. Racism is subtle. On the other hand, there is racism everywhere in the world. If you are a minority, you have to accept it. Silicon Valley is already much better in this regard. (Informant VL, interview with author, September 27, 2001)

Some Chinese are more observant and more vocal about racism in the workplace. They feel that good workers need to be rewarded regardless of cultural origin, accent, or ethnicity. All races and ethnicities should be allowed to pass through the glass ceiling and be promoted to the top. There should no room for racial discrimination at the top, nor at the bottom. These Chinese speak out against racial preference and advocate a complete meritocracy. Jerry Yang of Yahoo! is adamant about diversity. He said:

In the business I'm in, you get measured by how successful you are and how profitable you are and how fast you grow. You have no choice but to have a complete meritocracy and have the competition of the best ideas, best talent and the best people regardless of their backgrounds . . . you take the best of all backgrounds . . . working closely together as a team. You end up creating something where you can continually mine and strive for what's best in each culture. (dailynews.Yahoo!.com/h/nm/20010504/1f/entrepreneurs_chinese_dc-1.html)

It seemed then that all my informants agreed that in Silicon Valley (1) cultural diversity exists, (2) the glass ceiling is still there, and (3) education is needed for both Americans and Chinese in the area of human interaction.

THE WEN HO LEE INCIDENT

The experience of Dr. Wen Ho Lee touched many Chinese in Silicon Valley. They believed that he was wrongly accused as a spy and unfairly imprisoned. In a sense, his life echoes the lives of many Taiwanese Chinese. Wen Ho Lee was born in 1939 to a poor peasant family in Taiwan. He was one of ten children in the Lee family. When he graduated from middle school he was able to pass a competitive university exam and was admitted to Cheng Kung University. After he finished, he came to the United States to study at Texas A&M. He got his MS in 1965 and his PhD in physics in 1969.

Wen Ho Lee has two grown children, one a software engineer and the other a computer technician (*International Daily* February 19, 2000). Wen Ho is a family man who likes to cook and do housework. His hobbies are fishing, gardening, listening to music, and reading. But in December of 1999 he was accused by the U.S. government of being a spy. Then in September of 2000 he was cleared of fifty-nine charges derived from that accusation, and he pleaded guilty to a lesser felony count of "knowingly violating security rules in downloading classified nuclear data" (*San Francisco Chronicle* September 12, 2000).

The high-tech Chinese are familiar with the case of Wen Ho Lee. Many feel that Dr. Lee was targeted due to his race. Some Chinese were disappointed, and others angry with Dr. Lee's decision to accept the plea-bargain deal because they did not think he was guilty of any of the allegations of espionage that cost him his job and caused him the pain and suffering he had to endure. Because of the Wen Ho Lee case, some American politicians demanded close scrutiny of ethnic Chinese businesses in the scientific community and tighter controls of U.S. high-tech transfers and export. Some of the Chinese believe that these politicians were unfairly stirring up hatred against Chinese American high-tech personnel and their businesses. Their beliefs were a result of the conviction Chinese Americans feel that American society has a habit of distrusting and treating the Chinese as scapegoats since the California Gold Rush in the 1840s.

From the perspective of Chinese Americans as well as some insiders at the Alamos Lab where Wen Ho Lee worked, there was possibly a racial aspect to the case. Were Dr. Lee not a Chinese American, many Chinese argued that he would not have been singled out for investigation. They wonder why their heritage is a liability and they ask why this was a case of racial profiling. Many of the Chinese have served this country and fought for it. Yet, they felt they were being singled out for unusual and unfair treatment (*San Francisco Chronicle* August 13, 2001, A2). Despite such fears, some Silicon Valley Chinese believe that the best way to fight racism is through coalition building with other ethnic groups, and in this way to change the system by participating in it. They feel that more Chinese Americans must participate in the political system so as to give voice to the concerns and interests of the Chinese in Silicon Valley. Some, in fact, do run for electoral office and attempt to fight racism through the system.

GROWING ROOTS IN SILICON VALLEY

Contrary to the popular perception that the Chinese are foreigners who are not committed to their host country, I found that many of the Chinese are firmly grounded in the United States. Of the one hundred entrepreneurs for whom I have biographical data, most are seriously interested in community affairs. Many are highly dedicated to community activities and civic and local affairs.

For instance, Leonard Liu is California Motion Pictures Commissioner, David Lee is a regent of the University of California system, and Stanley Wang is a member of the Board of Trustees of the California State University system. Some Chinese are activists who participate in American politics through community involvement by running for political office or by supporting other Asian politicians and politicians who are sympathetic to Chinese American or Asian American concerns. They also participate in the valley's many professional and community organizations. When I interviewed them about their commitment, the majority told me that they wanted to establish roots in America. Their professed ideology is *luo di sheng gen* (establishing roots). Some even said, "If we don't stay in America, where shall we go?" or "We have lived in this country for such a long time. We work here and our children were born here. Our work is here and our family is here. Whether we like it or not, we are going to stay permanently in this country."

Occasionally, there are other voices, "Taiwan is very similar to the United States now. Whatever we have in the United States, Taiwan has also. The differences between the two are becoming less and less. I may go back to Taiwan to lead my life of retirement but it does not mean that I do not like America. If I do go back there it is because of my parents and my relatives." Others said, "Even if I want to go back to Taiwan, my children may not want to live there permanently. They were born and raised here in America. This is their country. For this reason, I will stay here." Several informants did tell me that they would return to Taiwan to stay there for good. However, an overwhelming majority of the Taiwanese Chinese prefer to stay in the United States permanently.

The majority of the Hong Kong Chinese and mainland Chinese immigrants whom I interviewed told me that they also wanted to stay in this country permanently. Many applied for citizenship as soon as they qualified for it. All the Chinese from Hong Kong and Taiwan have only one passport. They are anxious to purchase homes, and they want to have their homes in Silicon Valley. To this end, Chinese engineers, especially those who are married, are concerned about accumulating enough money for the down payment on their future home. On weekends, many Chinese families go to open houses to visit homes that are for sale. From 1999 to 2000 when the high-tech business was at its peak, one would see Chinese buyers camping out overnight in front of new houses, in order to be the first to purchase them. Once they have homes, their concerns then shift to mortgage payments and an education fund for their children. Many banks in Silicon Valley are familiar with the consumption patterns of Chinese Americans and have invented special banking products just for the them. After working for hours, these Chinese spend much of their free time on their homes, their families, and the education of their children. These are root-planting activities. In Chinese, one is said to be working to *an ju le ye* (to live comfortably in a house and happily establish an enterprise). In order to save money for their children's education, the Chinese are frugal about furniture, appliances, and automobiles. They do not change their cars frequently. Nor do they spend exorbitant amounts of money for household goods. They only purchase what they deem to be practical and durable. From visiting the homes of many engineers, I have noticed that the furniture they purchase tends to be quite modest. For those who are interested in entrepreneurship, they also save money for their future start-up company. Some may use part of their savings to purchase stock in the hope of accumulating money in the stock market. From these consumption patterns, it is easy to recognize that Chinese American engineers and entrepreneurs are planning for permanent settlement in the United States. They want to be established in Silicon Valley, especially in the communities that are known for their excellent schools, such as Cupertino and Los Alto Hills. Some of the younger engineers from mainland China told me that the price of housing in the valley is beyond their reach, with an average home easily selling for $600,000 in Cupertino and $1 million in the Los Alto Hills. They said to me that after they have accumulated sufficient savings and when they are ready, they may purchase homes elsewhere in the United States where housing is more affordable. But they do plan to stay in America! They definitely have accepted the ideology of *luo di sheng gen.*

POLITICAL PARTICIPATION AND THE CIVIC ACTIVITIES OF THE CHINESE

It is common knowledge that in order to fully participate in the larger society, ethnic groups need to have political representation. Knowing the importance of having elected officials to fight for their interest, the Chinese in Silicon Valley have sought to participate in local and national politics through (1) registering Chinese voters, (2) competing for political office at all levels, city and county, and (3) forming coalitions with other ethnic groups so as to elect politicians who are sympathetic to their concerns.

Globalization activities have not deterred the commitment of the Chinese to the United States. In San Jose, the registrar of Voter Registration Programs indicated that more and more Asians, including the Chinese, are voting. Former mayor Michael Chang of Cupertino told me that the Chinese are participating in local politics in increasing numbers. They normally start with school boards and move to city council elections. He said that the Silicon Valley Chinese are sympathetic to Chinese candidates in general. They also encourage and support both local and national Chinese politicians. Many Chinese politicians from out-of-state come to do fundraising among the Chinese of Silicon Valley, including Gary Locke (during his run for governor of the state of Washington) and S. B. Wu, former lieutenant governor of Delaware.

Chinese Americans are adamant in the fight for their rights. News about discrimination in business practices spreads quickly via e-mail in the valley. Racial slurs of white salesmen and other discriminatory practices are reported instantly. Supportive of the cause of Wen Ho Lee, many valley Chinese donated money for his legal defense. In order to safeguard their business and professional interests, they organize interest groups and associations. The high-tech Chinese of Silicon Valley are decision makers, movers, and shapers of their destiny.

Voter Registration

The Chinese in Silicon Valley are gradually realizing the importance of participating in elections, and they have started to organize voter registration drives. Kansen Chu, a Taiwanese immigrant, David Lee of the San Francisco–based Chinese American Voters Education Committee, and Michael Chang, the former mayor of Cupertino, have made great efforts to register Asian voters. David Lee said, "Asians are the fastest growing ethnic group in the county. They have no voice but they've reached critical mass. The conditions are ripe for greater representation" (Fan 1999).

In Santa Clara County, the heart of Silicon Valley, Asian Americans make up 23.4 percent of the county's population. However, not all of those eligible to vote have registered. Here is what Kansen Chu said: "Although we have big numbers here in terms of population, we don't have a strong voice unless we register and participate. Unless we are registered, we are an invisible group of people, as far as politicians or community leaders are concerned" (Fan 1999). Realizing the importance of voter registration, Kansen Chu and David Lee asked for help from the Chinese ethnic press, the *Sing Tao Daily* and the *World Journal*, which have a combined daily readership of 230,000. Apparently, their work was quite successful. For the March election of 2000 in Santa Clara, there were 23,244 registered Chinese voters who were immigrants from Taiwan, Hong Kong, and mainland China. Among registered Chinese voters, 11,050 voted, giving a participation rate of 47.5 percent (*Sing Tao Daily* May 6, 2000).

Elections

Chinese immigrants in Silicon Valley have learned that they need to have elected officials who will represent their interests, and so many Chinese now run for political office. There were two Chinese candidates for the Cupertino Union School District in 1997 and both won. One was Julius Chiang who was a manager of two bank branches. She graduated with a bachelor's degree from the University of California, Berkeley. The other candidate was Ben Liao, a software engineer with Apple Computer, Taligent, and HP. He graduated with a master's in computer science from Texas A&M University. In 1999 Barry Chang, a civil engineer, was elected as a member of the Governing Board of Cupertino Union School District. Meanwhile in the Foothill/De Anza Community College District and the Fremont Union High School District, Chinese American candidates, Kathryn Ho, Hsing Kung, and Homer Tong have been active participants in school elections.

Currently the mayor of Milpitas is Henry Manayan, a Filipino Chinese. Michael S. Chang, the former mayor of Cupertino City, is now a city council member. For the Santa Clara election of November 6, 2001, there were six Chinese Americans running for various political offices. Brothers Paul Fong and Alan Fong ran for Foothill/De Anza Community College District and Orchard School District. Ben Liao and Pearl Cheng ran for the Cupertino School District. Patrick Kwok ran for the city council of Cupertino, and Wei Wong for the city council of Palo Alto (*Sing Tao Daily News* September 20, 2001). Patrick Kwok, Ben Liao, Pearl Cheng, and Alan Fong won their elections. This is an indication of Chinese Americans' determinism to win and to ground themselves in the valley community.

Coalitions

In order to make an impact on the larger society, the Chinese in Silicon Valley realize that it is important to build coalitions with other ethnic groups that have common interests and have had similar experiences in the United States. For Chinese Americans, this means forming a united front with Vietnamese Americans, Filipino Americans, and Japanese Americans. (In official statistics, the Chinese and other ethnic groups are often lumped together as Asian Americans.) Some of the successful coalitions that have been formed with this in mind include (1) the Asian American Public Policy Institute of San Jose, (2) the Asian Americans for Community Involvement of San Jose, (3) the Asian Pacific American Consortium of San Jose, and (4) the Cross-Cultural Community Services Center of San Jose.

The Committee of 100

The Committee of 100 is a national nonpartisan organization composed of American citizens of Chinese descent. Members come from different walks of life but are generally successful citizens in the United States. The goal of the committee is to promote the interests of the Chinese in America by addressing important issues concerning the well-being of the Chinese community and issues affecting U.S.-China relations.

The Committee of 100 has some famous and highly accomplished Chinese Americans. Its membership includes well-known cellist Yo Yo Ma, celebrated architect I. M. Pei, and Chancellor Chang-lin Tien of the University of California, Berkeley. Quite a few Chinese American entrepreneurs from Silicon Valley are also members, including David Lam, George Koo, and Milton Chang. The committee aims to eradicate prejudices against and obstacles to the advancement of the Chinese in America. It has undertaken tasks such as helping to clear the name of Dr. Wen Ho Lee, and it has given awards to journalists who are helpful to the Chinese community. The Committee of 100 in its 2001 annual meeting, presented a Headliner Journalism Award to CBS correspondent Mike Wallace for an objective presentation of the case of Wen Ho Lee on *Sixty Minutes* (*AsianWeek* 22, no. 37, p. 8). The committee recognizes the achievements of Chinese Americans as well as other Asian Americans. The achievements of Norman Mineta (Transportation Secretary), Elaine Chao (Secretary of Labor), and Mike Honda (Congressman from California) have been recognized by the committee, as have the accomplishments of Chancellor Chang-lin Tien and Jerry Yang of Yahoo! The committee's work is an example of how Chinese Americans, including those in Silicon Valley, are anxious to establish roots in America.

The 80/20 of Silicon Valley

The 80/20 is a national, nonpartisan project devised by a group of concerned Chinese Americans. It was originally an attempt to create a block-vote among all Asian Americans in order to influence the 2000 U.S. presidential election. The organization hoped to unite 80 percent of all Asian Pacific American voters in the support of one presidential candidate. Such a block would be attractive to any politician, and it was hoped that the candidate who won the election with the support of this block would take an interest in the Asian community.

Silicon Valley Chinese are active in this organization. The 80/20, together with the Committee of 100, has sponsored the Flag Project, a movement to promote Asian Pacific American involvement in the patriotic flying of the flag on national holidays such as Memorial Day and Independence Day. The project is designed to show mainstream American society that the Chinese are also Americans. It is a tool used to inform the larger society that the Chinese are part of America and that they are just as loyal as other Americans.

Civic Duties and Voluntarism

Silicon Valley Chinese realize the importance of contributing to the community and participating in civic activities. On October 28, 2001, in Sunnyvale's Chinese Cultural Center, a seminar focused on Chinese voluntarism.

Seminar participants all agreed that it was meaningful and valuable to do voluntary civic work. In fact, the Taiwan-based Buddhist Compassion Relief Tsu-chi Foundation has shown the value and meaning of such civic involvement by being active in voluntary work. A spokesperson explained the foundation's position:

> Our master reminds us quite frequently that we are newcomers to this country. We have gotten a lot from this society and we should therefore give back to this society. Since we want to establish roots in America, we have to contribute our talents and our resources. The service of Tzu-chi transcends politics, religion and ethnicity. We want to be part of the mainstream society and want to help the mainstream society and their problems. (*Sing Tao Daily* October 29, 2001)

Chinese immigrants in Silicon Valley also believe that there are other benefits for the Chinese community in their voluntary work. These include the elevation of the status of the Chinese community. Charitable work is an important tool for community or public relations. When the seminar on voluntarism was offered, the attendance was good with more than one hundred people from the Chinese community present. They were eager to find out what they could do to help the less fortunate among themselves and in the larger society.

Paying Back the Community

The Chinese in Silicon Valley are concerned about paying back their community. This was particularly true in the 2001 election in which many Chinese city and school district officials were elected. As a further example of this concern, the Chinese in Cupertino decided to organize a Chinese buffet at Quinland Community Center to entertain the low-income and senior citizens of the community. Councilman Patrick Kwok, Councilman Michael Chang, Barry Chang of the Cupertino Union School District, and other elected officials served this dinner to low-income and senior citizens on December 18, 2001.

Professor Peter Lee of San Jose State University told me that the Chinese are learning how to organize voluntary services to help the less fortunate in the community. Chinese American students in local high schools are also looking for opportunities to help others by participating in peer tutoring and other community service projects.

CONCLUSION

From my study of the Chinese effort of establishing roots, it is safe to say that the Chinese in Silicon Valley invest a lot of energy in establishing themselves economically and politically in the United States. Their globalization efforts do not diminish their dependence on Silicon Valley. The transnational flow and cross-cultural networks and organizations that they maintain do not diminish the importance of place or traditional culture. On the contrary, these transnational networks are used to assist new immigrants in grounding themselves economically in the United States. There is also a continued dependence on the national institutions of the United States: elections, coalitions, political parties, and special-interest groups. My findings echo those of other globalization studies (Friedman 2002, Evans 1999; Escobar 2001). To be grounded locally and to reach out globally tends to be a better description of these new Chinese professionals and entrepreneurs. *Luo di sheng gen* (establishing roots), and *an ju le ye* (It is human nature to live comfortably in a house and happily establish an enterprise) are professed sentiments of the Chinese in Silicon Valley. This is also reflected in their interest and participation in local and national politics. The *New York Times* (January 3, 2004) has noted the eagerness of the Chinese to be part of America, and their success in making political inroads in Silicon Valley. To grow roots in a community requires journeys back to the ancestral land. This is an unusual kind of journey for new immigrants. They left their ancestral home to establish a new home. Now in order to fortify and enrich their new home in America, the immigrants have to return to their ancestral home once again. It is clear these new immigrants are actively engaged in shaping their destiny. This new way of searching for the American Dream is indeed novel to transnational migrants, but their activities are directed to building a new life in America.

Return migration is not solely motivated by a desire for wealth. There are other reasons for their temporary return. One was the economic recessions of the 1990s and early 2000s. Another is the glass ceiling phenomenon, which blocks the promotion of Chinese Americans, and the feeling of disrespect that accompanies this failure to be promoted. Third is the existence of *guanxi* abroad, the friendship, kinship, and other social ties that can be reactivated to launch business enterprises and that are abundant among many of the Silicon Valley Chinese. These relationships, if properly utilized, are highly rewarding financially and psychologically. As we have seen, many Chinese entrepreneurs have founded companies and transnational corporations through the use of *guanxi*. This kind of embeddedness (Kloosterman and Rath 2003) through the use of *guanxi* by return immigrants is important, but it has not been thoroughly studied by scholars of entrepreneurship.

This chapter has shown that globalization has certain aspects that may be worthwhile topics for future research. How has globalization created opportunities for the transnational migrant's entrepreneurship and employment? How has globalization provided ways for the transnational migrant to fight racism and obtain personal dignity? Many nation-based scholars who look at the movement of people in terms of one-way migration will need to reexamine such concepts as brain-drain, assimilation, community, ethnic entrepreneurship, and citizenship. The present study has found that among Chinese transnational migrants, discussion of the circulation of talent, jobs, and wealth is more meaningful than a discussion of brain gain or brain loss. Similarly, amidst political assimilation, there is cultural pluralism. Many Silicon Valley Chinese participate in domestic and national politics while still valuing their culture. Thus political assimilation and maintenance of cultural and ethnic boundary go hand in hand. Furthermore, the circulation of talent and the continuous back-and-forth movement of the Chinese transnationals do not necessarily mean that Chinese transnationals are not loyal citizens of America. In fact, data obtained from this research show that the majority of the Silicon Valley Chinese want to participate in American democracy and want to be treated equally. They want to grow roots in America *(luo di sheng gen)*!

The importance of human relations *(guanxi)*, that is, the successful use of cultural/ethnic and social capital (family, kinship, cultural values, and education), is important in the entrepreneurial activities of the Chinese. Immigrant and ethnic entrepreneurship depend on ethnic resources. These findings echo the results of numerous other studies (Min and Bozorgmehr 2000, 2003; B. Wong 1987; Wong, McReynolds, and Wong 1992; Yeung and Olds 1999; Ng and Wong 1998). The data obtained from this study also show that there is no lack of dynamism among the Chinese in Silicon Valley. Moreover, they use the opportunity and resources available to them, and are therefore actors and agents of their own destiny (Bourdieu 1997; Michel Foucault 1973, 1982). They should not be seen as middlemen, or as entrepreneurs who merely link dominant group producers and manufacturers to minority consumers (Bonacich and Modell 1980). As indicated in this chapter, Chinese entrepreneurs want to be producers, manufacturers, and participants in the global economy. However, to a certain extent, the "disadvantage thesis" of Light (1979), Auster and Aldrich (1984), and Jones, McEvoy, and Barrett (1994) still applies to some. The glass ceiling and other barriers such as language and racial discrimination, as indicated in this chapter, have driven some Chinese to be self-employed entrepreneurs in Silicon Valley or Asia, or to be return migrants.

Globalization and localization can coexist. Globalization does not necessarily imply political apathy or noncommitment to local culture, community, and national state. Not only is it that one can see the continued relevance of the national state in the inclusion and exclusion of minorities, one can also see how citizenship can be useful for the establishment of roots and the protection of minorities in the climate of globalization.

5

Globalization and Social Differences in the Community

Having examined the paradox of globalization and localization in the context of the Chinese in Silicon Valley, I will now deal with relationships between globalization and the members of the community in terms of diversity, career paths, employment, investment, and social equality. Mathews (2000), Braziel and Mannur (2003), Lewellen (2002), Inda and Rosaldo (2002), Marcus (1998), Kearney (1995), and others have pointed out that a flow of people, technology, political ideas, and media images does not necessarily result in homogenization. On the contrary, globalization maintains and creates social differences and heterogeneity. Globalization, as will be shown in this chapter, does not eliminate local and subcultural boundaries but actually increases diversity and accelerates social differences in the Chinese community of Silicon Valley. These differences are not immediately obvious to outsiders, but they are felt acutely by insiders and members of the community.

INTERNAL DIVERSITY AND DIFFERENT PATHS TO BEING AN AMERICAN

The Chinese in Silicon Valley are not a homogeneous community. Rather, they make up many subgroups distinguished by visa status and length of residence in the United States. Legally speaking, the Chinese in Silicon Valley become permanent residents in the United States by different means. One group is made up of locally born Chinese, known in the community as ABC (American-born Chinese). Many of these work in the high-tech industry as accountants, business managers, and engineers. Another group is composed of immigrants who came to the United States through the family reunion clause by being sponsored by family members, parents, siblings, or spouses. Some of these immigrants were already legal citizens or U.S. residents before they went to work in Silicon Valley. Members of the other groups, as discussed below, came to the United States as students or as temporary workers: F-1 student visa holders or H-1B visa holders. This group includes international students from Taiwan and mainland China since a vast majority of the Chinese engineers in the valley launched their careers as graduate students.

Those valley Chinese who came to America as students must have their legal status confirmed before they are permitted to work. Usually, once companies in Silicon Valley have recruited them, their employers will get them H visas. Later, the students are able to obtain green cards and finally, to become American citizens. Generally speaking, almost all the Chinese from mainland China and Taiwan working in Silicon Valley first arrived on H visas and later received their green cards and citizenship through naturalization.

In contrast to these migrant workers, many Hong Kong Chinese come here to join members of their American family or relatives who are already here. The mainland Chinese and Taiwanese Chinese who come here are not sponsored by nor are they dependents of Chinese American families. As newcomers without family links, the Taiwanese and mainland Chinese need to establish their new lives in America first. Once they are gainfully employed and established, they usually get married. Only after they gain their green cards, and obtain citizenship, can they then sponsor their parents and siblings from Taiwan or China. Through this system, a chain migration begins.

The Taiwanese and mainland Chinese differ from the Hong Kong Chinese in another way. Coming here first as graduate students, they tend to be older. In the case of the Taiwanese Chinese, they also have had to serve in the military before they are allowed to come to graduate schools in the United States. Both the Taiwanese and mainland Chinese students tend to study science and engineering in graduate school. Occasionally, some obtain an MBA. Suffice it to say that both the mainland Chinese and the Taiwanese Chinese are highly educated. Many come from prestigious universities like Stanford, the Massachusetts Institute of Technology, the California Institute of Technology, Harvard, and the University of California, Berkeley. Prior to their arrival in the United States, many Taiwanese and mainland Chinese were also students of prestigious universities in their homeland.

There is still another group of Chinese working in Silicon Valley. They come from different parts of the world such as England, Peru, Singapore, and the Philippines, and they are usually overseas Chinese on student visas who later find work in the United States. Some mainland Chinese come to the United States via England. Others are Filipinos of Chinese descent who migrate from the Philippines. In a sense, the Chinese community of Silicon Valley is a global community. Economic globalization and transnational migration have brought the Chinese from different parts of the world to Silicon Valley.

The economic globalization of Silicon Valley has created groups of different visa holders as the Chinese from Taiwan, Hong Kong, mainland China, and other overseas Chinese communities converge on Silicon Valley. The mainland Chinese are still newcomers and many are still trying to change from a temporary worker status to a permanent resident or citizen status. Thus, many of their professional associations focus on immigration issues. For the ABC, citizenship is not an issue because they are American citizens by birth. And for the Chinese relatives of American citizens, the final step to becoming an American is to pass a citizenship exam. Normally, after they have gotten their naturalization papers they will immediately apply for a U.S. passport and use it for international travel. Some will visit their homeland and others will sponsor their relatives to come to the United States. The commonality that links them is that they all would like to secure permanent residency and then eventually become citizens of the United States.

DIFFERENT PATTERNS OF ADJUSTMENT

The valley Chinese community is highly heterogeneous, having recent immigrant Chinese as well as fifth-generation Chinese Americans. Factors like time of arrival, birthplace, country of origin, age, family connection, level of education, work experience, and communication skill may play a significant role in their adaptation to American life in Silicon Valley. Their experience with discrimination varies and their social acceptance by the larger society also differs depending on where they came from and how long they have lived in the United States.

Concerning different valley attitudes toward discrimination and civil right issues, here is a characterization of the new immigrants from Taiwan and mainland China from an ABC perspective:

> Many of the new immigrants are relatively well-off, especially those entrepreneurs from Taiwan. Many have not experienced discrimination in the U.S. They are more interested in the education of their children and cultural preservation projects. The Taiwan, mainland and Hong Kong immigrants do not seem to be interested in issues like fighting for civil rights for everybody, including the civil rights of black and Latinos. It is not just for the Chinese Americans. These new immigrants are not interested in, for example, the mental Health Project of the Asian Community aiming at helping the Chinese, Cambodian and Vietnamese refugees. (Informant Y, interview with author, June 10, 2000)

Attitudes toward entrepreneurship also differ among the different groups of valley Chinese. Chinese from Taiwan started first as employees working as engineers. Some of them became entrepreneurs, founding and organizing start-up companies. After they became wealthy, they then became investors in and incubators of other high-tech companies. In the past five years the mainland Chinese have followed a similar path. This is not the case for the ABC. Many ABC prefer to work as professionals rather than become entre- preneurs. Proportionally, there are more new immigrants than ABC wanting to own their own business. My informants agree that, as compared to the ABC, there is more entrepreneurial spirit among the new immigrants. But some of them actually go on to start their own firm. Here is a typical state- ment from an informant:

> Chinese new immigrants like to have a business. That is a way to achieve their American Dream. They see that other people do it. They see colleagues who are no better than they are technologically and financially able to do it. If other peo- ple who are no better than they are can be entrepreneurs they think, "Why not give it a try yourself?" This is the mentality of many Chinese immigrants. (Infor- mant L, interview with author, September 19, 2001)

Immigrants are driven to succeed (Galbraith 1977). However, many of the Chinese immigrants whom I interviewed said that they feel they are already at the top of their field. In order to be successful and gain more recognition and financial reward from American society, therefore, they have to own a business. Through business, the Chinese immigrant can have more prestige and a greater financial reward. On the other hand, many of the ABC feel that being successful professionals in American society is the way to achieve recognition. They also have seen that their parents who ran businesses had to work too hard. "It is too much of a headache. I am doing quite well in my career. I don't need to have a firm. It is not worth it!" Globalization has not driven all the Chinese to change their attitude and become entrepreneurs.

CAREER PATHS

Chinese immigrants have a diverse interest in entrepreneurship, but career paths for foreign-born Chinese are basically the same. They differ only in terms of stages (see table 5.1). Most Chinese entrepreneurs and engineers in Silicon Valley come to the United States as students with I and J visas. Later they become employees or engineers, still later some become entrepreneurs, and finally some then go on to become investors in high-tech companies. Normally, when they were employed as engineers they got their status ad- justed to H-1B, so that by the time they have become owners or venture cap- italists they have already gotten their green cards and U.S. passports. Many Taiwanese Chinese have already achieved ownership or are now investors in other companies. But the mainland Chinese are still at the stage of being engineers or employees or establishing their firms. This difference in achievement is due to their later arrival in Silicon Valley. The Hong Kong

Table 5.1. Visa Status of the U.S. Chinese by Occupation

Occupation	Visa Status
Student	I or J visa
Employee/Engineer	H-1B visa
Entrepreneur	Citizen or permanent resident of United States
Investor	Citizen or permanent resident of United States

Chinese as a group also tend to have fewer PhDs among them, because most of them came to the United States originally for an undergraduate education. In terms of English-speaking competence, the Hong Kong Chinese seemed to be more at ease with the language than the other two groups. This is due to the fact that Hong Kong was a British colony. But although Taiwanese students may not be as fluent in their spoken English, they have good training in understanding, writing, and reading the language. The Hong Kong Chinese as a group are known to be successful in retail and wholesale businesses and in commerce, although there are some engineers among their ranks. In general, the Chinese from Taiwan and mainland China tend to be more prominent in the high-tech industry than the Hong Kong Chinese. To illustrate some of the social and occupational differences among the different Chinese, the following biographical sketches may be helpful. There are many more such cases that could be listed, but due to the limitation of space, I have chosen only a few illustrative representatives of career path patterns among the Chinese from Taiwan, mainland China, and Hong Kong.

ENTREPRENEURS AND ENGINEERS

Taiwanese

Winston H. Chen

Dr. Chen got his BS in civil engineering from Cheng Kung University, Taiwan. He got his MS and PhD from Harvard University. Upon graduation, he worked as an engineer for IBM in San Jose. In 1978, he became the owner and CEO of Selectron in Milpitas (Teng 1998). This company is a major producer of electronic equipment and computer products. The company went public in 1989, and has grown to more than 14 million square feet of capacity worldwide. The company has branches and offices in England, France, Germany, Australia, China, Japan, Malaysia, Singapore, and Taiwan. Dr. Chen became chairman of the board of Selectron in 1992. He later retired from the chairmanship of Selectron and became chairman of the Board of the Paramitas Foundation. He is now a member of the Board of Trustees of Santa Clara University (Teng 1998).

Denny Ko

Mr. Ko got his BS in mechanical engineering from National Taiwan University. He came to the United States as a student first to study aeronautical sciences at the University of California, Berkeley. After he got his MS, he went to the California Institute of Technology. He received his PhD in aeronautics and applied mathematics there. Upon graduation, he started to work for a number of companies. In 1976, he became the founder, chairman, and CEO of Dynamics Technology (DTT), and the company gained numerous government and industrial clients. DTT later expanded and took several companies under its wing, including Monolithic Systems and Gadzoox Networks. In 1982 Mr. Ko branched out to Asia. He was a cofounder and initial investor in Microelectronics Technology (on the Taiwan Stock Exchange), which became a global provider of microwave broadband subsystems. He is now a partner of Dyna Fund Ventures in Silicon Valley that provides funding to entrepreneurs building new companies (www.dynafundventures.com).

Lynn Liu

Ms. Liu graduated with a BS degree from National Taiwan University. She came to the United States to study engineering and got her MS degree from the State University of New York, Stony Brook. Upon graduation, she worked for NYNEX/New York Telephone, Columbia University, and MARCORP as a software engineer. In October of 2000 she founded Aicent, a wireless infrastructure company that provides a data roaming service for mobile operators in the Asia Pacific region. In her role as founder, Ms. Liu served as CEO and president of the company. She was also a cofounder of GRIC. Prior to cofounding GRIC, she was general manager and cofounder of the software division at Aimnet, a leading Internet service provider in Northern California. All in all, she has founded three companies (www.cina.org/WIB08252001.html). In Chinese, she would be referred to as *nu qiang ren* (a successful woman entrepreneur—literally, a strong woman).

Wu Fu Chen

After graduating from Taiwan National University, Wu Fu Chen attended the University of Florida, where he earned an MSEE degree. He later went to the University of California, Berkeley, to do his PhD work and to Stanford University to study business. He began work as an engineer, and later became a cofounder of fourteen companies in telecommunications equipment and components. Now he is an investor and partner of Acorn Campus. He told me that he has paid special attention to the global economy in the past five years and branched out his investment activities to Taiwan and mainland China.

Sio Chia

Sio Chia is one of the very few women scientists working in Silicon Valley. She graduated with a BS degree from Taiwan and later got her PhD in bio-chemistry. As a woman, she found it difficult to compete with men in high-tech Silicon Valley. She was laid off many times. She is presently a senior researcher at a biomedical research company in Silicon Valley. Chia said that she has no intention to run a start-up company as she is quite contented with her present position. She also said that biomedical technology is quite competitive and the equipment is expensive. Most scientists cannot afford to start up a biomedical company.

Mainland Chinese

Hong Chen

Chen is the cofounder and CEO of GRIC, a leading provider of Internet-based mobile office communications services (Zhang 2000). He graduated with a BS in computer science from Xian Jiaotong University in 1982 at the age of 19. After receiving his PhD in computer science from the State University of New York, Stony Brook, in 1991, like many other Chinese high-tech immigrants from mainland China he started to work as an engineer first and later became an entrepreneur. He founded Aimnet, an Internet service provider that was later sold to Verio. In 1994 he founded GRIC, which went public in 1999. GRIC is now a recognized expert and provider of global internet communications services, connecting more than three hundred of the world's top telecommunications companies in 150 countries. Chen serves as CEO and guides the globalization activities of the corporation.

William Yang

After graduating from Beijing University, Yang went to the University of Waterloo for a PhD. Like many other graduates, he worked as an engineer for a number of high-tech companies on the East Coast. He later got a job in Silicon Valley. Recently, with the help of his friends, he started Bayspec. His company is at an early stage. He and his friends work very hard, every day from 8:30 am to 9:30 pm. His company is still private, and it has sixty employees.

Sin An

An studied optical engineering and automatic control at Tsinghua University and holds a PhD in electrical engineering from the California Institute of Technology. After graduating, he was a research scientist and development engineer at a private research and development company specializing in optical technology development. Prior to his present position, Dr. An was a visiting scientist at the Jet Propulsion Laboratory in Pasadena, California, where he was responsible for space qualification of holographic devices. Currently he is contemplating starting a company with his friends.

Edward Zhao

Zhao is an engineer working for Delta Products Corporation. After graduating from Tsing Hua University, Beijing, he went to the State University of New York, Stony Brook, for a PhD and stayed on to work in the United States. He has worked for a number of high-tech companies and still works as an engineer. He is happy to be an engineer and has no intention of starting a company.

Daniel Xu

A graduate of Beijing University, Xu came to the United States to earn an MBA in business communication and an MS in economics research from the University of North Texas. He now works for a high-tech company and is an officer of the SCEA. He plans to open an international HR company to serve high-tech firms. He said that the entry of China into the WTO will definitely generate more international business ventures between Silicon Valley and China. With a background in business management and technology, and with his *guanxi* in China, he believes that he is in a good position to organize this global human resource company.

June Chu

Chu is an engineer from mainland China. She earned her MS in electrical engineering at the University of Oklahoma. She specializes in network software development and currently works as a senior software engineer at 3Com Corporation. Chu served the SCEA for three years beginning in 1998 as vice president of social activities and vice president of professional activities. She then ran for president of the organization in 2002 and won. The SCEA is the largest professional association in Silicon Valley with a membership of 3,500. It is concerned, among other things, with the promotion of entrepreneurship among its members. The association also helps its members participate in economic globalization activities in the Asia-Pacific region.

Hong Kong Chinese

David Lam

Dr. Lam graduated from high school in Hong Kong, finished undergraduate work in Toronto and received his PhD from the Massachusetts Institute of

Technology. After obtaining his PhD he worked for a number of companies. In 1980 he started Lam Research to make equipment to produce semiconductors. During the first year, he had fifteen employees. The company went public in 1984 and has since become a global leader in semiconductor capital equipment. Lam Research now has seven thousand employees. The company is global, doing businesses in different parts of the world. Dr. Lam has been a CEO for a number of other companies and is now also an investor. He is active in civic and community work, and in a number of public speeches he has advocated the hiring and promotion of minority engineers. He is also active in community activities and local politics. He was appointed by former U.S. President George Bush to serve on the U.S. Commission on Minority Business Development, and by California Chief Justice Malcolm Lucas to serve on the Commission on the Future of the Courts. He is a member of the Committee of 100. In 1993 he was appointed chair of the Silicon Valley Global Trading Center. He has also traveled to China with Ron Brown, secretary of commerce, to improve U.S. economic cooperation with China. David Lam is now a venture partner at Dyna Fund and is a board member of several high-tech companies.

Fred S. L. Chan

Mr. Fred Chan was born in Hong Kong. He came to the United States in 1968 to pursue his education at the University of Hawaii. After getting his BSEE (1972) and MSC (1974), he worked for Intel. He later founded AC Design (Teng 1998, 213). In 1985 he joined ESS Technology as president. The company offers comprehensive solutions for audio, video, modern, and home networking applications using the Internet. In 1992, he was appointed chairman of the board, and in 1994 he was appointed CEO (www.esstech.com/CorpInfo/management.shtm). ESS Technology has been named one of the best small companies in America by *Forbes* magazine. Mr. Chan established the Everlasting Private Foundation and the Chan Family Fund with the Community Foundation of Santa Clara. He is known to be an enthusiastic philanthropist in the valley community, and he has contributed scholarship funds to the University of Hawaii and Stanford University.

Milton Chang

Mr. Milton Chang completed high school in Hong Kong. He earned a BS in electrical engineering with highest honors from the University of Illinois. He completed his MS and PhD degrees in electrical engineering at the California Institute of Technology. Then he worked as a research engineer. Later he joined Newport Corporation and became its president and CEO. He was with the company for seventeen years and was responsible for taking the company public. He subsequently founded five other companies. In the development of each of these companies, he nurtured company capitalization from 0 to 50 million dollars. He is now an investor helping other start-up companies.

Pauline Lo Alker

Lo Alker was born in Hong Kong in 1942 and came to the United States at the age of seventeen with her family. When she was in college she majored in mathematics and music but also took courses in engineering and computer science. After graduating from college in 1964 she worked for a number of companies in the computer industry. She started Counter-Point Computers. in 1984. The company was acquired by Acer in 1987. She joined Network Peripherals in 1991 and is now CEO of the company (Liu 1995, 182).

Common Patterns among Chinese Entrepreneurs

In the above cases one sees a general pattern whether the entrepreneur comes from Hong Kong, China, or Taiwan. Usually these entrepreneurs arrived in America as students, and then gained employment in high-tech firms. Once they were established and had more confidence and experience in their field, they ventured into business, becoming CEOs of private companies, CEOs of public companies, and finally, investors and incubators. As mentioned above, there are more entrepreneurs and investors among the Taiwanese Chinese than among mainland Chinese. However, more and more mainland Chinese entrepreneurs are starting companies. Many of my informants predict that the number of entrepreneurs and investors from mainland China will eventually surpass that of their Taiwanese counterparts for two reasons. One is the fact that mainland Chinese engineers working in Silicon Valley now are younger and they form a much larger pool of talent. The second is that mainland Chinese engineers have been influenced by the recent economic reforms in China. They have been taught that "to be rich is glorious." There is a great deal of enterprising spirit among these young engineers. It is safe to conclude that at least 25 percent of them are constantly thinking and talking about entrepreneurship. How many of them will actually go on to become entrepreneurs is an unanswered question.

These high-tech professionals are decision makers. To find a job or to run a start-up firm, to sell or to acquire a firm, to localize or to globalize, to go or not to go public with one's business—all of these choices require critical decision making. When initiating their businesses, each one of these entrepreneurs had to bear certain risk. From interviewing such entrepreneurs, I have learned that they are innovators, risk-takers, profit maximizers, and eager participants in the global economy.

Chinese male engineers far outnumber female engineers, especially among the Taiwanese Chinese, due to the fact that female students in Taiwan tend to study business and the humanities while male students are encouraged to study science and technology. In mainland China both males and females are encouraged to study science and technology to help build a modern China. Modernization in mainland China is a national priority and equality of the sexes is emphasized.

These Chinese Americans are actively participating in economic globalization. As entrepreneurs, CEOs, and owners of companies in Silicon Valley, they are concerned with seeking production and sales outlets in different parts of the world. They would all like to have branch offices and market shares in North America, Asia, Europe, and Latin America. But not all of the Chinese in Silicon Valley are equally interested in the global economy. The decision makers of companies are more involved than employees in globalization activities. Thus, there is a difference in their participation in the global economy.

There are also other cases that do not fit into these three groups neatly. Jerry Yang of Yahoo! came to the United States at the age of two. He went to elementary school, high school, and the university in Silicon Valley. Other entrepreneurs came to the United States via another country. For instance, Jose Wong was born in China and educated in Macao. He migrated to Peru with his family, and he came to the United States to study at San Jose State University. Upon graduation he got a job in San Jose and is currently working as an engineer for Applied Materials in Silicon Valley. Another example is Mr. Li. He first migrated with his family from Shanghai to Hong Kong. He finished high school in Hong Kong and attended college in England. Upon his graduation from college, he saw in a newspaper an ad seeking engineers to work for Apple Computer in Cupertino. He applied for and got the job, and continues to work there. Silicon Valley, as a capital of high-tech, has drawn many talented Chinese from different parts of the world.

Thus we see that the globalization process has not homogenized the Chinese community. On the contrary, economic globalization and a transnational migration movement have created a community that is stratified in terms of birthplace, wealth, time of arrival, immigration status, and occupation. This phenomenon has been recognized by other social scientists (Appadurai 1996; Preyer and Bos 2001). What is unique about the Chinese in Silicon Valley is the fact that they are drawn from the same ethnic group but hail from different geographic areas under the reinforcement and constraint of diverse political systems.

The Taiwanese Chinese, the mainland Chinese and Hong Kong Chinese have been raised in different kinds of political-economic systems. The Taiwanese Chinese have been brought up under a capitalistic system. Conversely, a whole generation of young mainland Chinese, after being raised under a communist/socialist system, are only now learning about capitalism and free enterprise. The Hong Kong Chinese have been influenced by the British colonial and free-enterprise systems. Hong Kong has been important in global commercial activities for decades, and many Chinese in the San Francisco Bay Area, from Chinatown to the South Bay, are connected with Hong Kong in one way or another.

These three groups have integrated differently with U.S. society. In terms of electoral politics and running for public office, since the Hong Kong Chinese have a less pronounced foreign accent and are more Westernized than the other two groups, they are more electable. Michael Chang, a former mayor and current council member of Cupertino, told me:

> There are fifteen cities in Silicon Valley with ninety city council members. But there are only three Asians amongst them: Henry Manayan (half-Chinese/half-Filipino) in Milpitas; Hedy Chang in Morgan Hill; I am in Cupertino. Sunnyvale and Cupertino share the same school district. There are some Chinese serving on the school board. Immigrants getting elected are new. They need support from both Asians and non-Asians. It is easier for a Chinese to start from school board because of the perception that the Chinese/Asians value education and are good educators. (Michael Chang, interview with author, June 25, 2000)

He said that the Chinese have made some inroads into the politics of San Francisco but they had not yet been very successful.

> The Chinese have more Chinese voters to support them in San Francisco. Many of the elected ones were from Hong Kong. Lillian Sing, Mabel Tang, Julie Tang and others are from Hong Kong Christian schools. They are more Westernized. Hong Kong Chinese are more electable than the Taiwanese Chinese because of the fact that the Taiwanese Chinese have a heavier accent and are not as Westernized. Hong Kong Chinese are more acceptable to the voters. (Michael Chang, interview with author, June 25, 2000)

In the election of 2002, Taiwanese Chinese were elected to the college board and city council, so it seems that the situation has changed. However, as of this writing, I have not seen any Chinese from mainland China competing for political office in Silicon Valley. This is perhaps due to two major reasons. One is the fact that many of the mainland Chinese immigrants are not citizens yet. The other is time. They are the most recent newcomers and have not yet mastered the political and cultural systems. Given time, I presume that some of them will participate in the American democratic system through serving in public office.

On the issue of motherland politics, some of the Silicon Valley Chinese are pro-RPC (Taiwan), some are pro-PRC (mainland China), and some are neither. Some are for the unification of China and some are for Taiwanese independence. Some of the Taiwanese-born Chinese are increasingly critical of the KMT and openly talk about how the Taiwanese Chinese are different from the mainland Chinese. Some have "unbounded" their desire to have an independent Taiwan. A small minority goes as far as to argue that there is a separate Taiwanese culture (it is not just a Chinese culture), and these want to organize a Taiwanese Culture Heritage Foundation.

REGIONAL CULTURES OF THE SILICON VALLEY CHINESE

The Chinese in Silicon Valley differ from each other not only in their political outlook and their experience with the West; they differ from each other culturally as we have seen. There are differences in their dialects, foods, dress codes, social values, and political ideologies. But in Silicon Valley these three subcultures influence each other. There is a mixing of the materials of culture: food, drink, and linguistic expressions from Taiwan, Hong Kong, China, and even the United States.

The first-generation Chinese especially have a strong interest in keeping up their cultural traditions. They supported the construction of a Chinese Temple in the San Jose Historical Museum, and since 1980 have enjoyed access to more Chinese Schools, cultural classes, and Chinese-language classes in the valley. They have summer programs such as *Pipa* (a traditional Chinese musical instrument), folk dance, Chinese drums, handicrafts (arts and crafts), and Chinese painting classes. The first-generation community also sponsors cultural exhibits and activities. Its connection with Asia as a result of globalization helps in the maintenance of Chinese culture on the one hand and fosters hybridization of culture on the other.

All of the Chinese emphasize education, with the brightest Chinese students entering the fields of science and technology, but among the first generation, family, kinship, friendship, colleagues, alumni, and regional networks are also important. They celebrate Chinese traditions such as the New Year and the Mid-Autumn festivals.

Many Taiwanese Chinese have nuclear and even extended families in the United States. The mainland Chinese, as latecomers, may not have families in the United State yet but they long to establish them. All three groups have similar aspirations. They would like to acquire what are known as the "five valuables": money, automobile, spouse, house, and child. They call this the attainment of *wuzi* (five valuable things): *yinzi* (money), *chezi* (automobile), *chizi* (spouse), *fangzi* (house), and *haizi* (children). The Taiwanese Chinese have told me that they need money to survive and an automobile to get around. Those who are single are anxiously looking for marriage partners. They want to establish a family and hence they need a spouse because their parents always remind them about the importance of getting married and raising a family. Those who are married are anxious to purchase a house and have children. And once they have children, they become involved in the education of their children. It is widely known in Silicon Valley that the Chinese value education. In fact, many Americans are not at all hesitant to cast their votes in support of Chinese candidates running for school boards in the South Bay.

Chinese entrepreneurs in Silicon Valley are sensitive to current events. Many daily read two papers from two national perspectives. Typically, they like to read the *World Journal* and the *Sing Tao Daily*. They maintain connections with their families overseas or in the motherland through modern communication tools: telephone, fax, and e-mail. The major long-distance telephone companies have long known about the importance of intrafamily communication among the Chinese, and they target the Chinese in Silicon Valley as valuable consumers.

The Silicon Valley Chinese are in tune with modern technology. They use the internet to inform each other about the fate of other Chinese immigrants in Indonesia and different parts of the world. They also use high-tech means to voice their complaints about racism and to discuss problems faced by the overseas Chinese. They consult huaren.com periodically. Some use the site to conduct business in real estate and to market their financial products. They also use this website to discuss the ideas of a greater China, diaspora, citizenship, and other issues relevant to the Chinese around the world.

Taiwanese Chinese prefer to live in Cupertino. The richer entrepreneurs prefer to live in Los Alto Hills where the cheapest "fixer-uppers" start at a million dollars. The schools in Cupertino are thought to be excellent and real-estate values there tend to appreciate. This community is also very close to Stanford University where many Chinese families hope to send their children. The rich Hong Kong Chinese prefer to live in Hillsborough and San Mateo. The less affluent ones live in apartments in Sunnyvale.

Silicon Valley has an abundance of Hong Kong and Taiwanese products and consumer goods. Taiwanese coffee and Taiwanese food are served even in major supermarkets like Marina Foods in Cupertino. Hong Kong dim sum is available in many shopping centers in Milpitas and San Mateo. The mainland Chinese frequent Shanghai-, Beijing-, and Northern Chinese–style restaurants and they have their favorite professional associations. For their economic activities, they go to mainland China and to the places where they received their education, such as Beijing, Shanghai, and Tienjin. They have different demeanors and dress differently. They tend to live in San Jose, Milpitas, Fremont, Morgan Hill, and Santa Clara. As newcomers they may live in apartments first. Later when they have accumulated enough savings, they prefer to move into new houses in the above cities, which tend to be more affordable than houses in Cupertino, Los Altos Hills, Palo Alto, and Hillsborough.

As mentioned earlier, Chinese alumni associations in Silicon Valley are important in the organization of social and athletic activities. The different groups of Chinese tend to patronize their respective associations. Taiwanese graduates go to Cheng Kung, Taiwan, Jiaotong, and Tsing Hua University alumni associations. Graduates from mainland China tend to go to Beijing,

Fu Dan, Tsing Hua (mainland), and Jiaotong University alumni associations. The Hong Kong Chinese go to their high-school alumni associations. Socially they all have different roots and alumni networks. One of the reasons why there is this disparity or social segregation among the Chinese is the use of dialects. The Hong Kong Chinese prefer to speak Cantonese, while mainlanders speak Mandarin, and the Taiwanese speak either Fujianese or Mandarin. Another reason is upbringing. The valley Chinese immigrants were enculturated in different regional cultures. The members of these three groups of Chinese may talk about the detective stories, movie stars, and ethnic foods that are meaningful to them. Even in the case of dating, a Chinese girl from Hong Kong may want to go out with someone from Hong Kong for the sake of communication. Thus a common upbringing, common schools, common dialects, and common foods are important for social interaction.

Political distance among these three groups also exists. Certain topics are avoided, such as the policies of Chiang Kai Shek and Mao Zedong. But it is quite common for immigrants to talk about the politics of their mother country. During a Taiwanese election, some of the Taiwanese in Silicon Valley will discuss candidates of their choice although they may no longer vote in Taiwan. They were all concerned about the earthquake on September 21, 1999, in Taiwan in which over two thousand people were killed, and they are interested in kidnapping incidents and so on. One group is for Taiwan's independence. The other is for the eventual unification of Taiwan with China. In the case of the mainland Chinese, they may talk about an incident involving the collision of an American spy plane and a Chinese jet fighter, about the consequences of China's admission into the WTO, or about the bombing of the Chinese Embassy in Yugoslavia in 1999. In recent social gatherings, the mainland Chinese have been interested in discussing issues related to employment and insurance among expatriates working in China. All of the mainland Chinese are in favor of the unification of China and Taiwan. However, a small group of PRC Chinese are for democracy. They are members of the Silicon Valley for Democracy in China Association. Some were participants of the Tiananmen Square uprising in 1989; some are their sympathizers. The majority, however, are not political activists. The Hong Kong Chinese may want to talk about the political future of Tung Chee Hua, who was replaced by Donald Tsang in the summer of 2005 as Hong Kong's new leader.

There is a social distance between these three groups. They work together professionally but may not socialize with each other. The fact that they do not socialize together does not mean that they do not get along in the work place. On a professional level, they have cordial relations. In some of the professional associations, one can see crisscrossing membership. Speakers from one organization may be invited to speak at another. Thus, a prominent member of the Monte Jade Association (a majority of its members are from Taiwan) will give a speech before the SCEA (the majority of whose members are from mainland China). Professionally they interact with each other, while socially they maintain a certain distance.

In terms of establishing roots and fighting racism, they are supportive of each other. They want to fight for their rights and their equality in this country. When a Chinese is discriminated against, they will unify to fight. There was a case in which a car dealer shouted racial slurs and discriminated against a Chinese customer. Immediately an e-mail message was sent to other Chinese valley residents, whether they were from mainland China, Hong Kong or Taiwan. Likewise they were unified in the fight to seek redress for Dr. Wen Ho Lee. The community quickly established a website and organized a foundation to raise legal funds. They were able to raise $500,000 in legal fees for Dr. Lee. The goals of the foundation were to seek freedom for Dr. Lee and to work for getting justice for him. After Dr. Lee's release in September of 2000, the Chinese community felt much relief but vowed to continue to help him gain justice. Many of the Chinese people I spoke to feel that they have learned an important lesson from this case, and that they need to continue to fight racial profiling and racism. The case of Dr. Wen Ho Lee not only galvanized Chinese Americans, it inspired other Asian Americans to be vigilant in defending their civil rights (*San Jose Mercury News* September 14, 2000). The Chinese were also unified in their relief work after the September 11 terrorist attacks. As can be seen, the Chinese of the valley are united in many common causes but divided on certain issues related to their homelands.

KNOWLEDGE OF CHINESE CULTURE

Among the different groups of valley Chinese, Chinese cultural traditions are highly valued, and certain ideas and behavior are shared. On the other hand, the groups differ in terms of cultural knowledge and competence. Some group members speak several Chinese dialects, some speak two, some speak one, and some speak none. In the past, Cantonese was a lingua franca among the Chinese. Today in Silicon Valley, Mandarin is more commonly spoken among the Chinese. In general, the Chinese from mainland China and Taiwan can speak fluent Mandarin. Many Hong Kong Chinese have recently learned to speak Mandarin due to the fact that Hong Kong is now part of China. Many of the ABC can speak only Cantonese. Some older parents of the Chinese immigrants from Taiwan can speak only Fujianese (or a local Taiwanese dialect).

Not only does the ability to speak Mandarin vary among the Chinese, their knowledge of Chinese culture differs too. The Chinese from Taiwan, for instance, are well-educated in the Chinese classics and modern literature. Many in fact had a university education in Chinese prior to coming to the United States. The Hong Kong Chinese generally finished only high school in Hong

Kong. Their knowledge of Chinese is at the high-school level, and their writing skills in Chinese also remain at the high-school level. Of course there are exceptions, and occasionally some of the Hong Kong Chinese do go to the Chinese University of Hong Kong before they come to the United States.

The mainland Chinese are trained in simplified characters. Their training in Chinese classics, philosophy, and literature is also limited due to the fact that the Chinese government emphasizes specialized training. Only a few of them are trained in classical Chinese. Influenced by the Cultural Revolution, the PRC did not require university students to be well-versed in traditional Chinese poetry or prose.

There are subcultural differences among the mainlanders, the Taiwanese, and those from Hong Kong. Some of the Chinese even argue that there is a *Taiwan wenhua* (Taiwanese culture), a *Xiang Gen wenhua* (Hong Kong culture), and a *Da Lu wenhua* (mainland Chinese culture). Since the three regions share a similar base culture, strictly speaking, it is only appropriate to say that these three are subcultures. But even in the written language there are differences in the use of words and in the transliteration of phrases and foreign words into Chinese. That explains why the Mandarin-speaking Chinese from Taiwan prefer to read the *World Journal* (a Taiwanese paper), the Hong Kong Chinese prefer to read the *Sing Tao Daily* (originally, a Hong Kong paper), and the PRC Chinese will read the sina.com site in simplified characters. In terms of spoken language, the Hong Kong Chinese speak Cantonese and watch KTSF in Cantonese. Channels 17 and 32 (KPST) carry Mandarin programs. Since the Silicon Valley has more Mandarin speakers, Channel 66 is more popular in the South Bay.

In terms of enculturating their children into Chinese culture, there is often a conflict about standards and depth. In the various Chinese schools or Chinese curriculums, parents sometimes debate with other Chinese parents on the goals and standards of Chinese language education. Taiwanese parents tend to complain that the language programs are too easy or even useless for their children. They want to set higher standards in the teaching of language and culture. Parents of the ABC argue that the goal of Chinese education is to teach Chinese children something about their roots. There is an ongoing debate over whether traditional Chinese characters or simplified Chinese characters should be taught. There is also an argument about what kinds of textbooks to use. Should they use those published in Hong Kong, China, or Taiwan?

FORCES OF CULTURAL CONTINUITY

As part of their heritage, Chinese parents hope that their children will have a working knowledge of Chinese history, traditions, and social values, and that they will know the basic patterns of Chinese social interaction. Nevertheless, there is quite a bit of cultural retention among the valley Chinese in the areas of language, foods, and traditional festivals. This is the case even among the third-generation Chinese Americans. Many still speak their dialects at home. They address their relatives by traditional kinship terms and interact with each other according to traditional Chinese etiquette. Of course the first-generation Chinese in Silicon Valley read Chinese and often watch Chinese TV programs. They are adamant about transmitting Chinese cultures to the younger generation. This explains why there are so many private Chinese language schools in Silicon Valley. Some of these schools organize cultural tours to China or Taiwan. The teaching of Chinese calligraphy, Chinese dances, or Chinese martial arts to Chinese students as extracurricular activities is quite popular. Parents spend quite a bit of money just to make sure that their children will learn about their cultural heritage.

Chinese schools, newspapers, TV programs, and churches (Christian, Buddhist, Taoist) are all important agents for cultural preservation in the community. Travel to China and maintained family connections both act as important catalysts for the preservation of Chinese culture. In fact, some parents periodically take their children back to Taiwan or Hong Kong on vacation with the hope that their children will learn the language and refamiliarize themselves with Chinese culture. Some Chinese language teachers also make arrangements for young Chinese Americans to live with Chinese families in China or Taiwan in home-stay programs so that they can benefit from total emersion in the language and culture.

Chinese newspapers carry traditional and modern Chinese detective stories and love stories to attract young readers. Reading these stories helps them keep up in their reading knowledge. Many Chinese churches teach the important Chinese cultural values of family, Confucianism, and Chinese etiquette. Even in the preaching of the New Testament, a Chinese priest or minister may use Chinese proverbs or allegories to illustrate his points. These immigrant pastors also evoke the memories of their home countries and their past experience in China or Hong Kong. In doing so, a pastor can add more persuasion and warmth to and enhance acceptance of his church's teaching. In the Chinese Catholic churches, the love for ancestors is incorporated into the ritual of All Souls' Day. Often after the Sunday services there is a Chinese potluck or buffet and a celebration of a traditional festival.

Chinese TV programming has modern Chinese drama and historical stories. There are also Chinese language teaching programs in the valley, a Buddhist program, and movies from Hong Kong, Taiwan, and China. There are discussions of current events and news programs designed for the Chinese in America. Both Taiwan and mainland China broadcast such programs.

Despite these cultural preservation projects of the community, it is inevitable that many of the Chinese children are Americanized. Some of them are pressured to speak only English and to imitate the behavior of their

American peers. There is increasingly more intermarriage between the Chinese and the non-Chinese (whites, Latino Americans, Filipino Americans, and others). The forces of change are as strong as ever, and Americanization is thus an inevitable outcome. But even when the Chinese young have become Americanized, they still want to keep a certain familiarity with their cultural heritage. Multiculturalism and Americanization, from my observations in Silicon Valley, seem to go hand in hand.

CHINESE CULTURAL INFLUENCE IN THE LARGER SOCIETY

In multicultural Silicon Valley, one sees the cultural interactions of many diverse cultures. The Chinese have definitely left an imprint on valley society. Many Chinese festivals are celebrated, and major Chinese traditions have made inroads into the larger society. The Chinese New Year is celebrated with special foods, the Lion Dance, and the giving of *lishi* (*hung bao* in Mandarin) meaning "lucky money." In Cupertino, lion dancers and drummers are often non-Chinese. In the opening ceremonies of many business enterprises, the Chinese Lion Dance teams are invited to perform and to celebrate. Both Chinese and non-Chinese spectators enjoy their performances in Silicon Valley.

The Dragon Boat Festival has attracted Chinese as well as non-Chinese athletes to compete in its boat races. Traditionally in China the festival falls on the fifth day of the fifth month of the Chinese calendar. In Silicon Valley the celebration takes place during the summer months.

The Celebration of Confucius's Birthday has become a major event in many school districts in Silicon Valley. In the past several years, thousand of people have attended the Confucius Ceremony in the Chinese Cultural Center of Sunnyvale. The center is often filled to capacity with those watching a reenactment of traditional Confucius rituals. This is also an occasion for politicians to show their appreciation and hopefully win friends and potential voters. The governor of the State of California normally sends a special proclamation and greeting to the celebration. In 2002 Governor Davis, with the approval of the state assembly, declared September 28 Confucius's Day.

The traditional Chinese Mid-Autumn Festival is popular among the Chinese. In recent years, however, the non-Chinese in Silicon Valley, especially in Cupertino, have become aware of the festival. They call it the Moon Festival, and many have heard about and have tasted Chinese moon cakes. In 2001 Sandy James, the mayor of Cupertino, dressed herself in a traditional Chinese bridal costume to greet festival celebrants in Memorial Park of Cupertino. Additionally, in many of the high-tech offices one can see Chinese decor. American companies have Chinese scrolls on their office walls. Flags of China are flown in many buildings and government offices.

Asian restaurants are popular among the residents of Silicon Valley. There are Shanghai, Cantonese, Hong Kong, Vietnamese, Japanese, Filipino, and Indian restaurants. Both the Chinese and non-Chinese frequent these restaurants. In Silicon Valley one can find connoisseurs of Chinese food among these non-Chinese. Regional Chinese foods from Beijing, Szechwan, Hunan, Tainan, Hong Kong, and Shantung are all available. Chinese and non-Chinese alike go to Asian shopping centers like Ranch 99 in Milpitas to eat Chinese porridge or soup noodles. Chinese greens, egg rolls, and pot stickers are favorite food for parties. The principles of feng shui are used for architecture and interior decoration by many Chinese and non-Chinese in Silicon Valley, and the Chinese presence in Silicon Valley is also seen in housing styles.

There are numerous ethnic shopping centers in Silicon Valley. Many of them are run by either the Chinese or Japanese. However, there are many white and other non-Chinese customers. Chinese supermarkets in Fremont, San Jose, Milpitas, and Cupertino are full of customers, especially on Saturdays and Sundays.

In Overfelt Park of San Jose there are Chinese gardens where visitors can enjoy Chinese landscape design. In addition to the gardens and wildlife, one can view an impressive thirty-foot bronze and marble statue of Confucius that overlooks a reflecting pond. There is also an ornamental Friendship Gate with an inscription welcoming visitors: "Under heaven, one family. Welcome People from Far Away." The park has a Sun Yat-Sen Memorial Hall, a statue of Chiang Kai-Shek, and its Plum Pavilion. The San Jose Regional Parks, Conventions, and Arts & Entertainment Department manages it. In the park, one can see the practice of Tai Ji Quan (Chinese shadow boxing) and many of the devotees are non-Chinese local residents.

From material culture like food and clothing to worldviews and Chinese philosophy, from the Dragon Boat and Moon festivals to the Chinese New Year and Confucius's Birthday, one sees a greater acceptance of Chinese culture in Silicon Valley. The traditional melting pot or assimilation theory (Handlin 1972; Gordon 1964), which explained the Americanization process as a trickle down process dictating the direction of acculturation from the dominant society, needs to be revised. The data from my study indicate that ethnic groups' influence on the larger society often "trickles up" instead. Chinese traditions, food, and customs have been taken up by the larger society in Silicon Valley.

The Use of Chinese Language in the Public Schools

The school district in Cupertino, after much debate, has decided to offer Mandarin as an option for foreign languages. There are non-Chinese among the students who take Mandarin and, in fact, some of them speak better Mandarin than those of Chinese descent. In 2001 a non-Chinese person won a Chinese language contest organized by the Chinese Language Teachers Association of Northern California. The use of Chinese characters has become acceptable in Silicon Valley. Some non-Chinese students even learn Chinese calligraphy as part of their extracurricular activities in school.

Community and Interethnic Cooperation

There is also cultural syncretism. The Taiwanese, Hong Kong, mainland Chinese, and American cultures influence each other. Paradoxically, cultural diffusion and syncretism occur in food (vegetarian egg rolls, Chinese peanut butter sandwiches), music (Chinese words and American melody), mass media (English words in a Chinese newspaper), art forms (the Washington Square Dance), religion (Christianity with Confucian teaching), and feng shui with an American twist.

People adjust to their local environment and change their culture accordingly. They negotiate with their social and economic environments. They combine cultural components to create a new hybridized culture. Chinese restaurants that have hybridized cuisine call their cooking "fusion style." However, not all combinations are feasible. A hybridization has to stand the test of time.

Interethnic cooperation exists in Silicon Valley. It exists in business partnerships, in social and political joint ventures, and in social activities among neighbors. In many Chinese-owned companies, non-Chinese sales and marketing personnel are needed. There are also venture capital firms run jointly by Chinese immigrants and local financiers that support Chinese and non-Chinese businesses. Socially, one can see both valley locals and Chinese immigrants intermingling at social gatherings. In many business seminars, one will see Chinese-speakers and non-Chinese-speakers invited to make presentations. Politically, the Chinese community and its politicians may endorse non-Chinese men and women to run for public office.

Lester Lee, president of Recorte in Silicon Valley, noted that there is an interdependence among white, Chinese, Indian, Vietnamese, Mexican, and Jewish Americans of Silicon Valley. He as said that these groups need each other. The valley needs white marketing experts, Chinese hardware designers, Indian software developers, Vietnamese manufacturers, Mexican warehouse owners, and Jewish financiers. This apparently has been the case for the past ten years (Lee 2001). One can also see white Americans working for Asian employers, renting from Chinese landlords, and accepting Chinese engineers as their managers or colleagues.

There was a consensus among my informants that interethnic dependence is a trademark of Silicon Valley. My informants agreed with Lester Lee's assessment. For example, local politicians often need support from the Chinese community, and many Chinese entrepreneurs are willing to lend a hand to support candidates who are known to be fair and capable. During the re-election campaign of Mayor Sandy James in 2001, high-tech Chinese like the

CEO of Acacia Group, Mr. Chow, and Dr. Hsu of Cupertino, and a host of other prominent Chinese, were fund-raisers for her campaign (*Sing Tao Daily* October 23, 2001).

Conversely, many Chinese events and public forums, including the Chinese New Year Celebration, the Mid-Autumn Festival, and several nonprofit internet websites have white American sponsors. The Chinese community of Silicon Valley in general is well connected with the local community and the local residents.

Economically, it should be obvious that Chinese high-tech professionals have contributed to the growth of Silicon Valley. They still work in mainstream companies like Intel, HP, IBM, and Oracle, but Chinese American companies too are important have won prestigious awards for their respective specialties. Many of the companies owned by Chinese Americans create employment for Asian Americans and Latino Americans as well as white employees. Examples of these are Selectron, WYSE, and Lam Research. Each one of these has employed thousands of workers.

The real-estate business in the valley has been greatly stimulated by the infusion of Chinese immigrant professionals. Purchasing a home is the number one priority for Chinese families. As soon as they have accumulated enough money, they immediately look for a house. In the period from 1997 to 2000, one could spot long lines of Chinese engineers waiting to purchase houses in new housing developments in Fremont, San Jose, and Cupertino. Car dealers also take aim at Chinese customers and hire Chinese-speaking salesmen to facilitate business transactions. The presence of immigrant Chinese professionals has changed the economic valley landscape and increased interethnic economic transactions.

Immigrants influence mainstream culture and vice versa. There is a cross-fertilization of cultures. The traditional idea of the one-way assimilation by the host society of the immigrant culture is no longer true in this era of globalization. People are shapers, creators, synthesizers, and integrators of cultures. In Silicon Valley this kind of integration of cultures is particularly striking. Both Americanization and Asianization are taking place.

Unlike the immigrants who came to nineteenth-century America and who had to "give up their cultural baggage" and be quickly assimilated into the mainstream Anglo-Saxon culture, these new Chinese immigrants find themselves in a different time, place, and social environment. The immigrants who have come to Silicon Valley in the past twenty years are highly educated professionals and entrepreneurs. Meanwhile, some old-timers in Silicon Valley have not changed their attitude toward the Chinese. They still carry in their heads negative and racist images of the Chinese immigrant of the nineteenth century. They still think of the Chinese as laborers, laundrymen, and restaurant workers. These old-timers are shocked when they see the valley Chinese purchasing expensive properties in the most expensive areas of South Bay like Hillsborough, Los Alto Hills, Atherton, and Palo Alto. They are equally shocked to see so many Chinese people driving Lexuses, Mercedes, and BMWs. Some Chinese immigrants purchase homes and quickly remodel and enlarge them into mansions. A local may find these activities incongruent with their image of the Chinese. Or they may find it difficult to understand why these new immigrants are doing better than they are. There is certain amount of resentment and jealousy. "We have been here for so long. We could not even have what they have. They are newcomers and they are wealthy." This has a lot to do with a lack of understanding of the social and economic backgrounds of these immigrants from Taiwan, Hong Kong, and China. Some valley residents are not accustomed to see Chinese with PhDs and advanced degrees from elite American universities like Harvard, Yale, the Massachusetts Institute of Technology, and Princeton, or from elite Chinese universities like Beijing University, Taiwan National University, and Tsing Hua University.

Conversely, many of these same new immigrants experience culture shock in Silicon Valley. They have to learn how to adjust to Silicon Valley. At work, they have to learn how to express their opinions and defend their positions. The glass ceiling phenomenon is particularly frustrating. In PTA meetings, as parents, they have to listen to and understand school issues and take a proactive stand. They have to alter their perception of school teachers as untouchable authorities. When they go to eat in expensive restaurants, they have to learn how to speak quietly. When they purchase a car or a house, they are told to pay with a check not cash, even though many of them carry large quantities of cash and prefer to carry out transactions in cash. This kind of cash transaction is common in Hong Kong, China, or Taiwan but it is viewed in the United States with suspicion. The Chinese old-world habit of bargaining is sometimes perceived to be strange in America. During business meetings, many Chinese engineers are quiet and unexpressive for they want to show their respect for authority. Nor are they familiar with the rules of order that govern meetings. Because of this their behavior may be perceived by non-Chinese as uninformed and uneducated. Often Chinese high-tech people never drink or go out with their colleagues to socialize, and so are sometimes thought to be antisocial. In reality, they may never have learned how to drink alcohol. Nondrinkers in Chinese culture are considered good people. Some never learn how to make small talk or tell jokes in English. Others never learned that they are expected to go out to cafes or bars with their colleagues for the sake of social bonding and camaraderie. Indeed there is a problem of communication and cultural misinterpretation. In general, the Taiwanese Chinese who are educated in American universities are more Americanized than Chinese mainlanders who are new to the United States. Given enough time, it is conceivable that these cultural differences will diminish.

Similarly, when a Taiwanese Chinese resident enlarges his home so that he can accommodate his extended family, he may face objections from his non-Chinese neighbors. If that happens, he may become frustrated. He will think this objection is unreasonable and that Americans are inhumane in not allowing him to enlarge his home so that his parents can move in. For him, it is good to enlarge the home to accommodate his aging parents. For his American neighbors, it destroys the character of a small and pristine neighborhood to have a large home. They call it a "monster home" and criticize the remodeling as something extravagant and greedy.

Cultural misunderstandings exist in many such ways. Several years ago when Chinese parents wanted Cupertino schools to offer Mandarin, there were local residents who objected. In a school board meeting, someone shouted at the Chinese, "Go back to where you came from!" Another resident said, "What the hell, Mandarin in the schools? This is the United States." But the Chinese at the meeting countered that a voluntary Mandarin program would be good for students. They argued that learning two languages would benefit all students, regardless of their race or ethnicity. The Mandarin program was eventually approved by the school board in the spring of 1998 (*San Jose Mercury News* April 15, 1999). There was also the case in Los Alto Hills of a white homeowner who set up a big board with characters that were offensive to his Chinese neighbor. The Chinese neighbor thought that the sign looked like a Chinese tombstone, which is perceived to be bad feng shui. He went to the town hall and made a request for removal of the sign. But his white neighbor thought that it caused no harm and that the sign was artistic. Achieving multiculturalism is thus easier said than done. Education is needed to enhance cross-cultural understanding. In fact, in Cupertino an organization has been set up to facilitate communications between new immigrants and the locals. This organization is called the 5Cs—Citizens of Cupertino Cross-Cultural Consortium, and it has dedicated itself to the promotion of friendship and cross-cultural understanding among the city's ethnic groups. The 5Cs periodically organizes block parties, yard sales, and community forums to discuss racial and ethnic issues. The 5Cs hopes to develop unity in the midst of diversity. Many in the community told me that a lot of hostilities have been ironed out and cross-cultural communication has improved tremendously in recent years in Cupertino. My informants told me that in their experience Silicon Valley has improved in the area of cross-cultural communication. People tend to be more tolerant of each other nowadays because of the efforts made by local community groups and organizations like the 5Cs.

INSIDER VS OUTSIDER PERSPECTIVES

Social scientists have long recognized the importance of making a distinction between an emic (insider) and an etic (outsider) perspective. Sometimes these two are fundamentally the same and in fact, the two views may converge. Both insiders and outsiders may share similar views. However, most often there are differences. Some of these are due to either ignorance or irreconcilable disjunction in the use of paradigms. In Silicon Valley, questions that seem to be constantly on the table are the following: Are Chinese Americans more segregated in their economic activities? Are Chinese Americans a model minority? Are Chinese Americans more oriented to China and less loyal to America? Are Chinese Americans more globalized and less localized? Are Chinese Americans more Chinese and less American?

Many Americans have derived their assumptions of Chinese American economic segregation from traditional Chinese ethnic enclave businesses like grocery stores, restaurants, laundries, and gift shops. Many of these ethnic businesses are small in scale and are run by family members. And everyone who goes to Chinatown inevitably feels that Chinese businesses are segregated from the mainstream. Shopkeepers speak Chinese to each other and the organization, social etiquette, and interaction patterns seem to be "so Chinese" to the outsiders. Certainly there are firms run by family members and firms that hire only Chinese. However, in a place like Silicon Valley, there are very few Chinese-owned companies that hire Chinese workers exclusively. It is simply impossible for a large high-tech business to be totally self-sufficient and exclusive. Some firms at the beginning stage may depend on social networks for financing and may use friends and relatives as their labor source. However, as time goes on and the company grows in size, it will not be possible for the company to depend on family and coethnics entirely. The need for financial support is too great. When it comes to labor resources, any Chinese-owned high-tech company, with the exception of the very small ones, needs to depend on other Americans. This is particularly the case for Chinese companies that need nonethnic consumers for their profitability and survival. They always hire vice presidents, marketing personnel, and PR consultants who are well connected in the larger society. In fact, they prefer to hire white Americans who are highly skilled in communications. The owner of a Chinese company I visited in Silicon Valley was Chinese and he employed many Chinese engineering specialists. However, he hired a white American, who was a native speaker, to be an administrative assistant. His financiers were not Chinese either. I visited another Taiwanese equipment testing company in Silicon Valley where, to my surprise, all the blue-collar workers were either Indians or white Americans from the local community. At a high-tech investment company, I saw Chinese investors and partners conduct business with many non-Chinese firms. Although the company had almost all Chinese partners, the partners interacted with both Chinese and non-Chinese high-tech companies in Silicon Valley. At Incubic, an incubator company, the owner is Chinese but almost all the employees are white Americans, and the company does business with both Chinese and non-Chinese companies.

In order to participate in the Asia-Pacific market, it is natural for these Chinese firms to look for Chinese-speaking and trusted coethnics who can deal with that market. They would prefer to have capable Chinese friends, colleagues, and relatives head their overseas division. This is understandable because overseas work requires the intimate knowledge of a local culture and language. But even in this situation, white Americans are sometimes invited to accompany a company's overseas officials, who may need American legal and financial experts.

Outsiders may see that some Chinese companies have a solid core of people who came from certain schools and certain geographical areas. Again this is also understandable, for in Silicon Valley many companies do not use headhunters to recruit people since it is too costly. Besides, people hired through these means may not work out due to the company's lack of intimate knowledge of the candidates, who may only look good on paper. Many American companies use network hiring for the same reasons: to save money and ensure quality. Network hiring is particularly common when the job market is tight, and is commonly used regardless of race or ethnicity; it is not unique to Chinese-run businesses. The intrinsic nature of high-tech companies requires that they hire people who can do the job. Very few business owners are so irrational as to hire a relative who cannot meet the needs of a position.

In the manufacturing area, companies may have a group of Chinese employees working as assemblers. If one looks at the composition of the group very carefully, one will see that seldom are they related by blood or friendship. They are a mix of Vietnamese, Chinese from Guangdong Province, and Cambodians. To the average American, the assemblers will appear to be all Chinese. In reality, they are from different Asian ethnic groups. In Silicon Valley it is extremely difficult to staff an assembly line with just one ethnic group. And in any ethnic group there are some individuals who are highly talented and some who are not. Most of the decision making in hiring, from what I have learned, is not based on ethnicity alone. There are economic rationales to consider. There is a big difference between an enclave business where one can have one's family run the entire restaurant, and a big company for which outside help must be hired. In the high-tech business, cost, specialization, talent, and knowledge dictate employment practices. When a company has gone public, management and employment normally become highly institutionalized, and a professional staff will be chosen to run an HR department. The staff of this department will be careful to follow the proper procedures in hiring and other business practices. Often these professionals will not be Chinese. When a Chinese person is chosen, it is probably due to the special skills that this person might offer.

Hence, the outsider's perception that the Chinese hire only Chinese and that they do not contribute to creating jobs and wealth for the larger society is untrue. Immigrant businesses in the United States between 1983 and 1992 created more than 20 million jobs. Yahoo! for instance, cofounded by Taiwan-born Jerry Yang, benefits many Americans. Similarly, Oak Technology, Selectron, and other Chinese immigrant companies have created jobs, wealth, and employment for many of the non-Chinese residents of Silicon Valley.

Racial Profiling Problems

During the period from 1999 to 2001, there were two cases involving the Chinese that dominated national and local news in the United States. One was the case of Dr. Wen Ho Lee, and the other was the collision between an American spy plane and a Chinese fighter jet over the South China Sea. Due to these two incidents, many Silicon Valley Chinese felt that they were being profiled as spies, and that they were considered guilty by ethnic association. In fact, over the years this type of racial profiling has cost many Chinese Americans their careers. One engineer, Chih-Ming Hu claimed that he lost his NASA-related job in 1982 over his alleged ties to China. Hu worked as a realtor for awhile after he was fired. He has since worked for a number of high-tech companies and recently for Rendition, a Sunnyvale-based high-tech firm (*San Jose Mercury News* June 23, 1999).

In Silicon Valley a racist backlash followed the investigation of Dr. Wen Ho Lee. Lester Lee, said that Chinese engineers and scientists at that time were under a cloud of suspicion. His friends at Lockheed and Loral were looked at as suspects. Even he, the president of his own company, was being looked at differently. He said he found his non-Chinese employees at the time uncomfortably distant (*San Jose Mercury News* March 13, 1999). Engineers from mainland China suffered most from the impact of the case. In fact, some politicians in Washington, D.C., took this opportunity to call for stepped-up scrutiny of the ethnic Chinese business and scientific community in America.

In April of 2000 the collision of an American spy plane with a Chinese fighter jet and the aftermath of that incident also inflamed much bias against Chinese Americans in America and in Silicon Valley. Chinese informants in Silicon Valley told me that they sensed hostility toward them because of the incident. The *San Francisco Chronicle* (April 14, 2001; April 21, 2001) reported that a radio talk-show host in the San Francisco Bay Area, Don Bleu, used ethnic slurs on the air about Chinese Americans. Lumping together Chinese Americans with China and the mainland Chinese Government is a disturbing manifestation of racial profiling. Marshal Ginsburg wrote on April 14, 2000, about the persistence of racial profiling:

> Even the Bay Area, where Asian Americans are about 20 percent of the population and where people pride themselves on tolerance, has not been immune. Radio talk-show host Don Bleu spoofed the spy-plane standoff April 6 in what he called a "fry over." (Ginsburg 2000)

Ginsburg reported that the radio talk-show host, Don Bleu even called a restaurant in Chinatown and teased a Chinese person because of the spy plane incident. But the racial insults didn't end there. Cartoonist Pat Oliphant, a Pulitzer Prize winner, published a cartoon showing a buck-toothed Chinese waiter delivering cat gizzard noodles to a customer. Oliphant also made an ethnic slur about the Chinese. Many were shocked by this racial caricature, but others encouraged it. Some called for the internment of people of Chinese ancestry and some urged a boycott of Chinese restaurants. Some mocked Asian accents or telephoned people with Chinese last names and harassed them. This kind of behavior shocked many recent Chinese immigrants to Silicon Valley. They wrote to the newspapers and voiced their protest. They also worked through ethnic organizations like the OCA and other professional organizations demanding an apology. The radio station for which Don Bleu worked later offered an apology.

Outsiders might have thought these remarks were funny, or that they were just to provide laughs during a tense situation. The insiders did not think that way. In fact, some of them were worried about their lives in America, and feared that racial remarks and racial caricatures would lead to racial discrimination, persecution, and hate crimes. Some Chinese began to feel that this was a country that would never accept them. Some became enraged and vowed to dedicate their lives to fighting racism in America. It was a case of irreconcilable differences. The insider perspective is sometimes totally opposed to the outsider perspective.

Globalization Activities and Perceived Disloyalty

The world has changed economically and politically. It is no longer simply divided into a communist world and a free world. There are socialistic practices in the capitalistic systems. Likewise, there are capitalistic practices in the communist world. Furthermore, economic activities have gone beyond national borders. Modern communication and transit systems such as jet planes, the Internet, and fax machines have shortened, if not eliminated the time inherent to international communication and transportation. The stock market exchange systems of the world in London, Zurich, Tokyo, Taipei, Hong Kong, and New York are now intimately intertwined. The movement of money, products, and material has become globalized as well. This is particularly the case in the modern high-tech industry. The Chinese in Silicon Valley have typically enlarged their economic sphere to include the Asia-Pacific region. Many economists around the world have predicted that the twenty-first century will be the "Asian Century," and it is the Pacific territories that are particularly attractive to Chinese American entrepreneurs who have language and cultural assets in this region.

In the past fifteen years, many Silicon Valley firms have branched out into Europe as well as Asia. The economies of the Asia-Pacific region have been playing a catch-up game with the Western economies and thus have more room to grow. Economists have predicted that annual growth rates will reach double digits in China. In the high-tech area, China has a large market as well as a large labor pool. As a result, traveling to China, Taiwan, Hong Kong, and Singapore to conduct business has become quite common for the Western businessman (see chapter 4). In the next several years, this kind of business travel will intensify. However, constant traveling and frequent absences from one's home territory are sometimes perceived by American neighbors as a sign of rootlessness and of un-American sympathies. Some of these neighbors ask, "Why did they go to China to open up shops when they can open up shops here and benefit Americans?" Paradoxically, as these Chinese American entrepreneurs globalize their economic activities, they generate more money for their headquarters in Silicon Valley. In so doing, they generate more wealth to support more Americans in automobile manufacturing, real estate, the restaurant industry, banking and other service businesses. As I have shown, to achieve the American Dream a Chinese American may have to leave America and return to Asia many times over many years. This is a new breed of immigrant, these transnational migrants, and their mode of economic operation is globalization. Unfortunately, many scholars and officials, as well as non-Chinese residents of Silicon Valley, do not understand this changing world.

Government officials can seem particularly ignorant about the changing world. American immigration officials, at times, are disturbed by permanent residents who travel frequently overseas for business. They ask, "If you like this country, why do you leave it so often?" This question is often asked when immigrants are returning to America. They face tough questioning from immigration officials, and they have been threatened with confiscation of their green cards. Apparently, many immigration officials have not changed their worldview. It is inconceivable to them that people can have their roots in the United States and yet continue to travel to China or other parts of Asia strictly for business. Yet the modern economy requires constant international travel. My informants also mentioned that white Americans living overseas for years while working for multinational corporations seldom face questioning on residence or receive lectures on patriotism. Some of my informants told me that they are afraid to go through immigration in San Francisco because the officials there seem to be tougher and more provincial. Officials there are known to give lectures on loyalty and commitment to the United States. To avoid hassles, transnational migrants occasionally return to Silicon Valley via the international airports of Los Angeles and Vancouver.

My Chinese informants revealed to me that they had to answer embarrassing questions when they took the U.S. citizenship exam. Here are some examples: Will you shoot another Chinese if America is at war with China? Will you shoot your relatives and friends if they are on the opposite side? Why is there such an inclination of government officials to think that Chinese or Asian Americans cannot be patriotic? Some social scientists (Takaki 1989, 1993; Issacs 1980) contend that it is a die-hard white American paradigm to believe that Asians are different. Any nation and any people that can be seen as a threat to the superiority of white America is an enemy, evil and perilous. Ronald Takaki argues that white America has always considered Asia to be dangerous. The expression "yellow peril" was used to describe the immigration of the Chinese in the nineteenth century. The influx of Chinese immigrants was depicted then as an invasion, as the entrance of an alien and dangerous horde. David Wellman of the University of California, Santa Cruz, is even more explicit in his explanation, saying that "This country has always had a very racist attitude toward Asians" (*Los Angeles Times* April 30, 2001). He further predicts that negative sentiments will intensify as Asian Americans enjoy continued educational and economic success. Psychologists and anthropologists believe that deep-seated insecurity motivates many of these anti-Chinese activities. In the new global economy, China will emerge as a major economic power, and this presumably will further intensify negative sentiments toward Chinese Americans who have been labeled as strangers who owe loyalty to a foreign country. Many Chinese organizations in Silicon Valley are aware of this sentiment and are working hard to erase this stereotype about Chinese Americans. In order to dispel such stereotypes and in order to fight against racial profiling, the Chinese in Silicon Valley use their professional and civic organizations to strategize. They also write letters to the newspapers, elect Chinese officials, hold public demonstrations, and make use of the law and courts. Some Chinese Americans believe that the Chinese should integrate more with American society in order to gain better support from society.

In order to develop a true multicultural America, there is an immediate need to change this racist paradigm. The Chinese, as well as any other ethnic group in America, have made extraordinary contributions to this country. But they need the "others," those of different ethnic or cultural heritages and backgrounds. This is particularly the case in the new global economy. Immigrants with strong social ties to their mother countries are important bridges linking the United States with the rest of the world. Chinese Americans and other Asian Americans are indispensable bridges between the East and the West (Naisbitt 1995). They are culture brokers, mediators of various regional economic systems, and the links of political communities. Obliterating racial distrust, not only against the highly talented Chinese Americans in Silicon Valley who have made a commitment of establishing roots (*luo di sheng gen*) in the United States, but against all Chinese, can only benefit America.

Foreigners, Model Minorities, and Globalization

Despite their commitment to the United States, the Chinese are often seen as foreigners. Chinese immigrants and Chinese Americans, whether they are citizens or permanent residents, are treated as outsiders. Yet paradoxically, they are no longer treated as citizens of China once they have become U.S. citizens. When officials of the PRC attended functions in Silicon Valley commemorating September 11, 2001, they often commented on the patriotic fund-raising activities of the Chinese Americans. The Chinese Consulate in San Francisco praised their donations as the work of civic-minded American citizens of Chinese descent. The Chinese Americans were addressed as Americans and were congratulated for their commitment to their country.

Still, the image of the Chinese American as foreign is deeply rooted in the American psyche. Clearly, in order to develop a real multicultural society, much work still needs to be done. But ironically, there is an opposite attitude toward Asian Americans (including the Chinese), under which Asian Americans are seen as a model minority. But this seemingly positive stereotype can have detrimental effects as well on ethnic relations. It pits minority groups against each other. "How come your ethnic group cannot do it but the other group can?!" This attitude even encourages further discrimination against the Chinese Americans: "You are a model minority. Why should we help you!" It only helps unwittingly justify racism and the nonacceptance of certain groups.

My informants in Silicon Valley told me that race relations in Silicon Valley are probably the best when compared to race relations in places where they have lived before. Some Chinese entrepreneurs who are highly successful told me that the United States in how its people treat the Chinese is better than other parts of the world. "This place is the best. Racism is minimal. See we can make it here!" The less-successful Chinese immigrants see it differently. The following statement is quite typical among them:

> There is always a certain amount of racism. If you are a minority, you will always get discriminated against. It is unavoidable. We are less integrated into the mainstream U.S. society because we look different and the Chinese culture is different from Western culture. (Informant KL, interview with author, April 29, 2001)

A majority of the Chinese here feel that racism exists in American society. They also say that Silicon Valley, by comparison to the rest of America, is more tolerant. However even in Silicon Valley, they feel that they are often treated as foreigners although they are citizens of the United States by birth or through naturalization. Many are eager to use the ballot box to vote for public officials who are sympathetic to the interests of immigrants. Chinese American professionals are also quick to spread information through their professional organizations and the Internet about racial-profiling incidents and discriminatory treatments. They are no longer the passive receivers of unfair treatment.

CONCLUSION

The cultural mix of Silicon Valley is influenced by ethnicity, subethnicity, technology, globalization, and ideology. Many social differences in terms of its residents' social class, regional culture, knowledge of American or Chinese culture, and participation in the global economy still exist there. Technology and globalization do not homogenize culture and social differences but on the contrary, they accentuate intracultural and class differences among the Chinese.

Globalization necessitates travel. Entrepreneurs have had to expand their activities to different parts of the world. The reconnection of the entrepreneur with his or her homeland for business activities also generates a flow of mass media and material culture into the Silicon Valley Chinese community. This phenomenon has been recognized by social scientists who study transnational communities (Basch, Schiller, and Blanc 1994; Werbner 2002). In the valley one can see the latest movie on video, hear the latest Chinese hit songs, and taste the latest culinary inventions from Hong Kong, Taiwan, and mainland China. Globalization facilitates educational and cultural exchanges, hence promoting the flow of Chinese culture to the community. Thus, globalization does not cause the demise of traditional culture. On the contrary, it revives tradition and ensures the continuity of Chinese culture in the United States. Globalization in this sense does not produce homogeneity but rather social and cultural differences. For these reasons, cultural pluralism is also a by-product of globalization. Americanization or homogenization is not necessarily the result of the transnational flow as suggested by many authors (Appadurai 1996; Mcluhan and Powers 1992).

There is unity amidst diversity. The community created in Silicon Valley is both homogeneous and heterogeneous on different levels. Its members are united by their aspirations, their occupations, their involvement with technology, and their interest in finding a permanent place in America. They differ in their attitudes toward their motherland, as well as in their social and economic positions. Their attitudes toward the unification of China and the independence of Taiwan vary a great deal depending on whether they were raised in Taiwan or elsewhere. Silicon Valley has thus brought many politically diverse groups of people together who cooperate with each other on one level and do not cooperate with each other on another. The globalization that brought them together also disintegrates their unity via their connections with the old world.

Globalization has created a unique community permeated with Chinese culture outside of China proper. It is a modern case of a deterritorialized culture (Basch, Schiller, and Blanc 1994; Hall 1990; Gupta and Ferguson 1997). This community of high-tech professionals has made a choice: to make a living in America and to keep Chinese culture at the same time (*mei guo sheng huo, Zhongguo wenhua*). It is simultaneously a hybridization of elements from two cultures. A complete synthesis of these cultural elements still needs to be worked out! The Chinese diaspora in Silicon Valley, like many other diasporas in the world (Braziel and Mannur 2003), has become a site of contestations marked by hybridity and heterogeneity.

6

The Social Costs and Benefits of Globalization: Family Life and Social Adjustments

Economic globalization with its accompanying transnational movement has brought untold social cost and structural changes to the family. New opportunities and suffering go hand in hand with these changes. Specifically, participation in the global economy and transnational migration has had a great impact on the social life of Chinese high-tech workers in Silicon Valley. While some of these changes are beneficial, other are less so. This chapter demonstrates the indelible impact of these trends on family and social life and argues that the often assumed durability of Chinese family is not as resilient as previously thought. Transnationalism among these new immigrants has created new lifestyles resulting in the following four new family arrangements: (1) the matrifocal family, (2) the patrifocal family, (3) the nonparented household, and (4) the transnational extended family with members living in different parts of the world. This chapter will also show that the dispersal of the Chinese family is not always beneficial as claimed by Henry Yeung (1997), Kris Olds (1995), and Kwok-bun Chan (1997). However, these authors have focused their discussion on Chinese transnationals in the ASEAN (Association of Southeast Asian Nations) region where geographical, social, and economic conditions differ from those in the United States. In the case of the Chinese in Silicon Valley, one can see the loneliness of the children left by their transnational parents who return to Asia for business or employment. On the other hand, there are also Chinese who have developed transnational extended families that help them in maximizing economic returns for their family business; however, these are only a small minority (B. Wong 1988; Murata 2001).

Data obtained from fieldwork indicates that intrafamilial relations, residence patterns, and gender relations within the family have been altered as a result of transnational migration. The most obvious evidence of this is the uneven sex ratio of engineers in Silicon Valley. This and the phenomenon of a "bachelor society" are not uncommon in many transnational communities. For instance, there is a large population of single Filipina maids in Hong Kong (Parrenas 2001). The Silicon Valley Chinese, are highly educated and talented engineers, and they are the elite of their society. During the period from 1970 to 1980, most of the Chinese engineers in the valley were those who came from Taiwan as unmarried graduate students, leaving their parental families behind in Taiwan. After settling in Silicon Valley, they married their college sweethearts or other Chinese immigrants. Now, many of these Taiwan engineers have sponsored their parents to come join them. An influx of Chinese engineers from mainland China began in the late 1980s. In the past ten years or so (1990–2001), the number of these engineers migrating to Silicon Valley exceeded those from Taiwan. They were also younger, the majority of them being below the age of forty-five. Although during this time there was an increase in the number of female Chinese engineers from mainland China, the male to female sex ratio in the valley is still highly uneven at 7 to 1. As was the case with the Taiwanese students, the majority of PRC engineers are not married and have no family life.

Since there is this lack of family life, many associations specifically organize weekly activities in order to help Chinese bachelors in the valley deal with their loneliness. These associations have become substitutes for families. Colleagues and friends become quasi-kin. Still, loneliness and the lack of a family life are the most common complaints of mainland Chinese engineers. In many of the association gatherings and meetings I attended, I noticed that there were events and activities created especially for these young people, events such as parties for singles, social dances, and dinners. Social clubs abound: hiking, poetry, international folk dance, literature, and others. Sina.com and other business organizations have organized dating clubs and dances that attract participants from as far away as Taiwan. Then too, there are classified ads run by single Chinese men and women looking for partners of the opposite sex. Some ads are even placed by Chinese women who are still in China but who are looking for marriage partners in the United States.

With so many Chinese bachelors in the valley, the community has been labeled a bachelor society (B. Wong 1982, 1985, 1988). This highly resembles the situation in America's Chinatowns of the nineteenth century. However, there is a significant difference: female Chinese engineers today are a highly desirable element of this community. These young unmarried Chinese, male and female, are under enormous pressure from their parents. Chinese parents via long-distance phone calls and mail constantly remind even female engineers of the necessity of getting married. One engineer who graduated from UCLA with a master's degree said to me:

My parents keep reminding me that I am now thirty. They say that is not good. I should try harder to find a nice boy. They say after all I am not that young any more. They say that I should think about getting married and establishing a family. They want to have a grandchild. (Informant TT, interview with author, March 9, 2002)

This was a typical comment of many of my female informants. As for male engineers, some actually go back to China to look for potential marriage mates.

The extensive amount of traveling that Chinese entrepreneurs do has an enormous social cost. In particular, married men have to make many personal sacrifices. First of all, long-distance commuting is physically exhausting, especially when it involves seven to eight trips a year to Asia. This constant travel causes burnout and health problems. Long and frequent separations may lead to family problems, with the result that single-parent households among the affluent Chinese have become a noticeable phenomenon. At the same time, children can suffer from loneliness and this loss of parental guidance.

It is clear that globalization is responsible for the breakup of many personal relations. Engineers and entrepreneurs who are constantly absent from their home base are at particular risk. One male informant told me:

It is difficult for Chinese men to meet Chinese women in Silicon Valley. First, most of the men work in the high-tech industries where they have irregular working hours. Second, the sex ratio between the sexes is so uneven with seven men to each woman. The competition is tough. After you have a chance to develop a relationship, many find it difficult to maintain it because of overseas work or assignments. I lost my girlfriend that way because of my frequent travel to Asia. (Informant V, interview with author, September 27, 2001)

One of my female informants, Sharon Lee, told a similar story: participation in the global economy is hazardous to many Chinese engineers.

I had a boyfriend before. But he is like many other Chinese men who are anxious in establishing his career. He took off for China almost immediately when he experienced his first glass ceiling difficulty. Maybe boys are raised differently. They are more uncompromising. My friend was very upset. He wanted to go back to China because he felt that he was more appreciated there. I told him that he should not go since his job here is quite good and he can wait and find another job. But he just took off and split up the relationship. This is quite common among many young Chinese couples. It is a pity! (Sharon Lee, interview with author, March 9, 2002)

These stories about how return migration complicates romantic or personal relationships are quite abundant. Modern Chinese immigrants differ significantly from their predecessors.

In the lifestyle of highly educated professionals and affluent businessmen operating on the global stage, many new challenges arise as the identity of the family itself is severely compromised. Furthermore, in response to changing economic opportunity structures in the world, Chinese immigrants have broadened their employment from traditional ethnic niche and professional occupations into global businesses, and, many have taken on the mantle of the global, transnational worker, conducting business in different parts of the world. For some Chinese immigrants, long-distance commuting has become common. Some are required by their jobs to live temporarily in one country and to conduct business in another; they have become transnational nomads in the modern world.

GLOBALIZATION AND THE NEW SOJOURNING LIFESTYLE: HOMES AWAY FROM HOME

While it is true that some engineers and entrepreneurs from Silicon Valley go back to Asia with their families, the majority, if they return, go alone to work. The purchase of condominiums by overseas Chinese in Shanghai or Beijing is becoming a common phenomenon. It is their home away from home. "What they are" is affected by "where they live." A home away from home has an effect on people. Many globalization scholars have discussed this phenomenon (Portes 1997; Ong and Nonini 1996; Wu, McQueen, and Yamamoto 1997; Yamashita, Din, and Eades 1996). To understand these global actors and transnational migrants, one has to examine their lives in their permanent homes as well as in their lives away from those homes. Globalization has given rise to a multi-sited ethnography or a macro-anthropology (Hannerz 1996; B. Wong 1997; Burawoy 1991). The following is an examination of several sites in Asia that have become temporary homes for the Silicon Valley Chinese.

Taiwan

In the Asia-bound movement there have been several waves. The first wave took place in the early 1980s as Taiwanese engineers returned to Taiwan to develop the semiconductor business. Taiwan then had the capital but not the technology, so it was a perfect marriage between the two. The engineers had technological knowledge, and Taiwan had financial capital just waiting to be used in developing an industry.

The second wave came during the early 1990s when Taiwan already had a high-tech infrastructure in place. What Taiwan then lacked were high-tech experts. Other events and happenings in the United States such as a severe recession in the early 1990s, American society's refusal to completely accept the Chinese, the glass ceiling effect, and greater opportunities in Taiwan all helped contribute to this second wave of returnees.

The third wave, made up of high-tech engineers with high salaries from Silicon Valley, left for Taiwan between 1994 and 1995. These engineers returned to Taiwan primarily to (1) participate in the further development of the semiconductor industry, and (2) take advantage of exceptional offers and opportunities in Taiwan. On the Hsinchu Scientific campus, research facilities, condominiums, and other technical support centers were built to attract Chinese engineers from Silicon Valley. Examples of these repatriates include Peter Chen, Rick Tsai, and Genda Hu, all originally from Taiwan, though they had acquired advanced training at American universities and had worked in Silicon Valley. Many of those who returned to Taiwan actually had families still living Silicon Valley. These high-tech engineers would return to the United States quite frequently to visit their families. They were the so-called astronauts, shuttling between countries.

According to many of my Chinese informants in Silicon Valley, the Taiwanese government played an active role in enticing the Chinese to return to Taiwan to work in the semiconductor business. In 1980 Mr. Lee Guo Ding of the Taiwanese legislature established five scientific divisions to serve and coordinate scientific personnel in Washington D.C., Los Angeles, Houston, San Francisco, and Chicago. The Taiwanese government also sent scholars to the United States to learn technology management and to coordinate scientific exchanges between Taiwan and the United States. In 1984 a Science Division of the Taiwanese government was established in Silicon Valley, with a head office that is now located in Santa Clara. The Science Division is itself under the direction of the Taipei Economic and Cultural Office in San Francisco. Its facilities include a meeting room and a library that provides information about investment, research, and business in Taiwan. The division also publishes a newsletter and encourages the development of professional societies. The Monte Jade Science and Technology Association was established in 1990 under the Scientific Division. Both of them have sponsored trips to visit China.

China, Greater China, and Other Regions of Asia

In the 1980s Asia had the so-called four little dragons: Taiwan, Hong Kong, Singapore, and Korea, which acted as suppliers of cheap labor and a large consumer market. In the 1990s the four little dragons became part of the United States' economic sphere. Many Chinese engineers from Hong Kong, mainland China, and Taiwan were recruited to work in Asia as expatriates. In the 1990s China started to become a key player in the high-tech world, which may not be surprising because the highest-ranking officials in the national governments were engineers. As such, they understood that science and technology bring material benefits to the nations that are willing to develop them. Chinese Americans in Silicon Valley also understood this, and some took the opportunity to work in China, while others were sent by American companies to work in Asia as expatriates; still others went there to be entrepreneurs. Steven Ting, for example, went to China to organize a research center for Nortel, Mr. Y. M. Ting brought Oracle to Asia, and Mr. Shi went to China to establish a computer business.

Jumping on the bandwagon, Hong Kong established its own Silicon Valley, and called it the Cyberport (*San Francisco Examiner* November 19, 2000, B1). Korea and Malaysia also developed their own regions similar to Silicon Valley. Malaysia calls its version the Multimedia Super Corridor. But Taiwan, by far, has been the most successful in its attempt to duplicate the success of California's Silicon Valley. All these Asian countries have been trying to lure high-tech experts, especially the ethnic Chinese, from California's Silicon Valley.

THE TRANSNATIONAL CHINESE

Language ability, cultural knowledge, and informal social networks are important for economic globalization. Some businesses, such as Nortel, Cadence, and Oracle, understand the importance of transnational joint ventures. Chinese American entrepreneurs and high-tech personnel have served as vital bridges to the creation of this globalized industry.

Steven Ting graduated with multiple degrees: a BS in electric engineering from Cheng Kung University, an MS in mathematics from Missouri State University, and an MS in electric engineering from the University of Cincinnati. Ting left Silicon Valley and went to China in 1993 to work for Nortel as a vice CEO. His position required much travel in China. As an expatriate he was allowed to relocate to Beijing from Silicon Valley with his family. In addition to his regular salary, he received numerous perks: transportation, accommodation, and education and living subsidies. He moved one-third of his furniture and household goods to China, leaving two-thirds in storage in Silicon Valley (Teng 1998, 435). Ting's responsibilities included the establishment of research and development centers, the transfer of technology, and sales and marketing. As one of the pioneers of high-tech joint ventures with China on behalf of Nortel, he was chairman of the Board of Trustees of Shanghai Nortel Semiconductors, and he shouldered other responsibilities.

Another pioneer was Sherman Ting of Oracle. He helped globalize Oracle technology in Asia, Japan, Taiwan, and mainland China. Sherman Ting graduated from the Department of Geology of Taiwan University. He received an MA in computer science from the University of Pennsylvania, then worked for Intel and later for HP. In 1987 he went to work for Oracle, but returned to HP to help the company generate substantial profits. Ting was invited to Taiwan in 1992 to give a speech on his success. When he returned to the United States, he proposed that HP organize an Asia-Pacific division. He then traveled to Japan, Taiwan, and mainland China to organize branches for the company. He also helped establish a branch of his own company in Taiwan in 1992, and cooperated with NEC, Fuji, and other Japanese companies. In 1997 Sherman Ting was able to arrange meetings between high-ranking officials of Oracle and the vice premier of China, Li Peng. Network components and software produced by Oracle were introduced to Asia due to the efforts of Ting (Teng 1998, 447).

Mr. Chris Xie is an example of those who have recently returned to China. Xie left China in 1993 to attend the University of California, Riverside, to study computer science. After he finished his education, he started a peer-to-peer computing company in 1998. Like many PRC Chinese, he started the company from his Sunnyvale apartment. Through friendship connections, Xie teamed up with a partner, Zhao Guobin. They eventually went back to Shanghai to found Green Tea Technologies, which they originally intended to establish in Silicon Valley. The reasons for their return to China were quite simply economic. They could not get seed money from Bay Area investors. However, on the other side of the Pacific, they were able to get funding from a Shanghai biotech company, through which business contracts, cash grants, and rent-free office space were also acquired. Green Tea Technologies now has offices in three cities: Shanghai, Beijing, and Shenzhen. Recently, it signed an agreement with Dawning of Beijing, which has a $12 million contract to put computers in public schools all over China. Meanwhile, Chris Xie keeps his apartment in Sunnyvale, while traveling frequently between China and the Bay Area (*San Francisco Chronicle* January 2, 2002, B1).

All of these China returnees kept their roots in the United States (and Silicon Valley) when they went to Asia for business. The modern economy requires their physical presence on many continents. However, they have not become rootless commuters living in space. They are aware of their roots in Silicon Valley and they actually miss the United States. Jennie Chen, who left San Jose to run an HR software company in Shenzhen, said, "I miss the lifestyle in the Valley, where you can just drive to Yosemite on the weekend" (*San Francisco Chronicle* January 2, 2002).

Modern transnationalism demands that immigrants develop and sustain multiple social relationships spanning different geographic, political, and cultural borders (Bash, Schiller, and Blanc 1994; Rosaldo 1989). This concept of transnationalism differs significantly from the hitherto traditional concept of immigration. The concept of unidirectional immigration movements that proceed one-way from mother country to host country requires rethinking. During the period from 1940 to 1970, many scholars (Handlin 1972; Gans 1963; Gordon 1964) believed that immigrants experience initial uprooting, make gradual adjustments to the host country, and eventually settle down and become members of the host society (assimilation). However, current reality is much more complex. Transnational migrants experience more obstacles in adjusting and readjusting to both host and home societies due to the fact that they are constantly crossing and recrossing borders. The social cost incurred by transnationalism is demonstrably high. Transnational migrants have to negotiate, create, and maintain various social relationships—family, kinship, friendship, gender, and other network relationships—in two or more communities or countries. Intrafamilial relationships that include husband-wife, sibling-sibling, father-child, and mother-child relationships are altered and sometimes destroyed in the process.

TRANSNATIONALISM AS A NEW WAY OF LIFE

Transnationalism has necessitated a series of changes that include a change in residence patterns, social relations, gender relations, and parent-child relations. It has also altered relationships between immigrants and their receiving countries. The uprooting of social, economic, and cultural connections has created new family patterns.

In the past twenty years the Pacific Rim countries have become an important economic arena (see chapter 2). This geographic region covers many different countries, and these have become mutually linked in the manufacturing and distribution of goods and services. The rapid economic development of China, the political situation in Asia as a whole, the uneven economic development of the third world, and the transformation of the Western economies from manufacturing to high-tech and service industries, are all factors that affect the activities of Chinese transnationals. Chinese immigrants who arrived after the 1990s found that America was not a paradise for everyone. The concept of the American Dream needed to be redefined. Typically, after much soul-searching many Chinese immigrant families decided to opt for a transnational lifestyle, and in doing so they accepted that they might have to return to Asia or to travel to different parts of the world to seek their financial fortune. However, the majority of these transnational migrants have preferred to make their permanent home in the United State (chapter 4). Some of these families prefer America because of the better educational opportunities available to their children there. Some like the physical environment; others favor America's political system, political stability, and the personal freedom it allows them (B. Wong 1998a). Transnationals travel for economic success. With a good job, and the high income or profits they obtain from Asia, these immigrants hope that they can eventually settle comfortably in the United States and send their children to desirable schools or universities there. Social mobility thus requires that the family breadwinners or wage earners commute internationally.

The High-Flying Astronaut

The term *tai kong ren* has many meanings in Chinese. One connotes an astronaut; another indicates an airline frequent flier. In Chinese there is also a colloquial usage of the term *tai kong ren* meaning a "wife without her husband" or vice versa. In the context of this book, *tai kong ren* or *astronaut* simply refers to the transnational migrant who travels internationally for his or her livelihood. Estimates from my informants suggest that as many as one out of four of the twenty thousand Chinese engineers and high-tech personnel in Silicon Valley travels extensively between Silicon Valley and Asia on business. The home base of these astronauts is now the United States rather than Asia as was common in the nineteenth century. Due to the high proportion of male to female engineers, those who travel as astronauts are usually men. But in the case of a woman who does travel, her husband will stay in the United States with their children. And in some situations, both husband and wife travel as business partners, and have residences in different parts of the world. They sometimes call themselves "modern nomads." They reside half a year in Taiwan and half a year in the United States. However, this is not common. By far the most common astronaut is a husband traveling back and forth between the United States and other parts of the world.

My informants told me numerous stories of itinerant businessmen traveling between the United States and Hong Kong, Taiwan, or China who found themselves entangled in new social relationships. As it turned out, some of these men even started two families, one in the United States and one in Taiwan (or China). A husband would then have one wife in one country and another in a second country. Though bilocal polygamous households have been created through transnational migration, this pattern is not the norm.

Through my research I found several major family patterns among the transnationals commuting between the United States and Asia: (1) a matrifocal family headed by the mother, (2) a patrifocal family headed by the father, (3) a nonparented family or household, and (4) a transnational extended family with members living in different parts of the world.

FAMILY PATTERNS OF THE TRANSNATIONALS

Transnational immigrants, whether rich, poor, or middle class must travel long distances and undergo family separation, emotional upheaval, and disruption of the social lives of their children, parents, and friends. Of course, Nobel Prize winners, university presidents, white-collar workers, blue-collar workers, and paupers may also suffer these upheavals. But transnationalism as a way of life is an option chosen by individuals under the reinforcement and constraints of the global economy.

The phenomenon of returning to one's country of origin has recently caught on among recent immigrants to the United States. Major newspapers in the United States note that some of the country's most distinguished immigrant scientists and professionals (who have enriched the West with their talent and contributions) are returning to Asia. Although many young Chinese students and professionals continue to come to the United States for a university education and employment, more and more of them are returning to Asia where job opportunities are expanding. At the same time, their families often continue to live in America.

As we have seen, their motives for returning home are complex. But these Chinese immigrants fear that the economic potential of the United States is limited. Its growth is inhibited by high costs, high wages, and low productivity. By contrast, China and Taiwan's economies are growing, and their proximity to the burgeoning Asian consumer market may hold greater promise. Furthermore, the U.S. recession of the early 1990s affected California more than many other states. This was due to the fact that California is home to the defense and aeronautics industries, which were particularly affected by the recession. The loss of these industries magnified the recession's economic effects on other sectors of the California economy such as real estate, tourism, and the retail industry. In addition, the accompanying loss of consumer purchasing power affected many Chinese businesses. Small businesses, large firms, and professional personnel were affected. At the same time, the economies in Asia were experiencing unprecedented growth. These developments triggered a reverse immigrant exodus, especially during the period from 1990 to 1995 (*New York Times* February 21, 1995; *San Jose Mercury News* August 22, 1993). Then in the period from 1999 to 2001 we again saw a wave of return migration as a result of another recession.

Among less-educated newcomers to the United States, returning to Asia or other parts of the world to seek employment during the recession of the early 1990s was an adaptive strategy. Many traveled to South Africa, Central America, Thailand, Nepal, Saudi Arabia, or China where they had social or economic connections. Among newly arrived immigrant families in the 1990s it was common to see one or both parents in a constant state of departure or arrival. This was, indeed, the life of an astronaut.

Matrifocal Families

Carol Stack, Gregory Guldin, and a host of other authors have discussed the formation of matrifocal families. A matrifocal family refers to a family made up of a mother and her children. Thus, it is a single-parent household. This family type is the result of migratory labor. In her work on African Americans, Stack demonstrates that the matrifocal household is an adaptive mechanism. With their father's absence, the children have to depend on their mother and her social network for survival (1974). Guldin in turn describes how the Fujianese Chinese in Hong Kong live and garner support from their mothers, rather than their fathers, who are forced to travel to the Philippines to make a living overseas (1977). Matrifocal families existed among the Chinese in the past when families were separated by the immigration exclusion laws of the United States (B. Wong 1985). The U.S. Immigration Act of 1924 specifically prohibited the entry of Chinese wives. Chinese immigrants had to return to China to marry and sire children. They then returned to the United States. Their families in China continued to be tended by the wives they left behind. However, that situation has been reversed among today's Chinese transnational migrants. Chinese wage earners still leave their families behind, but now they leave them in the United States. In these matrifocal families, the men travel back and forth between the United States and other countries. In such cases, the fathers may return once or twice a year to visit the family. Instead of developing a father-son bond, the dominant dyadic relationship is that of mother-son. This is a change from the traditional Chinese kinship pattern, which emphasizes the father-child relationship in a patrilineal kinship system (Hsu 1983). Among transnational Chinese families today, the communication between a father and his family is more often carried out via telephone and e-mail rather than by face-to-face interaction.

Another significant negative outcome of the transnational lifestyle is that some transnational migrants on leaving their children and spouses behind acquire a new sense of freedom. They suddenly become "bachelors" who are free and undisciplined in their daily regime. After work they frequent restaurants and entertainment establishments. Their eating and sleeping habits are entirely changed. Then when they return to America, they find their families boring. Their children have become strangers to them and vice versa. Intrafamilial relationships can be devastated by this constant separation. A traditional, complete, nuclear family household has now become an incomplete, mutilated one. The children are emotionally tied only to their mothers, and this bond persists even after the child's reunion with their father.

Some transnational migrants return to Taiwan to head major divisions of a company, while others became directors or vice presidents overseas. In Taiwan's Hsinchu area, some of these astronauts live in the business park in luxurious condominiums paid for by their companies. Their living facilities are no different than some of the California condominium communities. I saw tennis courts, swimming pools, and golf courses located on site. There are up-scale restaurants, and many companies and research facilities have their own dinning rooms. In the government-sponsored research facilities where these astronauts work there are organized weekend movies, dances, and shows. The most difficult time for the astronauts is during traditional family holidays like Chinese New Year and the Autumn Moon Festival. During these holidays, astronauts tend to feel lonely and isolated. The Chinese New Year is particularly hard for them since many of the restaurants are closed so that their employees can be with their families. Homesickness is a necessary byproduct of the astronaut lifestyle.

The decision to return to Asia is often initiated by the husband but it is usually with the consent of his wife. After considering the financial advantages, the husband then departs with the reluctant blessing of his wife. Take Mr. Chung, for example. After graduating from National Taiwan University, Mr. Chung came to the United States for advanced study, getting an MA and a PhD in computer science at the University of Illinois. He then found employment in Silicon Valley. He purchased a car and met his future wife in San Jose where she was pursuing a master's degree in business. They married, purchased a home in San Jose, and soon had two children. Thus far Mr. Chung had followed the ideal career path for a Taiwan engineer. In Silicon Valley, among the Taiwanese, it is called *wu zi dang ke* (five successful steps to be completed). After getting a job, the five steps are, in order: (1) earn money, (2) purchase a car, (3) get married, (4) purchase a house, and (5) have children. Chung did all these valued and desired things as a Taiwanese PhD graduate student in America. He then worked until 1997 in Silicon Valley as a project manager. With the booming semiconductor industry in Taiwan, he was given the opportunity to return to Taiwan to head a division at a company in Hsinchu. After discussing this with his wife, Chung decided that the opportunity was too good to pass up. He was offered stock, a company apartment, travel allowance, and a salary comparable to what he was already receiving in the United States. An additional bonus was that the tax rate is much lower in Taiwan, while the responsibilities, being broader, provided an opportunity for Chang to eventually become vice president of the company.

His wife, on the other hand, felt that it was impossible for her to leave her job in America. After receiving her MBA from San Jose State University she had found a position of responsibility in a financial institution in Silicon Valley. The family home was situated in a desirable Los Alto neighborhood and their children were doing well in school. So she and Mr. Chung decided that the family would stay in the United States while he went to Taiwan. Mr. Chung commuted between Taiwan and the United States for four years. He has since returned to the United States, but other Chinese astronauts continue their frequent travel career. And nowadays, the commuting has become even more complicated. Some astronauts must travel to three or more destinations—the United States, Taiwan, Hong Kong, and mainland China, for example—all in one trip.

The lifestyle of the astronaut has become an established trend, especially during the last ten years. Consider the experiences of the Tsenshau Yang and Samuel Liu families as reported by the *San Jose Mercury News*. Mr. Yang, an engineer in his late thirties, moved from Taiwan to the United States for study. After obtaining his doctoral degree in engineering at Stanford University, Yang stayed on to work in Silicon Valley. However, in 1993 he returned to Taiwan to work as vice president of a start-up company designing integrated circuits. His wife, Shyun, and their two children, still live in Cupertino. For Yang, Taiwan offers better opportunities in his field, but for his wife, an accountant, finding equivalent work in Taiwan is difficult. Yang returned to Taiwan with the blessing of his wife. She said, "I didn't want him to come to me in ten years and tell me he regretted not starting his own business . . . But now, I am beginning to regret it because he is not home most of the time." Yang comes back to visit his family several times a year (*San Jose Mercury News* August 22, 1993).

Another Taiwanese engineer, Samuel Liu, had a similar experience. After receiving an American education and working as president of a Silicon integrated systems firm for a number of years, Liu returned to Taiwan to take over a troubled semiconductor company that had made him an attractive job offer. Liu is able to return home seven times a year to see his wife and children, but he misses his family most of the time (August 22, 1993). As we can see, this mode of adaptation is not without its perils. Other families are not as lucky as the above three. In some astronaut families, children go unsupervised and experience problems in school and at home. Some of these children join gangs. Other families experience emotional and marital problems. Indeed, new immigrants must pay a high price if they choose to lead this lifestyle.

Patrifocal Families

Patrifocal families are those headed by a male single parent—something relatively new and rare among new Chinese immigrants, but it does exist. These families consist of a father and his children who live together as a social unit. Children in this kind of household derive their emotional support mainly from their father rather than from their absentee mothers. Both patrifocal and matrifocal households come about because of the need for economic betterment. Relatively speaking, matrifocal households are more numerous than patrifocal ones. This is probably due to the fact that men are the traditional wage earners in most families, especially in the high-tech industry. And in Chinese culture, it is more acceptable for a husband than a wife to travel overseas to seek employment (Hsu 1983). However, with equality in education and greater economic opportunities for women, it is now possible to have patrifocal Chinese families with fathers as house-husbands. This represents a change in traditional Chinese kinship because the husband has now assumed the wife's role. The women's liberation movement and the improved education and social capital of the Chinese woman have encouraged her to sometimes adopt a nontraditional sex role. Transnational migration can change the sex roles of its participants as well as the kinship system of the Chinese.

Burton Pasternak, Carol Ember, and Melvin Ember (1997) observe that the development of residence rules or patterns has much to do with the division of labor by gender. George Murdock (1965) notes the same phenomenon. The division of labor by gender does account for residential variation. In the case of Chinese immigrants, matrifocal households develop when men's careers necessitate long distance travel; and when women commute internationally for a living, patrifocal households develop. In either case, a separation between spouses and between parents and children results. These separations can cause human and emotional suffering.

Among the new Chinese immigrants, there is another new breed of women and wives: *nu qiang ren* (in Mandarin) or *nuey keung yan* (in Cantonese). This phrase means "strong women [who are extremely talented]." At times these wives may have better *guanxi*, social capital, or professional training than their husbands. These wives may have had high-paying jobs in Hong Kong or Taiwan prior to their migration to the United States. After their arrival here, however, they become impatient with the downward social mobility they are experiencing as the result of not being able to find suitable employment. So they return to China or Hong Kong to look for better economic opportunities. Here is the story of one such woman.

After much brain-storming and discussion, Mrs. A decided to leave Silicon Valley to go to Hainan Island to help with the development of a power plant. She left San Francisco and leased a hotel room in Hong Kong. From Hong Kong, she traveled to Hainan Island to conduct her business. Hong Kong was her business center; the United States was her home. Mrs. A returned twice a year to see her family. Her husband was an engineer and was in charge of raising their school-age children. Here was a reversal of the traditional gender role, with the man running the household, instead of his wife. He had to go to work daily, supervise the children's schoolwork, and do household chores. He was the head of the family, the wage earner, and the homemaker all combined. Because of this, the children became more connected to their father than their mother. However, the family was unhappy with this separation. After being gone for three years, Mrs. A successfully completed her business project and returned to the United States with much acquired wealth. The family then purchased a large house in the San Francisco Bay Area. Mrs. A believed they had suffered enough, and she vowed not to travel anymore.

This case of a temporarily separated patrifocal household had a happy ending. But it is a kind of separation that was almost unheard-of in traditional Chinese families of the past. Now it occurs often in modern Chinese immigrant families. Demonstrated talent and greater education on the women's part and trust between a husband and wife are important factors in the success of such risky adaptive ventures. Both patrifocal and matrifocal households can disintegrate. In my fieldwork I saw families torn apart because of family separation. This was particularly the case when the husband and wife's relationship was strained prior to one of their departures for Hong Kong or other parts of the world. In this case, the marriage often ended up in divorce.

Nonparented Households and Parachute Children

"Parachute children" are children left in a foreign land with little or no adult supervision. For the Chinese immigrant in the United States there are many reasons for treating one's children as parachute children. One is the perceived advantage of the education available in America. Due to stiff competition for limited space in Asian universities, many parents believe that their children will be able to attend a better university in the United States than in their country of origin. Curiously enough, there is the perception that American grade schools and high schools are better than those in Taiwan. Some parents feel that there are too many exams and too many hurdles for young students in Taiwan. Additionally, in order to go to universities, their children have to study day and night and complete extra *ngu pu* (cram courses). These cram sessions are in the evening and on Saturdays or Sundays after regular school hours, and they are intended to increase a student's chance of being admitted to a good university. As in Japan, Taiwan, and Hong Kong, students face this "examination hell" as part of their matriculation process.

A second reason why Chinese parents might employ this strategy is political and economic. Parents are worried about the political stability of Asia. Many believe that investing their savings in a U.S. property that their children can live in and watch over is a sound financial move. In the case of a disastrous political or economic change in Asia, they believe they can always fly back to the United States and live a comfortable life in a comfortable home. In other words, a home and legal residency in the United States are an "ace in the hole." "Plan before it rains," or "Don't wait to dig a well until you are dying of thirst"—these were the commonly quoted Chinese sayings given in response to my questions. Political instability between China and Taiwan is still a cause of great uncertainty. Many Taiwanese Chinese feel safer if their children and other assets are in the United States. Another reason for leaving one's children in the United States is avoidance of the mandatory military service imposed on Chinese males in Taiwan. All in all, educational opportunity, pursuit of wealth, and the perceived political instability of Asia are the major reasons that motivate parents to resort to this kind of adaptation.

The resulting nonparented household is another new phenomenon among Chinese transnational migrations. Some well-to-do Chinese immigrants from Hong Kong or Taiwan, after obtaining immigrant visas and green cards, set up a household for their children and then leave. The children remain behind in America to pursue their education. These parents will typically have purchased a house and found a school for their teenage children. Sometimes, extracurricular activities are also arranged for them. Whenever possible, relatives or friends are instructed to visit or keep an eye on these children. In reality, the supervision is often nominal. After the arrangements are made, the parents return to their homes overseas. This has lead to the parachute children phenomenon. Such children are on their own when it comes to schoolwork, housework, social activities, cooking, and playing. It can be expected that while some of these teen-age children are doing well, others are not. Loneliness and a lack of parental supervision create problems. Gangs bully some teenagers. Other children have problems with friends.

Not all of these parachute children are from astronaut families. Ranging in age from eight to eighteen, some were sent here by affluent parents in Taiwan via arrangements with travel agencies (at a stiff price). Others came here on tourist visas or F1 student visas to stay in a boarding house or in the home of a relative. Some parachute children came to the United States with their parents on family reunion visas under a provision of the 1965 Immigration Law. Still others came to the United States with parents who had E2 investment visas (granted to a family that invests $1 million in the United States). In Silicon Valley, most of the parachute children are such for one of those three reasons, but in general, parachute children come from relatively affluent families. No one really knows the exact number of parachute children in the United States but there are estimates that at least thirty to forty thousand such cases come from Taiwan alone.

Parachute children started to appear in the United States in the mid-1980s following the United States' recognition of the PRC. Parents of these children had great anxiety that Taiwan would be turned over to China. The second wave of parachute children came after 1987 when the U.S. Supreme Court ruled that public education could not be denied to illegal immigrants.

It is to be expected that not all the parachute children will do well under such circumstances. In fact, the majority have language problems when they first arrive, and consequently have difficulty getting along well with their American peers. Homesickness is common. Frequently, these children and their parents cease to have anything in common. Often, on the occasion of family reunions, the children and their parents cannot even engage in ordinary conversation with one another. The children's ties to the family are weak and exist only in economic terms.

Sometimes younger children may live near an aunt's or uncle's household in the United States. The authority figure in this case becomes the uncle. This pattern resembles a modified version of the avunculocal residence pattern of the Trobriand Islanders (Pasternak, Ember, and Ember 1997). A designated authority figure (the uncle) checks on the children and reports back to their parents.

TRANSNATIONAL FAMILIES AND GLOBAL BUSINESS STRATEGIES

The world has become smaller due to modern transportation and communication systems. The commuting time between continents has been reduced. What was once considered a collection of independent and often isolated states is today an interdependent world. Processes of production now span national boundaries, and items of consumption may be assembled in more than one country. As modern communication and transportation technologies have seemingly shortened the distances of international travel, some citizens have become transnational migrants, living their lives across multiple borders. It is no longer rare to have extended families with members traveling and residing in different parts of the world.

The transnational extended family refers to a large family headed by a patriarch. As a family it is a collection of many nuclear ones, with members that are often scattered across the United States and other parts of the world. Transnational extended families are not units of consumption, but rather units of economic activity. Extended families may coincide with family firms, and a transnational corporation may have several branches in different parts of the world administered by several children and their families. The headquarters of this corporation may be run by the founders and patriarchs of the family in Hong Kong, Taiwan, or Singapore.

Many economists see a negative role for the family in business, and argue that particularistic social relations like kinship can inhibit economic development and retard productivity. In contrast, I find that kinship is important for international business. The studies of Gallo and Sveen (1991), Whyte (1988), and B. Wong (1998a) also suggest that family and kinship can be engines for economic growth and the internalization of business in a global economy.

Chinese family firms have been important for the economic activities of the Chinese in the Philippines (Amyot 1993); China (Redding 1990; Yang 1994); Southeast Asia (Weidebaum and Hughes 1996); and the United States (Wong, McReynolds, and Wong 1992). However, the development of transnational extended families among the Chinese is a relatively new phenomenon. A joint family venture, with various world branches run by family members and their spouses, is becoming a necessity in this global economy. In these ventures, strategic information is kept within the family. Decisions can be made quickly because of the centralization of authority and control. In certain circumstances, the chiefs of these family businesses can also delegate decision-making powers to family members in different local offices.

The Transnational Extended Family

The transnational extended family applies only to the very rich. In this case, Chinese businessmen enlarge their family businesses by going global, thereby enlarging their sphere of economic activity and developing transnational networks to capture a larger market share. Diversifying and globalizing family businesses into different fields and locations has become a common response of wealthy Hong Kong business people to help cope with globalization trends. Employing this strategy can also help them gradually move capital from one place to another during or in the wake of a crisis.

Multinational corporations have been created by Chinese businessmen to develop shopping centers, office buildings, and other commercial real-estate businesses. The multinational corporations build residential housing as well.

This type of business venture is a recent phenomenon among the Chinese from Hong Kong, Thailand, Taiwan, and the United States. For example, Alexander Lui owns Anvil International Properties in San Francisco and is on the Board of Directors of Furama Hotel Enterprises in Hong Kong. Lui is also on the Board of Directors of Trans Pacific Bancorp in San Francisco, and it is reported that the Lui family has investments and development interests throughout Asia and Indonesia (*San Francisco Examiner* August 20, 1989). Another example of the phenomenon is Anthony Chan. The Chan family has extensive investments in China, and he himself has been a general partner of WorldCo since 1972. He and his partners developed a twelve-story office building on Sutter Street in San Francisco, and have built shopping centers across the Bay Area and especially in the South Bay Area. These Hong Kong businessmen have connections and businesses in different parts of the world. Moreover, they have personal contacts in various Chinese communities throughout the world. Then there is Robert Chan Hing Cheong, former chairman of HK-TVB, a Hong Kong cable company. Cheong has many connections in San Francisco, including a former schoolmate, Deputy Mayor James K. Ho. With his international contacts and his financial resources, Chan Hing Cheong has become a successful commercial and residential real-estate developer in Northern California. The Wang Family of Pantronix in Silicon Valley has companies in the United States, the Philippines, and Taiwan. WYSE of Silicon Valley, another example, started by a husband-and-wife team and their friends, also has diversified its business into Taiwan, Hong Kong, and China. The Liu Family runs Sun Moon Star and Addonics in both Taiwan and the United States. They are now marketing their products through Best Buy, Wal-Mart, Staples, Fry's, and The Good Guys in Northern California.

    The movers and shapers of these big Chinese businesses and multinational corporations are small in number. They do not represent the majority of Chinese immigrants. Suffice it to say that class differences exist among the Chinese immigrants of Silicon Valley. Some Chinese immigrant capitalists possess both the power and the money to pursue global business strategies which are otherwise available only to very wealthy Americans. There are only about two or three dozen Chinese families in the Bay Area who participate in such large scale international business ventures. Most Chinese immigrants must return to Asia for similar employment opportunities.

    Some immigrants use their connections in China and other parts of Asia to establish international trading companies. They sell heavy equipment, medical instruments, and local U.S. products in China while purchasing consumer goods from China to sell on the U.S. market. Many grocery stores and restaurants in Chinatown need foodstuffs and products from China. These are supplied by immigrant importers. Other Chinese products are produced in Canada and shipped by land to bypass United States regulations or to gain tax advantages. For instance, Chinese-style sausages are made in Vancouver or Toronto by Chinese businessmen. Similarly, it is easier to import shark fins and other marine products from Mexico than from Asia.

There are positive and negative aspects to membership in an affluent transnational family. The data obtained from this study suggests that family members can facilitate the internalization of their family businesses. As exemplified in these cases, rich, transnational, extended families have used adaptive responses to economic globalization. With trusted family members overseeing economic transactions in different parts of the world, these international family firms can achieve greater control over and more economic gain from their vast economic empires. However, some transnational family members are unhappy with their newly fashioned lifestyles. Some must travel constantly, thus creating a separation between themselves and their spouses and children. Some complain about their lack of "grounding." They comment that they are not tied closely to any nation or community. Some feel isolated from their parents and siblings in Hong Kong, Taiwan, and elsewhere. Discontentment and isolation are part of the social cost of transnational migration.

THE GLOBALIZATION OF DATING SERVICES

As stated, in the high-tech community of Silicon Valley there is a severe shortage of eligible women for marriage. Universities in Taiwan have produced very few female engineers. As a result, there are very few Taiwanese female graduate students studying engineering in the United States. A few female software engineers from the PRC have recently appeared, but people still mock Silicon Valley as a bachelor society resembling that of the nineteenth-century San Francisco Chinese community.

Realizing the shortage of females in Silicon Valley, many young women in Taiwan, Tienjian, Beijing, Shanghai, and other parts of Asia have placed classified ads in local valley Chinese newspapers indicating their availability. Some conduct their search for marriage partners online. Sina.com in fact has a special dating service (yuan.sina.com). It is a highly popular e-dating service, and through its websites in China and Taiwan Sina.com has been promoting this long distance dating service. In the summer of 2000, Sina.com organized a party for Chinese bachelors in Silicon Valley. The information about this party was disseminated by overseas websites in Asia. To the surprise of many, young women in Taiwan saw the information and came by international flight to attend the party. Because of the phenomenal success of its first matchmaking party, Sina.com decided to hold another one on June 30, 2001, at the Four Points Sheraton Hotel in Sunnyvale. Only unmarried singles were eligible to attend. The admission was limited to sixty men and sixty women, and the per person price of admission was fifty dollars. According to my informants, the party was filled to capacity.

The *International Daily News* and other ethnic newspapers carry special sections dedicated to matchmaking. A typical example of a woman in Shanghai looking for a marriage partner in the United States:

> Shanghai young girl recruiting marriage partner. 39-years-old. Height, 1.64 meter, gentle and talented. Looking for American male, citizen. Age, 40–60 with stable income who is interested in life-long partnership. Send letter to Ms. Yu Sheu Fang. 144 (37) Second Stone Gate Road, Shanghai. (*International Daily News* July 24, 2001)

Similar ads are run by men looking for women as marriage partners. In general, there are more women from Taiwan and mainland China looking for Chinese Americans to marry than vice versa. The American citizenship of the partner is an important consideration.

High-tech companies have long seen the lack of suitable Chinese partners as a problem, and they have tried to facilitate the social lives of their workers by organizing parties during the weekend or on Fridays. Recognizing the same need, a number of media companies advertise on the Internet to attract Chinese girls from overseas to come to Silicon Valley to attend these social events. We should not be surprised that intermarriage between Americans (those of Chinese descent or not) and Asian citizens has increased as a result of international travel. Even courtship and matchmaking have become globalized through the Internet and the Chinese ethnic press.

THE GLOBALIZATION OF SOCIAL LIFE

In this predominantly high-tech immigrant community, even social activities take on an international character. There are international Chinese folk dance clubs, bridge clubs, golf clubs, hiking clubs, and even Latino dance parties organized by the various alumni associations. Alumni associations have close contacts with their counterparts in the United States, Taiwan, China, and Europe. They hold joint activities, such as the annual Chinese American Athletic Tournament of the San Francisco Bay Area, which is normally held at De Anza College. Representatives from different alumni groups attend the event. At times it looks like a pan-Chinese activity, and at times it looks like an international event with Chinese from different parts of the world.

The best-organized alumni association, by far, is the National Taiwan University Alumni Association, which has many clubs and committees. It has a club for singles, a drama club, a bridge club, an Audio/Visual Club, a social welfare club, and a host of others. The National Cheng-Kung University Alumni Association of Northern California is also well-organized. It won nine events in the Chinese American Athletics Tournament of the San Francisco Bay Area in 2000. It has organized seminars on literature, investment, and even feng shui for its members. Like other associations, it has annual picnics and social dances, and it pays special attention to technological and business opportunities. The association participated in the 1999 World Alumni Carnival in Atlantic City where alumni of Cheng Kung University from different parts of the world gathered.

The Tsing Hua Alumni Association of Northern California has sponsored summer teaching programs in Beijing, a Valentine's Dance Party, the Cupertino-Hsinchu Friendship Cities Program, the China Flood Relief Fund, and other activities. The Beijing University Alumni Association of Northern California has organized activities such as a Chinese New Year Celebration, e-commerce seminars, music seminars, a PRC National Day Celebration, table tennis and badminton tournaments, Entrepreneurship Day, and social parties with the National Taiwan University Alumni Association. It has Internet links with the Beijing University Alumni Overseas, Beijing University in China, and the Beijing University Alumni Association of Southern California. Similarly, the Fudan University Alumni Association of Northern California has its alma mater situated in Shanghai. The association organizes picnics, seminars on investment, and other business activities. Although it is not as large as the other alumni associations I've mentioned, it maintains a website and provides assistance to alumni in need.

The Chinese in Silicon Valley are different from the Chinese in any other ethnic enclave. These high-tech professionals have little or no interest in gambling. They enjoy visiting restaurants, playing video games, participating in athletic activities, and traveling. As a result of their interest in tourism, there are many local and international travel companies set up in Silicon Valley to serve them. They are interested in domestic tourism. As a result, tour buses leave the valley regularly for Yellowstone National Park, Lake Tahoe, the Grand Canyon, Los Angeles, San Diego, and other popular tourist destinations. Whenever the Chinese of Silicon Valley take a vacation, they like to visit Taiwan, Hong Kong, Japan, and China. Some travel with the entire family to visit their home countries. Traveling to Europe is popular too. There are bilingual tours specifically set up for Chinese travelers in Europe. Thus, the Silicon Valley Chinese have globalized even their recreational activities. The world has become not only an economic field—it is also a large playground for their social activities.

GLOBALIZATION AND THE ABC

The ABC are highly Americanized. Many choose schools and careers according to personal interests. However, some of them are still influenced by their parents' wishes, and these decide to become engineers or scientists. Here is a statement from one informant:

> I told my two sons that they could do whatever they want to do. For practicality, I advised them to study engineering. I said to them that they can always make a living if they are engineers. Engineering should be their base. After they are done with engineering, they can pursue what they wanted to do. They did.

One went to Stanford and the other went to Cornell. My older one is pursuing a graduate degree in computer science. My younger one is trying to transfer to another field from engineering. He said he was bored by engineering and is now trying to study psychology. It is OK with me. (Informant L, interview with author, September 19, 2001)

Another parent told a similar story:

My children were born here and are much Americanized. I have a son and a daughter. When they were younger, I told them to do whatever they wanted to do. There is a future in every field. I told them to do something that will help them make a living. I did not tell my children to get an A in every subject. But I told them that they have to get at least one A just to feel how good it is. They followed my advice. They both did well in school. One chose to be a computer scientist. The other got an MFA in arts administration. They both did well and I am proud of them. (Informant C, interview with author, October 19, 2001)

Some of the ABC of high-tech engineers learned Mandarin and Chinese culture from home and from their Saturday Chinese schools. These children are seen by corporate headhunters as highly desirable bilingual professionals. Some have been recruited to work in China, Hong Kong, Taipei, and Singapore where they command six-figure salaries plus housing, travel, and dependent allowances. The ABC tend to travel with their families. They told me that they are treated very well by their firms and live in posh apartments in the scenic Repulse Bay Area of Hong Kong. Another expatriate told me that he and his wife and baby lived in the penthouse of a Hong Kong Hotel facing the beautiful harbor. The rent was paid by their company.

Not all of the ABC are happy with their transnational existence. They miss their homes in America. Their life in Hong Kong away from America is a transitory existence. They believe that it is good for them to have the opportunity to live overseas, but they plan to return to the United States permanently. Some of the ABC are no longer accustomed to the Chinese style of business. They do not feel comfortable with the business mentality in China and the emphasis on *guanxi*. There are also practical problems such as the education of their children and the maintenance of their properties in the United States. Some of my informants said that as soon as their children started school, they would like to transfer back to America so that their children would not experience any discontinuity or a disruption of their education. As for their houses in the United States, although the ABC may have rental agents or property managers to take care of their real estate, they are still concerned about this upkeep. The longer they are away, the more worried they become. They also feel homesickness for America where their parents have already established roots. This longing to return to America is common among Chinese American expatriates.

GLOBALIZATION AND PERSONAL RELATIONS

Globalization has created but also changed interpersonal relations. It has created interpersonal social relations that now span the globe. The transnational elite, the CEOs, CFOs, and high-ranking officers of multinational corporations now have more information about the different markets in the world. They also have many more connections with people in different localities. These connections turn out to be instrumental in obtaining talent, cheap labor, and other economic advantages. Observing their entrepreneurial activities, I found that personal closeness and personal connections can become exploitative, going hand in hand with class exploitation. In the context of the global economy, this kind of practice is strictly business because it maximizes profit.

The transnational elite may benefit from newly found connections or *guanxi* due to their strategic position. Thus, a CEO who has offices in China and Silicon Valley may have access to local employment markets and can tap into labor resources from each place to benefit his company. Say that the CEO of a start-up company has a branch in Beijing. There he might become acquainted with a talented engineer in IC design. They become friends, and later the CEO helps this engineer obtain an H visa and come to work in the company's Silicon Valley headquarters. Not knowing the economic disparity between Silicon Valley and Beijing, the engineer may simply accept the salary offered to him. Upon his arrival in the United States, the engineer finds out that his pay is considerably lower than that of others in a comparable position in Silicon Valley. In this case, the CEO benefited from his knowledge and his connection in Beijing. He got a super engineer at a low cost. However the engineer, from his point of view of, feels that he has been taken advantage of. We see here how globalization created a personal closeness that crossed national borders and could be used for economic maximization activities by the transnational elite. Knowledge, information, and international experience become assets for the transnational entrepreneur.

On the other hand, many PRC Chinese would consider such an offer of employment in the United States a *prestation* (gift) because it is an unusual opportunity to work in Silicon Valley. Even with the knowledge that their salary will be lower than other American employees, these Chinese engineers may still accept the invitation for the sake of learning more about the world (*jian shi yi xia*). It is an opportunity for them to visit a place they have always heard about—a world renowned high-tech capital. It may also be a stepping stone to greater opportunities. One of my informants, Mr. Liu, observed:

> Quite a few young Chinese from mainland China think about establishing a start-up company someday. I think it is about 25 percent of the newcomers/engineers. This is not the case among the Chinese who are older than forty-five. Why? The older Chinese are not influenced by the new economic reform of China. "To be

rich is glorious" is something many young Chinese believe in. That is the reason why they work. When they have extra money, they invest in the stock market. They want to make more money and save more money so that they could start their own business. (Mr. Liu, interview with author, March 9, 2003)

When I asked him whether he would start his own business one of these days, he nodded affirmatively. (He arrived from China just six months ago.) He continued:

> My wife and I are now working. We live in an apartment and have purchased a car strictly for transportation. We carpool every day to save gas and avoid additional automobile expenditures. When I find an angle or something special, I will try to start my own business. (Mr. Liu, interview with author, March 9, 2003)

Many young Chinese engineers from mainland China consider Silicon Valley a place full of entrepreneurial opportunity. This explains why some job candidates are still glad to accept an initial salary that they know is lower than the salaries of their American colleagues. From their point of view, they have much to gain from the opportunity to leave China and come to America. They believe that they may "make it big" in America, just like their sponsor or boss. The economic activities of the Silicon Valley Chinese in China have created personal relationships, employer-employee relationships, and friendships in the office environment. These can be converted into immigration sponsor-sponsored relationships as well as patron-client relationships. Such relationships contribute to personal closeness and class exploitation, and at the same time they offer a potential economic opportunity to young Chinese immigrants. From interviewing my informants, I have a sense that many of the Chinese in China would prefer to work for Chinese American entrepreneurs or American companies. This is principally due to the fact that it offers them an opportunity to come to the United States. In this way, globalization creates personal relationships that can be instrumental for obtaining overseas employment. Conversely, Chinese American entrepreneurs in China are able to recruit low-cost personnel to work in their companies in Silicon Valley. This helps them lower company expenses and generate more profit.

THE RIPPLE EFFECTS OF GLOBALIZATION

With so many single-parent and parachute children households due to the long-distance travel and prolonged absences of transnational wage earners, there is a great need for baby sitters, house sitters, and property managers. Many ads for childcare workers are placed in the Chinese newspapers of Silicon Valley. The workers are given room, board, and a monthly salary to take care of the children of the wage earners.

Those wage earners who take their families overseas on business with them then need real-estate professionals to sell, rent, or manage their properties in the United States. The boom economy of the mid to late 1990s created prolonged absences for some valley residents and gave rise to a large group of Chinese American real-estate professionals in Silicon Valley.

International travel and commuting between immigrant homelands and Silicon Valley have increased the flow of cultural material into the valley, such materials as Chinese books, videos, music, furniture, and household goods that come directly from Taiwan, China, or Hong Kong. Economic globalization is facilitating cultural connections. Returnees to the homeland communicate to those there the demand in the valley for certain goods, foods, and professionals from Asia. For example, the Hong Kong–style cafes and Taiwanese–style fruit drinks that are popular in Silicon Valley are imported from Asia. Interestingly, even some of the high-tech items sold in the valley, like cell phones and cell phone covers, are imported from Taiwan or China because their designs and decoration will be more appealing to the valley Chinese. Specialists in religion, feng shui, Chinese painting, calligraphy, folk dancing, and martial arts also flock to Silicon Valley. In this way businessmen and engineers from Silicon Valley play the role of agents for cultural borrowing. As in anthropology we have seen how missionaries, soldiers, and traders have played an important role in culture changes, so in this modern era we see global workers and business people assisting in the cultural changes in Silicon Valley.

During the time of prosperity in Silicon Valley from 1999 to 2000 when the dot-com economy was at its peak, many Chinese flocked to the United States in the hope of participating in the good life of America. Globalization engendered the movement of people around the world. Two kinds of international movements may be of particular interest to social scientists. One is the entry of pregnant women into the United States. The other is the global movements that result from the activities of smugglers of illegal immigrants. According to one report, "snakeheads" (illegal immigrant traffickers) are often arrested before they are able to smuggle people into the United States (*China Press* May 13, 2000). There have also been reports of the importation of child laborers to make up for labor shortages in certain regions of the world (*International Daily* May 12, 2000).

An increased number of pregnant Chinese women commonly enter America. These women come to the United States on tourist visas shortly before their due dates. Upon arriving in the United States, they stay in prearranged housing, either with relatives or in private housing for which they pay a certain amount per month. The cost of such housing in the Los Angeles area, according to a press report, is about $1,000 a month. After the birth of the child, the housing fee then goes up to $3,000 per month. Delivery charges range between $2,500 and $3,000, and when surgery is necessary, the cost can be as high was $10,000 (*Zhongguo Daily* January 27, 2000). Why do these women from Hong Kong and Taiwan spend so much money to have their children born in the United States? Their move is a calculated one. According to U.S. law, citizenship is bestowed, jus soli, on individuals who are born in this country. Furthermore the Chinese child, being an American citizen, will someday be able to sponsor his or her parents' immigration to the United States. It is difficult to obtain statistics on the number of these births taking place in Silicon Valley. But according to my informants this kind of calculated citizenship birth does exist, making it an unexpected effect of globalization!

THE ENTRY OF CHINA AND TAIWAN INTO THE WTO AND ITS IMPLICATIONS FOR THE CHINESE IN SILICON VALLEY

China and Taiwan's entry into the WTO was a frequent topic of conversation in Silicon Valley, with celebrations among the valley's various professional organizations. The SCEA organized a big party to celebrate China's successful entry because it was seen an event whose importance went beyond economic considerations. Many of the valley Chinese felt that it was an occasion for them to express their ethnic pride. They felt that the position of the Chinese had been elevated internationally, because China was now recognized by the world's largest trade organization. Although the Chinese from China and Taiwan maintain a certain political distance, they do appreciate each other's membership in the WTO, and they believe that Taiwan, mainland China, and the United States will reap economic benefits from these new memberships.

The benefits will result from two principle changes. First of all, the three-way trade link between these countries will be strengthened. This will be particularly true in the case of the computer industry, which will find the strengthened links not only beneficial in trade but also in manufacturing and research. Many companies already have research and development offices and manufacturing plants in each location. For example, Acer Computers of Taiwan has branches in both Silicon Valley and China. Similarly, some Silicon Valley companies, such as HP and Apple Computer, have offices in both Taiwan and China. Secondly, China has a large consumer population and a huge market, and U.S. auto, computer, insurance, banking, telecommunications, and Internet firms have been waiting to set up operations in China. With those business operations more rigorously regulated according to international rules and agreements (as a result of China's entry into the WTO), many American businesses hope that they will have a level playing field on which to meet their Chinese competition. This optimism is felt especially among the Chinese in Silicon Valley, for they expect to play a significant role in the bridging of the economies of Taiwan, China, and the United States. Psychologically, many Chinese feel that finally their ancestral land is moving rapidly toward the top. China is no longer looked down upon by the world as a poverty-stricken and famine-infested third-world country. Another benefit specifically for China is a greater ability to export textile, apparel, shoes, and toys to the United States. The Silicon Valley Chinese hope that their talents, skills, and cultural knowledge will give them a head start in exploiting China's large market, thereby providing them with opportunities to get rich, not from the United States, but this time from their own homeland (*San Francisco Chronicle* February 17, 2002).

The entry of China into the WTO is also said to be good for Silicon Valley because it will drastically reduce tariffs on computers, semiconductors, and all Internet-related equipment from the current average of 12 percent to zero by 2005. China will allow foreigners to own up to 49 percent in Chinese telecommunications, Internet, and financial services companies, that percentage rising to 50 percent two years after China's entrance. It is believed that these moves will help Silicon Valley companies generate higher profits, whether they are Chinese American companies or not. In fact, all Silicon Valley companies lobbied the U.S. government to assist China's entry into the WTO (*Silicon Valley News* May 14, 2000; *San Francisco Chronicle* May 12, 2000). For all these reasons, the successful entry of China into the WTO in December of 2001 was a joyous occasion for the many Silicon Valley Chinese professional organizations dealing with the high-tech industry.

Young Chinese American professionals have also started to look eastward. Some of these American Chinese professionals, who now have bilingual and bicultural backgrounds, are in demand. According to Heidrick & Struggles, an executive search company, there is a great deal of demand for talented people with multicultural backgrounds. This particular firm was at one point looking for high-tech engineers to serve as general managers for a number of Taiwanese companies, and after much effort they could locate only six candidates. Tony Scott of Trans-Pacific, a venture capital company, has said that bilingual skills and a bicultural background are absolute necessities in Asia-Pacific economic transactions (*Sing Tao Daily* December 8, 2001).

The trend of the ABC going to Asia to look for jobs started in 1997. Matt Miller notes that at this time many young Californian Chinese were going to Hong Kong, Taiwan, and China to look for employment. But their reason for was not just the money. Some went to avoid the glass ceiling of discrimination. Miller finds that many multinational corporations in Asia need managers who can understand the local environment.

It is this gap the U.S.-trained Asians are hoping to fill. This type of migration is nothing new; Asians in America journeyed across the Pacific throughout the past century. But there are several wrinkles today. As they search for economic opportunity, some younger people are also traveling to Asia to reconnect with their heritage or reunite with families. For others, it's a well-paid adventure.

Many see it as a way to avoid the so-called glass ceiling they believe keeps them from competing for upper-management positions in the U.S. (Miller 1998)

With China's entry into the WTO, Chinese Americans want to return to have a first-hand look at China and to reconnect with their ancestral land, at least for a short time. Many in Silicon Valley now want to learn Mandarin to prepare themselves for this odyssey. In fact, those Chinese companies engaged in international trade demand absolute fluency in both English and Mandarin. Furthermore, if one has these skills, he or she will be paid handsomely. As a result, there is a wave of interest in learning Mandarin in Silicon Valley. Even Cantonese-speakers are now studying Mandarin, which will result in many more open doors for these young Chinese professionals.

There are other benefits to be expected from China's entry into the WTO. It may spur foreign investment in China. Some also see the possibility that with economic freedom there will be more concern for human rights issues. The entry of China into the WTO also raises other issues like health insurance, taxes, and retirement benefits for the Chinese who work in China, Taiwan, and the United States. Some further believe that the WTO's stringent business rules will reinforce the rule of law and diminish corruption in China. Others argue that WTO membership will help diminish China's pollution levels, which would be of benefit to everyone.

Since Taiwan and the United States have been doing business with each other for a long time and economic transactions between the two countries have been regularized, Taiwan's entry into the WTO will probably not create much change in the United States. However, Taiwan's membership does have an impact on the people of Taiwan. Hence, it is also a cause of heated conversation among the Chinese in Silicon Valley. Businesses in Taiwan such as recycling, textile manufacture, transportation, bicycle manufacture, and electronics will reap benefits. In the long run, the domestic electronic appliances, pharmaceutical products, and paper products industries will suffer. For Taiwan, agriculture, steel, and financial services will suffer as well as the automobile industry. The Taiwanese government, in order to compete with the PRC for market shares, may be forced to relax its policy on accepting the sales and distribution of foreign products. Taiwan will probably have more economic exchanges with mainland China and in fact, will compete with China for international markets. With increased competitive trade between the United States, China, and Taiwan one will see an even greater movement of people and products between them. Currently the Silicon Valley Chinese travel to both Taiwan and China. It is hoped that the historical hostility between these two countries will be further reduced by this recent development. In Silicon Valley there are discussions now on the possibility of unification. This is also perhaps the result of on-going business contacts.

SUCCESS AND FAILURE

Some transnational migrants become successful because of their participation in the global economy. One told me that when Japanese computer chips were cheap and the exchange rate between the Japanese yen and American dollar was good, he imported them for the computers made in Silicon Valley. He did this for about ten years and made a fortune, but pulled out of the business in the mid-1990s when the Japanese yen became too high. Some Chinese American expatriates now working for Canadian or American firms in China told me that they were highly valued and highly paid. Their benefit packages include all kinds of benefits: housing and transportation allowances, and education for their children. As a result, they have amassed substantial savings. Recently, companies have reduced the hiring of expatriates from America due to the high cost. They prefer to hire local staff instead with only one or two expatriates assisting the staff. Engineers who return to China to work for Chinese companies have told me that taxes are low in China. Although the salary may not be as high as that in America, their purchasing power is greater. They are thus able to save more money there than in the United States. But it must be said that not all transnational employees or entrepreneurs achieve this success. Some entrepreneurs do not have the right contracts, or they are not able to maintain their production facilities and make quality goods. Furthermore, the globalization of one's family firm may lead to family disharmony. Josephine and Alan Smart have noted these fractures within overseas Chinese family businesses (1999). Some of those who fail in their overseas business ventures must come home to Silicon Valley to start all over again. Tales of both success and failure are prevalent in this community.

THE PRICE OF SUCCESS

Paradoxically, in order to achieve the American Dream, the transnational entrepreneurs that I've described have to go overseas. Having made their fortune, they then return to Silicon Valley. Some purchase larger houses upon their return, while others enlarge or expand their existing houses. These so called monster homes occasionally give rise to conflicts with neighbors. Many valley residents have lobbied for the passage of an anti-monster home ordinance. A point needs to be made here. Not all of these monster homes are owned by returnees. Some are owned by rich people who have recently acquired wealth in Silicon Valley, but not all of them are Chinese, just as not all Chinese American returnees are successful in their overseas business or work. During my travel to Asia, I was told by informants that competition in Asia is quite keen. In December of 2000 I was briefed by the manager of an industrial expo in Hsinchu, Taiwan, who told me of Chinese American industrialists who had lost all their investments. As a result of their losses some became psychologically ill. Suicides also have been known to occur after disastrous business failures. Economic globalization does not guarantee financial success.

CONCLUSION

As the world gradually develops into a single production system, many Chinese businessmen and educated professionals are deciding that they want to be players in the global economy. The center-periphery model of the global economy (Wallerstein 1989) can no longer depict their boundary crossings and transnational economic activities. Their mode of operation involves the use of transnational social networks that are comprised of family members using advanced technology, electronic media, and global capital (Appadurai 1996; Braziel and Mannur 2003). Some have built international social networks that respond successfully to the changing economy of the world.

Nuclear families, extended families, and non-residential extended families continue to exist among the Chinese transnational migrants in Silicon Valley. Young or old, the first- and second-generation Chinese Americans still consider family important. However, among some immigrants, transnationalism has created a new structural arrangement: the mutilated nuclear families that have been transformed into patrifocal or matrifocal families, nonparented households, or transnational extended families. Overseas spousal employment has increased the number of single-parent households. Marital strain and problematic parent-child relations are a frequent result of these mutilated households. As a way of life, transnationalism has a high social cost.

We have seen thus far that extended families do not atrophy or disappear in contemporary societies. On the contrary, they are still used as tools by Chinese businessmen and others to adapt to economic globalization. We have also seen that the relatively durable Chinese institution known as *family* is subject to change. As a social institution, the family has been shown to be diverse and fluid. But this fluidity means that the concept of the fixed, unitary, and bounded culture and its one-sided influence on that family is outmoded. The Chinese family can and has changed in our transnational world, because family types and relationships are being influenced by the cultural constraints and reinforcements of globalization.

7

Globalization and Ethnic Identity: How Does Globalization Affect the Identity of the Chinese in Silicon Valley?

The traditional static model of analyzing ethnic identity in the context of a narrowly confined national state is no longer accurate. Because the movement of overseas Chinese does not follow a linear path from the sending country to the receiving country, their activities are often transnational and circular, crossing the boundaries of many nations, and it is therefore necessary to assume a larger territorial framework or global context. The forces and conditions that shape social formation and ethnic identity creation are complicated and multifaceted. The identity and identities of the Chinese in Silicon Valley are intimately linked to issues relevant to culture, state, social ties, family, and business practices.

Globalization affects the identity formation of the Chinese in two different ways. First, it promotes the resurfacing and repackaging of regional cultures and ethnicities. The Chinese who are drawn to Silicon Valley come from different parts of China and the world, and each place has different political ideologies and subcultures. Michael Kearny (1995), Katherine Tehranian (1998), and Hurbert Hermans and Harry Kempen (1996) have found a similar development in transnational communities as a result of globalization. The second effect of globalization on ethnicity is hybridization. Aihwa Ong (1999), Anthony King (1995), Arjun Appadurai (1998), Linda Basch, Nina Glick Schiller, and Christina Szanton Blanc (1994), Ulf Hannerz (1996), Ted Lewellen (2002), and others have also recognized this phenomenon. In the case of the Chinese in Silicon Valley, we have seen a mixing of regional Chinese cultures as well as a synthesizing of Chinese and American cultures.

In this chapter, I will focus on three groups of factors that affect the selection and development of the ethnic identity of the Chinese in Silicon Valley: global factors, local factors, and the social, economic, and political practices of the sending countries.

GLOBALIZATION AND CHINESE CULTURE: EMERGENCE OF SUBETHNICITY

Not much has been written about the fluidity of ethnic identity and its relationship to time. From the 1960s to the 1990s, the Silicon Valley Chinese tended to identify themselves as Asians or Asian-Pacific people. After the turn of the millennium, the ethnic identification of the Chinese started to change. This change was not driven by the changing racial categorization of the federal government, but rather, the Chinese started to identify themselves by the names of the regions from whence they came. They started identifying themselves as Hong Kong, mainland, or Taiwanese Chinese. There were reasons for this reemerging of regional identification. Beginning in 1980, these three immigrant groups each started to coalesce in Silicon Valley as a result of globalization and the global economy. During the 1990s, each group gradually reached a critical mass in America: they had many coethnics with which to identify. But cultural and especially language differences worked to segregate these groups.

The Chinese from Hong Kong speak Cantonese. Taiwanese Chinese high-tech people speak Mandarin to each other at work but at home may speak Fujianese to their parents, spouses, children, and in-laws. Mainlanders do not necessarily come from the same region and are not a homogeneous group. Some are from Beijing, some Tianjin, some Shanghai, Harbin, Sichuan, or Zhejian. In public, they speak Mandarin. When they are with their friends from the same city or region, they speak individual dialects like Shanghainese, Sichuanese, and Beijingese.

Regional cuisine differences also work to identify and separate each group. For instance, people from Taiwan miss their Taiwan porridge and Tainan noodles and Tainan beef. As a result, Silicon Valley has many Tainan restaurants to meet the culinary demand. The Chinese from Shanghai area may want to have their special pot-stickers, and the Sichuanese may miss the hot taste of Sichuan foods. Hence, regional Chinese restaurants sprang up in places like Sunnyvale, Freemont, Santa Clara, San Jose, and Cupertino. Prior to the 1990s, a critical mass of coethnics did not exist to sharpen the distinction among the various regional groups of Chinese. As a result of the influx of new immigrants from different regions of China, these regional groups were now able to develop their subethnicity. This demarcation of subethnic differences makes sense only among the Chinese, acting as a signal to each of them about their subethnic differences. Knowing that someone is from Taiwan or Hong Kong may be useful when one is communicating with them. In a word, subethnic identity informs intra-ethnic interaction.

In residential areas one can see a similar pattern emerging by which people of the same subethnicity prefer to live together. Near the twin Pacific Rim plazas in northern San Jose, there are streets called Taipei Drive, Shanghai

Circle, and Hong Kong Drive. People from different regions frequent different grocery stores and restaurants. They need different ingredients for their regional cooking, and periodically they prefer to go to restaurants where they are served their childhood favorites: red bean ice, tapioca and other tropical fruit drinks, or Hong Kong–style Western food.

Their subcultural differences are also reflected in their consumption patterns. Hong Kong Chinese may look for their favorite CD produced by musicians from Hong Kong, while Taiwanese Chinese may look for their favorite video programs and the *World Journal*. Different consumer tastes give rise to a variety of ethnic stores. There is multiculturalism among the Chinese, making their community more colorful and enriching. This diversity within the community should not be interpreted as a balkanization or as conducive to conflict, since there is a common culture shared by all Chinese. The following is a sentiment shared by all of my Silicon Valley Chinese informants:

> They like Chinese traditions and Chinese heritage. Their homes are decorated with Chinese arts, paintings and artifacts. The new immigrants like to send their children to Chinese school. My estimate is there are ten thousand Chinese kids attending the Chinese schools after the regular public schools to learn Chinese language, arts, painting, dance and music. (Informant JL, interview with author, April 29, 2001)

Michael Chang, who has been chair of the Asian American Studies Program at De Anza College since 1989, made a similar statement:

> All the immigrant Chinese in Silicon Valley like to maintain Chinese culture in America. Some professional artists from Chinese mainland are invited here to teach Chinese music, dance, painting . . . It is good because they are the experts doing what they know best. Parents also appreciate the talents of these people and send their children to learn from these experts. (Michael Chang, interview with author, June 12, 1997)

Chinese immigrants identity themselves as bearers of Chinese culture. They love their cultural tradition and hope to pass it on to their children.

As we have seen, these Chinese immigrants have no desire to return to China permanently, and an overwhelming majority of them are establishing roots in the United States. For economic reasons they may travel to Asia to make a living, but they prefer to return to the United States. Nor do they want to fence themselves in to maintain a moral community or to isolate themselves from the larger society. They speak Chinese and prefer to interact with other Chinese in a Chinese way. They want to keep their heritage and tradition, but this does not preclude their interaction with local non-Chinese. Hence, the Chinese diaspora is a cultural diaspora. One informant put it this way:

The majority of the Chinese I know, whether they are from mainland China or Taiwan, like to keep their Chinese culture. If they are here for a long time, they may forget about their Chinese culture. In general, the culture they want to keep is Chinese. Their ideology is, "keeping Chinese culture but living in America [*wenhua zai zhongguo, sheng huo zai mei guo*]." (Informant WL, interview with author, February 7, 2002)

Appadurai uses the concept of cultural flow to discuss the complexity of globalization. In his formulation he includes five dimensions: (1) the ethnoscape, (2) the mediascape, (3) the technoscape, (4) the financescape, and (5) the ideoscape. What is most relevant to our discussion here is the ethnoscape, which refers to the landscape of persons who constitute the shifting world in which we live. These persons are tourists, immigrants, refugees, exiles, guest workers, and other moving groups and individuals who constitute an essential feature of the world and who appear to affect the politics of nations (Appadurai 1996, 33). The landscape of persons that constitutes the Chinese in Silicon Valley is composed of many subcultural groups. These different groups have different political ideologies and maintain different attitudes toward their ancestral land and host country. Their existence in Silicon Valley has an effect on local politics (see chapters 4 and 5).

The ABC

Although cultural hybridization is taking place in Silicon Valley, another current is also in the making. The ABC in recent years have developed more interest in their roots. Among them, there is a growing current of interest in Chinese culture. Through the social memory of their parents, they have learned about their home culture and ancestral land. In fact, the first-generation Chinese may even make arrangements for and encourage their ABC children to visit their homelands in Taiwan, Hong Kong, and China. The Junior Monte Jade Professional Association, which was founded specifically for second-generation high-tech engineers, has a program to facilitate such visits to China. These second-generation ABC engineers want to visit high-tech places in Hsinchu (Taiwan), Shanghai, Shenjian, and Beijing. Additionally, cultural events, historical monuments, and famous scenic places are included in their visits. The engineers feel that the famous cultural scenes and places their parents talk about are essential to their cultural education.

Many formal and informal trips are organized by travel agencies, organizations, churches, and schools in Silicon Valley to help the second-generation Chinese visit Taiwan or China and learn Mandarin. Mostly first-generation Chinese immigrants, who are anxious to have their children learn Mandarin, run these organizations. Parents do not mind sending their children, who are only middle- and high-school age, to stay with relatives or friends overseas. Those who do not have such family and friends can also find sponsor families in Taiwan or China to house their children. This total immersion is supposed to be an ideal way to acquire the language.

What has motivated the learning of Chinese recently among the ABC is the opportunity to enhance their careers. Many of them have been taught that China is going to make a giant step in economic development. Some have even heard that fully bilingual speakers of Chinese and English are paid very well and are in demand by many international businesses in Asia. In fact, there are many of these ABC already working in Asia and being paid well with housing allowances and other bonuses. Thus, learning Chinese is not just to please one's parents; it enhances one's career too.

It is extremely difficult to write about the cultural identity of the ABC as there are so many variations. The retention of Chinese cultural heritage depends so much on family enculturation. Some ABC have a shallow knowledge of Chinese culture; others have a deep appreciation. Some can speak Mandarin and Cantonese. Some have already lost their ability to speak Chinese and have only "restaurant Cantonese" with which to order food. However, common to them all is the fact that they speak English fluently and are Americanized in their dress code, speech, value orientation, and interpersonal interaction patterns. Immigrants from China or Taiwan can easily detect who is an ABC and who is not, and vice versa.

The Taiwanese and the China-Born Chinese from Taiwan

The people of Taiwan can be divided into many groups. The ethnographic classification of Weiming Tu (1996, 1172) differentiates them as *wei sheng* (other provinces), *bendi* (local), *hakka* (guest people), and indigenous people. Huang Huang-hsiung (Tu 1996) on the other hand, classifies the Taiwanese as indigenous peoples (*yuanzhumin*), Fulo (a combination of Fulao and Helo, the Han people who lived in Taiwan before 1945), and the *hakka* and new settlers (*xinzhumin*—the new mainland immigrants since 1945). While these classifications may be appropriate for the Chinese in Taiwan, they are not appropriate in Silicon Valley. The consensus among my informants was that there are principally two subgroups of Chinese from Taiwan (see table 7.1). One group is made up of the Taiwanese who are natives of Taiwan province. The members of the other group are called *wei sheng ren* (people from other provinces), meaning mainland-born Chinese or children of mainland-born Chinese who have lived in Taiwan since 1945.

Table 7.1.   The Chinese from Taiwan

Taiwan Ren (Taiwanese): Chinese who are natives of Taiwan; children of the Taiwan natives.

Wei Sheng Ren: Mainland-born Chinese or children of mainland-born Chinese who have lived in Taiwan since 1949.

Among the Taiwanese who were born in Taiwan, some of them have a certain nostalgia about their homeland. Their uncles and aunts, childhood friends, and other relatives may still be in Taiwan and doing well. Some are afraid that their good life may change if Taiwan is unified with China in the future. This group of people has ideas similar to the ideas behind the Taiwan independence movement; they would like to maintain the status quo of Taiwan indefinitely. These are called *Tai-Du*. For them, Taiwan is a morally superior place. They also like the Taiwanese culture, arguing that Taiwan has developed a distinct culture with input from the Portuguese, the Dutch, the Japanese, and China. However, even among the *Tai-Du*, very few of them plan to relocate to Taiwan permanently. What they want is: *Meiguo sheng huo, Taiwan wenhua* (American living, Taiwan culture).

The Taiwanese in Silicon Valley are the Chinese who were born in Taiwan and whose parents were inhabitants of Taiwan before the mainlanders came after 1945. At home many of these Taiwanese speak *Min Nan Hua* or *Tai Yu* (Fujianese). Some of them speak Hakka at home. This group of Taiwanese-born Chinese also learned Mandarin at school. However, after migrating to the United States, some of they want their children in the United States to learn Fujianese or Hakka. The Taiwanese-born Chinese feel that they are different from the China-born Chinese. In 2001 there were about ninety Chinese schools serving twenty thousand Chinese children in northern California. In Silicon Valley there are at least ten thousand Chinese children who go to Chinese schools. Among these schools the majority teach Mandarin, with only about nine schools teaching Fujianese, and one school run by the Hakka Association teaching Hakka. According to the *Sing Tao Daily* (December 12, 2001), three of the nine schools teaching Fujianese were run by churches, five were private schools run by Taiwanese, and the Taiwanese Hometown Association administered the other. The teaching of Taiwanese dialects in Chinese schools is significant because the parents who send their children to these schools feel that the Taiwanese people are different from other Chinese peoples. The parents feel that it is more practical for their children to learn these dialects so that they can communicate better at home.

Even when they learn the Chinese written language, which is the same across its dialects, the second-generation Chinese often learn grammar and syntax through their own spoken dialect. They learn Chinese history and Chinese poems too. Since the characters of the language are the same for all the Chinese, including the Taiwanese, one can argue that Taiwanese culture is actually a subculture of broader Chinese culture. Tu believes that the so-called mainlanders and native Taiwanese share enough of a common racial, national, religious, linguistic, and cultural heritage to be considered of the same ethnicity (1996, 1132). On the other hand, Taiwan has its own local peculiarities and dialects. In the past twenty years, Taiwanese self-identity has also been used to indicate the difference between the Taiwanese Chinese and the Chinese of the PRC (Tu 1996; Bosco 2004; Brown 2004).

The China-Born Taiwan Chinese (*wei sheng ren*)

The *wei sheng ren* of Taiwan feel that they have been misunderstood by many. Some came to Taiwan with their parents who were fleeing China and communism in 1949. They speak Mandarin and received their elementary and university education in Taiwan. When they came to the United States, they had to struggle to achieve success financially. They were not always rich. Many of them told me that they came to the United States with hardly any support from their families. They had to work summer jobs to support their U.S. education. After many years of hard work, they finally settled in Silicon Valley. The members of this group of Taiwanese had a very solid education in Chinese language and culture and were raised to appreciate the Chinese way of social interaction. They want to maintain their Chinese background while living in America, because they like American houses, technology, and affluence. They would like to keep their Chinese heritage and impart some of it to their children.

The Chinese from Taiwan came with passports issued by the government of the Republic of China. Their national day is celebrated on October 10, and it is known as Double-Ten (*sheun shu jie*). Their national flag is the one used by the *Kuomintang* government (the Nationalist Party). In the past, the *wei sheng ren* were against communism and socialism, but today some are not necessarily against it and in fact, are for the unification of Taiwan with China. Others are for the independence of Taiwan, and others are for democracy. The Taiwanese do business with mainland China even though politically they may not like its communist system of government. They separate the issues of politics from economics. Similarly, they separate the issue of cultural heritage from politics. A survey conducted by a Taiwanese Internet magazine, www.bwnet.com, estimates that there are 300,000 Taiwanese Chinese businessmen living in the Shanghai area. Professor Jenn-hwa Wang estimates the number to be around 1 million (2004). Some of these businessmen are in fact from the United States. The magazine also points out that there is a difference between the Taiwanese Chinese in Shanghai and their counterparts in the United States. The Taiwanese Chinese in Shanghai want to take advantage of the economic growth in China, but they have no intention of establishing roots in Shanghai as their counterparts intend to do in the United States.

The Mainland Chinese

Many of mainland Chinese who work in Silicon Valley plan to use it as a safe haven. This explains why they do not want to go to China before they acquire their green cards or U.S. citizenship. They like the democratic form of government in America, the educational system, and the living conditions. At the same time, due to economic declines in the United States and the growth of opportunity in China, they may periodically go back to China to work but always retaining their American residence, as we have seen. They say, *Zhongguo zheng qian, Meiguo sheng huo* (to make money in China but live in America).

Out of this group, some are against the current government in mainland China and want to have democracy. In fact, there is an organization called Silicon Valley for Democracy in China. Some are sympathetic with the current administration, while others express the hope that China will implement more reforms and grant more freedom to the Chinese people. In the valley there is also a small group of followers of Fa Lung Gong (which is considered by the PRC to be a cult). The mainland Chinese in Silicon Valley support a mixed bag of political ideologies.

The Hong Kong Chinese

In Silicon Valley there are two groups of Hong Kong Chinese. One group came here through the family reunion clause of American immigration law and joined their relatives in the San Francisco Bay Area (B. Wong 1994). These Hong Kong Chinese high-tech professionals in Silicon Valley tend to be connected to the Chinese community in the city of San Francisco. On the weekends they go to visit their relatives in Chinatown or in the city's other Chinese neighborhoods. The second group of Hong Kong Chinese came to the United States on student visas to attend college or graduate school. After graduation some found employment and applied to stay in the United States permanently. The Hong Kong Chinese speak the Cantonese dialect and prefer to eat Hong Kong–style Cantonese food. Many of the restaurants in Silicon Valley name their restaurants after famous Hong Kong restaurants in order to attract clientele from the region. The hair salons, grocery stores, video stores, and newspapers of the Hong Kong Chinese are specifically geared to their needs. The Hong Kong Chinese argue that they have their own local culture: *xiang geng wen hua*. They have their music, movies, food, dialect, clothing, and style of business. Most of my informants from Hong Kong told me that they are interested in visiting Hong Kong on vacation but not for permanent resettlement.

The Chinese homeland has something to offer each of these four groups of Chinese immigrants, for it is the ancestral land of Chinese culture. And it is also a place of economic opportunity, especially for those Chinese in the high-tech industry. But when these Chinese travel or return to China, their home there is only a temporary home, a "home away from home." This trend is the opposite of that followed by the immigrants who came to the United States in the nineteenth century. Those were the Chinatown settlers who were only sojourners in the United States, and who were hoping to return to

China, the homeland, to live out an elegant retirement. Today many Silicon Valley Chinese want to live and die in the United States. My informants told me that more and more Chinese transnationals are bringing the remains of their ancestors from China to the United States to be buried. This is another indication of their commitment to the United States. Their permanent home is no longer in their ancestral land but in the United States.

Applying the concept of diaspora to describe the Chinese in Silicon Valley is problematic. First, they have not built a real or imagined wall to separate themselves from the larger society. Second, they want to be part of America and to be accepted by the larger society. Third, they do not consider Silicon Valley their place of exile. On the contrary, it is their desired home. Fourth, their love for Chinese culture does not imply that they would like to return to their homeland permanently. But on the other hand, the concept of diaspora has a certain utility and implies a sense of identity and a yearning for certain cultural ideas.

When it comes to the question of whether globalization has obliterated national or cultural identity, the answer is clear. After examining the data, it is safe to conclude that globalization does not erase local, ethnic, or cultural identification. On the contrary, globalization has opened up opportunities to confront diversity and to accelerate the development of regional, national, and local identification.

HYBRIDIZATION

The role of succeeding generations is significant in the understanding of any ethnic identity. The first generation has migrated to the new country and therefore it has a greater social memory of the old culture. As time goes on, that social memory can gradually diminish. By the second generation, culture and language retention are further removed from the original culture. Second-generation Chinese do not always observe the traditions of first-generation immigrants. One of the obvious losses is in the fluency of second-generation Chinese and their ability to write and read. In Silicon Valley many second- and third-generation Chinese can speak Chinese and watch Chinese TV programs without difficulty. But when it comes to reading and writing, their knowledge has become rusty. Meanwhile, their knowledge of the dominant culture is more complete and their English is better. Another phenomenon at work here is the mixing of the Chinese and English languages, sometimes called "Chinglish." In vocabulary as well as sentence construction one can hear and see the mixture of the two languages, though normally the valley Chinese speak Chinglish only to other Chinese speakers. Hybridization occurs also in the Chinese American diet, resulting in peanut butter egg rolls, Chinese chicken salad, and steak Kew—just some examples of the hybridization of Chinese and American food items.

Rituals may also be hybridized. On the afternoon of a couple's wedding day there may be Chinese wedding rituals, and in the evening, American rituals. The bride and groom may change their clothes for the two occasions. The bride may wear the red *cheong sam* (a long Chinese gown slit to the thigh) in the afternoon, changing into a white wedding gown later. Guests will be given barbecued pork and American-style wedding cake to take home, and there will be *Li shi* or *Hung Bao* as well as American-style wedding presents given to the newlywed couple. The hybridization of funerals also occurs. We see Chinese flower bouquets with Chinese characters written on white ribbons. Or there will be an American ensemble playing Christian music. In architecture occasionally one will see beautiful American-style houses decorated with Chinese doors. The hybridization of two cultures is carried out with elements from both cultures. In itself, this cultural reconstruction or construction is a creative act and hence has its own authenticity. The participants in this creative act work in a new and meaningful way with the knowledge, cultural ideas, and sometimes the social memories of their old-world culture.

To return to marriage, I should note that there are more and more intermarriages between the Chinese and non-Chinese. This is particularly the case among second-generation Chinese Americans in Silicon Valley. A valley Chinese may marry a person of Latino descent, and marriages between Chinese and whites or marriages between Chinese and blacks also occur. The children from these mixed marriages not only carry genes from both parents but are sometimes raised in two cultures. Thus, there is hybridization in both the genetic and cultural sense.

Laws in many states once prohibited intermarriage between whites and Chinese in America, but the U.S. Supreme Court lifted this barrier in 1967. From San Francisco to San Jose, and from the Peninsula to the East Bay, it is not uncommon to meet children born from mixed marriages. Intermarriage has obviously found more acceptance in Silicon Valley. Among the highly educated Chinese parents in Silicon Valley, one sees less resistance to intermarriage or the mixing of cultural traditions. One parent said:

> My children can do what they like. They can pursue whatever careers they want to. But I told my children that they have to do well whatever they are doing. They should do whatever they want to do with a passion. The can marry whoever they want too. The second-generation is dating the non-Chinese. There are mixed marriages and mixed blooded children. You could see the amalgamation of ethnic groups and cultures that way. It is a kind of hybridization. There is nothing wrong with it. This is Silicon Valley! (Informant D, interview with author, March 9, 2002)

Among first-generation valley Chinese and those who came here as children, some are still inclined to marry their Chinese compatriots. However, the reality is such that some have no choice but to marry a non-Chinese person.

As mentioned earlier, the male to female ratio of the valley Chinese is 7 to 1. There are many Chinese engineers who simply cannot find a female counterpart. Some return to China to marry former sweethearts and then sponsor them to come to the United States. Others will take a non-Chinese spouse. Not surprisingly, interracial dating is more common among the second-generation valley Chinese than among the first-generation.

Mixing cultural elements taken from the Chinese culture and other cultures also occurs. The Taiwan-style Chinese Boys and Girls scouts are organized in Cupertino with Chinese symbols and American insignia. The troops are frequently invited to participate in Asian Pacific Heritage Week as well as Hispanic Heritage Week in San Jose.

Hybridization occurs on regional levels as well. Within the Chinese community of Silicon Valley, there are mixtures of elements from different regional cultures. In Santa Clara's Chinese Rice Stix Restaurant, one sees the hybridization of Chinese dim sum items that include Chinese-style Portuguese egg tarts, Chinese-style Portuguese chicken, tapioca pearl teas, Northern Chinese dumplings, small (short) grain porridge, and sticky rice pork dumplings. These dishes are hybrids from several regional cuisines or national traditions. From martial arts to lion dances, one sees the hybridization of the northern and southern Chinese styles. These hybridized styles are accepted in the United States in general and in Silicon Valley in particular.

Hybridization does not imply the disappearance of a local culture. The Chinese people know the origins of many of their cultural practices but they deliberately do not make an issue about any practice's origin or authenticity. Neither will they degrade the hybridization of these practices. They feel that they are now culturally tied to the United States as well as China. They celebrate Chinese festivals like the New Year, the Dragon Boat Festival, and the Autumn Moon Festival, and American holidays like the Fourth of July, Thanksgiving, and Christmas. These customs are practiced and embraced by Chinese American families. One informant said, "The mixing of these cultural practices is just as ordinary as washing one's face and driving one's car" (Informant JL, interview with author, April 21, 2001). It is no longer a conscious event. It is part of their hybridized culture.

Another kind of hybridization takes place in the mixing of different lifestyles and cultural values. One mainland Chinese engineer in Silicon Valley told me that he likes American democracy but Chinese culture. He likes American houses, universities, and the country's physical environment. But in terms of social interaction, he likes the Chinese way. He thought the Chinese way was more humane and personal. This is what he said:

The Chinese way is more subtle. Americans are too frank. They do not care what you feel. They just shoot their mouths. But I like their emphasis on equality and democracy. I think I prefer living the Chinese way but exercising my political rights the American way: w*en hua zai zhongguo, zheng zhi zai mei guo* [my culture is Chinese but my politics is in America]. (Informant W, interview with author, March 9, 2003)

What he said echoes the sentiments of most new immigrants from China. But some Chinese recognize that there are some Americans who are as personal and warm as the Chinese are.

THE LOCAL FACTORS OF ETHNIC IDENTITY FORMATION

Local factors such as the size of the Asian population, its political dynamics, the length of residence of the Chinese of that population, and its acceptance or nonacceptance in Silicon Valley influence the identity choices of the valley Chinese. Additionally, "place entrepreneurs" also play a role in the construction of ethnic identity. These place entrepreneurs, while serving the Chinese Americans, also fashion and market their condominiums and supermarket products according to their imagination, with input from both Chinese and American culture. In doing so, place entrepreneurs are reinventing Chinese culture and marketing ethnic products with Chinese cultural themes that are acceptable to the transnational migrants living in America. This phenomenon has been recognized by scholars like Christopher Mele (1996) and Alejandro Portes (1996).

One effect of globalization is the necessity of constructing one's identity according to local conditions (Winland 1988; B. Wong 1998a, 2001b). In doing so they often create an identity according to what they think Chinese culture should be. It is a creation of identity within an imagined community (B. Anderson 1991). More discussion on the creation and reconstruction of ethnic identity will follow later in this chapter.

Identity Questions and Demographic Factors

The issues pertaining to a migrant's ethnic identity are complex. They evolve with the length of the migrant's residence in the receiving country and his or her birthplace, age, generation, personal success, property ownership, and citizenship. Identity is also affected by whether the migrant has children born in the new country. In terms of identification, some migrants distinguish cultural identification from political identification. Some identify with one culture, for example Chinese culture, while others prefer to have a hyphenated identity like Taiwanese American or Chinese American. Social scientists have debated for years whether ethnic identity is subjective or objective. Fredrik Barth (1969) and a host of others (Novak 1972; Greeley 1971; Glazer and Moynihan 1970) tend to emphasize the subjective aspects of ethnic identification. Prior to the 1960s, most people believed that objective characteristics determined ethnic categorization. Recently some social scientists, reacting against subjective categorizations, have argued that ethnic identification is influenced by both subjective and objective factors (Gladney 1999; Jenkins 1996). In Silicon Valley we find both these factors at work in defining ethnic categorization. A further complication arises from the Taiwan independence and China unification issues. What is going on in the politics of the mother country affects the ethnic identity of the Taiwanese Chinese in the valley. Any discussion of the ethnic identity of the Chinese will be highly fluid and emotionally charged. One informant told me that I should not ask people this question of ethnic identity because it is private and personal. She also said that this question requires a maturation process. Each immigrant to America has to work out his or her ethnic identity there. However, after interviewing many informants at great length, from their answers some patterns emerge on the topic of ethnic identity.

Asian American Identity

Historically, the use of Asian identity to form coalitions started in the 60s with the civil rights movement. When Chinese professionals started to move to Silicon Valley in the 1960s, the Asian population was numerically quite small. Then during the 1980s Silicon Valley saw the infusion of a large number of Vietnamese. But it was difficult for Asian Americans to have any political impact until their population reached a critical mass in the 1990s. In recent years, Silicon Valley has became highly globalized with transnational migrants from all over the world especially from Asia, and some Chinese now feel that there will be more protection for them if they are part of a larger group. These Chinese want to use their Asian identity to form this larger coalition. In order to have representation and a voice in the larger society, they say, it is advantageous to use a larger population base in order to develop an Asian coalition. Using Asian American identity as a basis for such a coalition and uniting immigrants from China, the Philippines, Korea, and Japan has certain advantages. Numerically speaking, the builders of this coalition hope to gain more voters by using the Silicon Valley region to form an ethnic block.

In official statistics and government documents, all peoples from Asia are listed under one category: Asian. In certain situations the government links Pacific Islanders with other Asians as well. For instrumental purposes the Chinese are also lumped together with other Asians. Such an inclusion is often used to satisfy certain statutory requirements or entitlements.

There are certain physical and cultural characteristics shared by different Asian groups. It was once hoped that if one group broke a racial barrier, the others would also benefit. However as time went on, more and more Chinese from different regions of China arrived, and they started to form organizations like the OCA. Using the Chinese identity to unify all Chinese has become an option only recently. However in Silicon Valley not everyone agrees with the idea of using the Chinese identity in this way. One Chinese community activist commented:

> Asian identity, Asian coalition . . . are important because all the Asians encounter common prejudice and share common traditions and interests. They want to change how other[s] think about them. They also want to change people's attitudes toward the black[s] and Hispanic[s]. We are for the civil rights of everybody. It is not just for the Chinese Americans. This is the reason why I have a problem with the OCA. (Informant Y, interview with author, April 29, 2001)

Another elected Chinese American official said:

> We don't have the votes from the Chinese. It does not make sense to use the Chinese American identity to unify among ourselves. In Silicon Valley, the Chinese with other Asian voters will develop a formidable voting block. It is good to have some influence than no influence. (Informant C, interview with author, June 10, 1997)

The development of Asian identity and its use for politics is an example of how objective factors and practical considerations dictate one's choice of identity.

Many Chinese agree that an Asian identity does exist. The Chinese share certain cultural characteristic: strong family sense, interest in their children's education, personalism. They also share similar consumption patterns: enjoyment in purchasing electronic items, Asian foods, and real-estate property. Therefore, some argue that there is a de facto similarity among them. They share more with each other than with non-Asians. For Asian supermarket builders and housing developers, this assumption makes perfect business sense. Mr. Chester Wang, a developer and high-tech investor, told me how he envisioned the formation of Asian identity. Many years ago he decided to build Asian shopping centers in the San Francisco Bay Area. He said he went to census maps and picked out the pockets of Asian population in the Bay Area first. He looked at the demographics and found six Asian population concentrations. One was in the city of San Francisco, the second was in San Jose, the third one was in Fremont, the fourth in Milpitas, the fifth in Daly City, and the sixth in the Oakland-Emeryville-Berkeley-Richmond area. He then found available land accessible to highways around these pockets. So far, he has built five shopping malls in the Bay Area. Out of these five, four are in Silicon Valley. He did not build one in San Francisco. He said there is no need to build one there because the city has a large Chinatown which is in itself a big "shopping mall." Each one of these Asian shopping malls has a supermarket (Ranch 99 or Lion City) serving Asian consumers. Each one of these also has a variety of Asian restaurants (Chinese, Japanese, Filipino, and Vietnamese). And of course each has a variety of stores and banks to serve the day-to-day needs of their Asian consumers. These four shopping centers do a bustling business. On Saturdays and Sundays they are so crowded that they resemble little cities in Asia. People congregate in the halls before and after shopping. Children play video games and parents talk to their friends. Grandparents talk to their in-laws and neighbors. One can see face-to-face interaction at these malls. Mr. Wang said, "See! Marketing goods to Asian consumers make sense. There is an Asian culture and there are things for all Asians. It makes sense to organize an Asian shopping center!" (Mr. Chester Wang, interview with author, October 24, 2001). Chester Wang is only one example of a place entrepreneur.

In their political activities, Asian American politicians tend to solicit votes from other Asians. At universities there are Asian American Studies programs. Socially, when Chinese, Japanese, Filipino, or Vietnamese people get together, they use an expression like We Asians to describe themselves. Many white people, who cannot distinguish one sub-Asian ethnic group from another, use the term *Asian* for them all. So, the term *Asian American* has practical, social, political, and economic significance.

Length of Residence, Success, and Identity

Among Chinese immigrants there are two interrelated factors affecting their assumption of identity. One is the success factor. The other is the length of their residency in the United States. Immigrants who are successful tend to have been in Silicon Valley longer. The following informant's statement represents the opinion of many in the community:

> Do they identify with the U.S.? It depends on how long they have lived here and how successful they are. People who are here longer than five years, they probably like to stay here for good. People who have their children born here and have bought their homes, they would prefer to stay in the U.S. and identify with the U.S. (Informant X, interview with author, February 7, 2002)

This informant further qualifies his statement with the length of residence consideration:

> For young people who are here for a short time (shorter than five years), when they go back to China, they probably do not mind staying there for good. Some just go there to work. However, they normally do not go to work in China if they do not have their green cards. U.S. is just like their safe haven. If anything happens in China, they would quickly return to the U.S. (Informant X, interview with author, February 7, 2002)

Another informant said that acceptance by the larger society is essential. Many informants agreed with her. This is what she said:

> Some mainland Chinese engineers find it difficult to be accepted by the mainstream society. English is a factor. Their communication skills are not sufficient

for them to have real exchange with the Americans. Glass ceiling is another factor. That is the reason why some returned to China for employment. Those who have been around here for a while and are accepted by their American peers and bosses would like to identify with the U.S. (Informant L, interview with author, September 19, 2001)

There is also a class factor related to an immigrant's length of residence and success. The successful immigrant engineers or businessmen tend to be those who have been in Silicon Valley for a while. This was correlated by my interviews. I noticed that in general, the long-time valley residents tended to be more successful financially. They are the ones who live in the large homes in Los Altos Hills. These are the entrepreneurs who tend to identify with the United States and who are members of the Committee of 100 and other prestigious organizations. Anthony Giddens (1991, 1999) and others have also recognized the importance of social class in the formation of social identity.

Entrepreneurship and Ethnic Identity

Place entrepreneurs such as real-estate developers, supermarket builders, and mortgage brokers can have a subtle influence on the formation of ethnic neighborhoods and ethnic identity. They appropriate, package, and market their products with an ethnic flavor. They also encourage their clients to value certain cultural items. At the inauguration of Chinese stores, banks, supermarkets, and social services, the place entrepreneur will invite a Lion Dance team to celebrate the event. Place entrepreneurs will guide home purchasers to certain neighborhoods with Chinese neighbors. They will direct the Taiwanese Chinese to Cupertino and Freemont, the mainland Chinese to Sunnyvale and so on. They name certain streets or certain areas with Chinese names.

Place entrepreneurs also know how to tap into the market of their ethnic consumers. They build large supermarkets in areas with Chinese concentration. Here is one developer's strategy:

When we built shopping centers, we pulled out the census map and the probate data. We need information about the demographics. We had to find out the ethnic Asian pockets. After we built the shopping centers, we found out that many more Chinese are trying to move in to those areas. So, we built condominium near the shopping centers. (Informant W, interview with author, February 7, 2002)

When creating a Chinese shopping center, place entrepreneurs make an effort to serve and attract ethnic consumers by offering essential ethnic goods. For instance, one entrepreneur told me that he had to find the right stores for his shopping center. These were regional Chinese restaurants, Chinese herbal stores, Vietnamese noodle shops, Hong Kong beauty shops, Chinese bookstores, a Chinese baker, and a Chinese supermarket. He told me that those are the minimal ingredients for a Chinese ethnic shopping center. He also said that when a shopping center had all these basic stores, he could easily get more customers to buy the houses he built nearby. Thus, successful packaging of ethnic shopping with condominium development is important for the place entrepreneurs. They are, in fact, developers of ethnic neighborhoods and communities. They can then say, "Go to that area. It is highly ethnic, convenient, and is the best for Chinese people!"

Ethnic shopping centers not only attract Chinese consumers. They often symbolize Chinese culture. Tour companies are starting to bring tourists to many of these shopping centers for sightseeing and shopping. There are now new houses catering to Chinese engineers near the McCarthy Ranch Chinese Shopping Center in Milpitas, the Little Taipei Shopping Center of Fremont, and the Berryessa Shopping Center in San Jose. One developer told me:

> With available land, one can build a shopping center and some new houses in places like Berryessa. The high-tech companies like to be near each other for support. The Chinese CEOs and high-rank officials like to live close to their companies but the engineers and other workers do not live close to their work place. For one thing, it is very expensive. They would go to live in the new area with new homes with shopping convenience. That was the reason why we built in Freemont, San Jose, and Milpitas near the Chinese shopping centers that we built. (Informant W, interview with author, February 7, 2002)

Real-estate entrepreneurs therefore package their products around the shopping center. They are the definers and shapers of what goes into a Chinese shopping center. They are not just the builders of ethnic neighborhoods but also the definers of ethnic identity. That entrepreneurs have invented culture for profit has been noted by other social scientists (Mele 1996; Ibarra 1976, 2001). What is unique about the place entrepreneurs in Silicon Valley is that they attract customers and tourists from the homelands (Taiwan, Hong Kong, and mainland China) of the high-tech engineers for whom they build. The local real-estate business in Silicon Valley has became a global business. One real-estate entrepreneur told me this:

> When we built the shopping center, we noticed that many older Chinese congregated and socialized in the mall. They came from the nearby housing area. They told their old friends or neighbors in Taiwan that they should come over here because their children also work in Silicon Valley. They said that it is great to live in this area because they did not need to drive and they could buy just about any Chinese things from the shopping center. They could converse with other Chinese and meet their friends in the shopping center. They told us to build more houses. We did. In fact, we had inquiries and purchase requests from Taiwan, Hong Kong and even Southeast Asia. (Informant W, interview with author, February 7, 2002)

Ethnic entrepreneurs in real estate have done much to create and perpetuate the image of the Chinese in Silicon Valley. Traveling to Japan, Taiwan, Korea, and Hong Kong over the past several years, I have constantly received inquiries and comments about the "successful" and "rich" Chinese community in Silicon Valley. In conversations, many of these Asians talked about their own experiences in shopping and dining in the Asian shopping centers of Silicon Valley.

Flexible Citizens or Multicultural Americans

The Chinese working in the high-tech industry have to be sensitive to the global economy for a number of reasons. First, Silicon Valley is the leader in high tech. Many countries around the world want to learn from the leading experts in the field. Second, the world has become the new arena for economic activities. What is produced in Silicon Valley is demanded in many different parts of the globe. Lastly, Silicon Valley has talent as well as products. It can outsource this talent and these products, as well as the research that created them, to certain parts of Asia such as Singapore, Hong Kong, Shanghai, and Beijing. In those areas, American expatriates are needed, at least as those countries build their information technology infrastructure, to conduct joint ventures or technology transfers. In other words, Silicon Valley entrepreneurs and engineers are needed to traverse national borders to perform their role in the global economy, thus constituting the modern technoscape (Appadurai 1998). While it is true that there are multiple passport holders who have no loyalty to any nation or country, an overwhelming majority of the Chinese Americans who travel internationally and who reside temporarily outside of the country are solidly committed to the United States.

A local historian and long-time resident of Silicon Valley observed that Taiwanese entrepreneurs travel frequently and sometimes maintain two houses: one in the United States and one in Taiwan. However, she said that most of these Taiwanese Americans still prefer the United States to Taiwan. Here is what Connie Yu, an activist and a writer, said about Taiwanese Americans:

> All they want is a safety net. Sometimes, a child may live alone here. His or her relatives would check on the child. You could say that many Chinese live and commute in two places. This is a new way of making a living. There is a pan-Pacific economic union. The husband may spend three months in Taiwan and three months in Palo Alto. What do they do in Asia? They are engineers, entrepreneurs and wealthy businessmen. They are selling products in two places: Asia and the U.S. They may live in two places but America is their home. They paid a lot for their house. A Taiwan couple just moved into my neighborhood and paid a lot of money for the house because they believed the feng shui is good. They also believe in America! (Connie Yu, interview with author, June 10, 1997)

Michael Chang, the former Mayor of Cupertino, echoed what Connie Yu said about the transnational Taiwanese Americans and mainland Chinese businesspeople and engineers:

> They may want to go back to China or Taiwan, but not forever. They want to establish roots and settle in the U.S. permanently. They return to Asia principally to visit relatives or to do business. Many are used to the American environment. Children grew up in the U.S. and are not comfortable with Asia. Economically, Asia may be more ahead now, but not environmentally. Some of Chinese engineers or businesspeople say they just cannot put up with the traffic and pollution any more in Beijing or Taipei. (Michael Chang, interview with author, June 12,1997)

Other informants agreed. Whether they are from Taiwan, Hong Kong, or mainland China, the Chinese want to establish roots in America. The so-called return migration is for business purposes only. Frequent zigzagging across national borders is a new way of life in the new global economy. Another expert informant concurred:

> During the recession in 1993, a noticeable number of Chinese went back to Asia for better economic opportunity. They kept coming back. What made them come back here is the quality of life and their family. Most of them left their wives and children here. Some went back to Taiwan with the entire families. Most of them have citizenship and properties in the U.S. They brought houses in Milpitas, Sunnyvale, Cupertino, Los Altos, or Palo Alto. (Informant ST, interview with author, March 9, 2002)

Those who travel back and forth are not always happy about this new mode of existence. One entrepreneur complained that the nomadic life style is hard for children:

> The money made is OK. Not great. There are difficulties. Not enough holidays with family. My family gets angry. Children are alienated. They have four major adjustment problems. First, growing up is a challenge; second, growing up as an Asian in America is a challenge; third, growing up not having parents in one place; fourthly, growing up being immigrant is hard. (Informant MC, interview with author, March 9, 2002

The Host Country

An ethnic group's identification with its host society has a great deal to do with its treatment by the host-country majority. In a comparative study of the Chinese in Lima, Peru, and New York City, I was able to isolate factors that were affecting the differential assimilation of the Chinese in the two cities. These were social, economic, political-legal factors emanating from the host

societies. The existence of interethnic institutions, an open economic opportunity structure, and the absence of unfavorable laws against the Chinese
helped the assimilation of the Chinese in Peru (B. Wong 1978). Joe Tan also
argues that an ethnic group's loyalty toward its adopted country depends on
its treatment by the larger society. He lived in Malaysia but he went to New
Zealand and became naturalized there. He said:

> There is a well balanced symbiosis between New Zealand and me. As a citizen,
> both New Zealand and I are winners. New Zealand provides a balanced and fair
> environment that enables every citizen to contribute and receive with fair oppor-
> tunities. This helps to improve the nation as a unit with good cooperation . . . Love
> for one's nation, whether it be native or adopted, is a two way symbiotic process.
> Do not expect any citizens and ethnic minorities to respect the government or the
> dominant ethnic majority when they are discriminated or restricted or forced to
> assimilate their culture. (Tan 2001)

Historically, there were at one time many legal restrictions and laws against
the Chinese in the United States. The Chinese were not allowed to enter many
occupations. In New York State twenty-seven occupations, which included
attorney, physician, bank director, chauffeur, dentist, embalmer, liquor ven-
dor, and pawnbroker, were legally off-limits to the Chinese until the 1940s
(B. Wong 1978), not to mention the Chinese Exclusion Law of 1882 that denied the admission of the Chinese to the United States in the first place.

After 1965 many changes took place. These included the enactment of
new immigration laws, and acts providing voting rights, equal opportunity,
and affirmative action. In the past twenty years, the Chinese have been
specifically invited into certain professions and certain geographical areas in
the United States. Many Chinese students, engineers, and scientists were recruited to Silicon Valley to work in the high-tech industry. The quota of
H-1B visas was enlarged. This explains why so many highly educated Chinese flocked to Silicon Valley.

Although unfavorable laws have been revoked and many discriminatory
practices have been removed, in certain areas Chinese still meet obstacles.
According to some, there is subtle discrimination against those Chinese seeking financing and housing. Some Chinese entrepreneurs find it difficult to
borrow money to start a business. Chinese house buyers have been shocked
to find out that there were still archaic ordinances about ownership of homes
in the South Bay Area. Some old deeds specifically prohibited ownership of
certain homes by blacks or Asians. These ordinances or restrictions, when
discovered, were quickly corrected, but the fact that they existed shocked
many Chinese immigrants. They also feel that they have to continue to fight
for equal treatment and equal rights. In general, they are pleased that unfair
treatment against the Chinese has decreased. In Silicon Valley the Chinese

immigrants are anxious to become permanent residents and naturalized. This indicates that they want to be part of the United States. Critics might argue that the Chinese merely want the convenience of having green cards and citizenship papers. However, from my research I have learned that the majority of them want to establish roots in America. *Luo di sheng gen* is the ultimate goal. This is reflected in their desire to always return to the United States, which they regard as their permanent home. The purchase of properties, the continual sponsorship of family and relatives to come to the United States, the participation in politics and community activities, and the desire to have their children educated in the United States are also indicators of their commitment. They are not the sojourners of the nineteenth century who used this land to make money and then returned to China to settle permanently (B. Wong 1997). Social, economic, and political acceptance of the new immigrants has induced their loyalty and commitment. They call themselves Chinese Americans, and make use of the OCA and other civil rights organizations in Silicon Valley in order to participate in the American political system and to establish roots in the new land (see chapter 4). According to voter registration records in the county of Santa Clara for the year 2000, there were 23,244 voters of Chinese descent, and 47 percent of them voted in the March 2000 election (*Sing Tao Daily*, May 6 and May 20, 2000). These numbers represent a large increase over the years.

The appointment of Elaine Chao by President Bush to lead the Labor Department was a joyous occasion for Chinese Americans. The local Chinese ethnic press in Silicon Valley expressed its appreciation as well as ethnic pride, and Ms. Chao was welcomed by Chinese and non-Chinese community organizations whenever she visited Silicon Valley. The success of Chinese American politicians in U.S. society in general and in Silicon Valley in particular indicates the acceptance of the Chinese in American politics. This acceptance in turn encourages greater participation by the Silicon Valley Chinese in local politics. Six Chinese Americans were elected to various school boards and city councils in Santa Clara in 2001.

Many government offices have started to recruit Chinese Americans to work in their agencies. These include the INS, the FBI, the IRS, and other law enforcement agencies. These are gestures of acceptance that make the Chinese feel that they are part of U.S. society. Acceptance invites further participation and identification with the larger society. One informant summed up the feelings of many:

The more the Chinese are accepted by the mainstream society, the more they identify with the U.S. From my observation and my experience, the Chinese get along well with their white coworkers. In the work place, they get along well. Diversity is a characteristic here. (Informant L, interview with author, September 19, 2001)

Another informant, who is a local historian, told me that recent Chinese immigrants do not experience as much discrimination as their forebears. She made this comment about how the good life in America induces the commitment of recent Chinese immigrants:

> The Taiwan and mainland Chinese do not participate so much in the fight against racism as we old timers activists did, that is because they do not suffer as much as the old timers. They can make money quickly and purchase nice houses right away. They don't feel the need to participate in many of the Asian Civil Rights organizations. They like Chinese culture on the one hand but want to stay here permanently on the other hand. Some of those who are successful simply deny that there is any discrimination at all in American society. They love America. (Informant CY, interview with author, March 9, 2002)

One thing is clear from the above: decreased discrimination, the acceptance of the larger society, economic opportunity, and financial success induce immigrant identification with a host society (Tan 2001; Wang, personal interview, 2002; Liu, personal interview, 2002; B. Wong 1978).

The situation for second-generation Chinese Americans and those Chinese who came to the United States as young children differs from that of the first generation. In Silicon Valley, the ABC who have received all their education in America and have socialized from childhood with their white American peers feel differently. They identify entirely with the United States. This is also the case for the Chinese who came as children. They have been Americanized in their up-bringing. Both of these groups feel differently than their parents do. Although they have been indoctrinated by the older generation with the importance of Chinese culture and of keeping one's roots, they do not have the same passion as their parents for their ancestral land. Some in fact no longer speak Chinese. They may not even marry within the group. They may or may not follow in the footsteps of their parents in their careers. American values of individualism, self-fulfillment, and social mobility are embraced. They want to be treated equally in American society. For them, it is important to identify with the Unites States, and they want to be totally integrated with mainstream society. A recent emphasis on multiculturalism, however, has encouraged some of them to trace back their roots and to acquire a knowledge of the Chinese language and culture.

EXTRATERRITORIAL FACTORS AND IDENTITY: THE SENDING COUNTRY

U.S.-China Relations

The destiny of Chinese Americans historically has been affected by U.S.-China relations (B. Wong 1986; Lowe 1998). When the United States needed the Chinese immigrants, they were welcome. They were recruited to build the trans-Pacific railway, to develop the western frontiers, and to work in the gold mines. During World War II, China was the ally of the United States, and Chinese Americans were treated relatively well. After the war, communism was an enemy of the United States and therefore, communist China was automatically an evil empire to the United States. Chinese Americans were then suspected of being a fifth column. During the Korean War, Chinese Americans in Chinatown were identified by Americans as the enemy. Americans would blame the Chinese, stating that "your son killed my son in Korea"; and during the Vietnam War, the Chinese were called "gooks." But in 1972 when President Richard Nixon visited China, China became suddenly a friend in the eyes of Americans. This political rapprochement continued to bloom in the 1980s. Maurice Mesiner comments on why in the Wen Ho Lee incident there was such fury over alleged Chinese spying at U.S. nuclear facilities:

> The deterioration of Sino-U.S. relations in recent years has been accompanied by a revival of old racial stereotypes. The relatively positive and human images of Chinese encouraged by President Richard M. Nixon's 1972 rapprochement with China, which then blossomed in the 1980s, have faded at an accelerating pace in the 1990s. With China no longer vital as a strategic partner in the post-Cold War era, U.S.-China relations have foundered over a host of real and manufactured issues: the future of Taiwan, trade imbalances, controversies over human rights, fears over deployment of Chinese ballistic missiles and murky tales of Chinese attempts to influence U.S. elections, as well as these current allegations about nuclear espionage. (Mesiner 1999)

From 1990 to 2000, U.S.-China relations deteriorated. China was painted again as an evil empire. The media turned to stereotypes again in discussing the spy plane incident near southern China in 2000. This incident unleashed other stereotypes as well. International conflict was suddenly transformed into an ethnic and racial conflict. Talk-show hosts and the mainstream media in the San Francisco Bay Area as well as in different parts of the United States ridiculed Chinese Americans. Many Silicon Valley Chinese expressed great dismay over the treatment of the Chinese in the press. It should be obvious that the international relationship between a host country and the mother country of an immigrant ethnic group can affect the destiny of that ethnic group.

China and the Overseas Chinese

An ethnic group's relationship with its mother country or land of origin also plays a role in that group's selection of an ethnic identity. Since most of the Chinese in Silicon Valley came from one of two countries, the PRC or the Republic of China (ROC), they have to deal with their relationship to these two places of origin. The United States officially recognizes only one China. The ROC is represented in the United States by the Taipei Economic and Cultural

Office. However, on Taiwan passports and other official documents, the name Republic of China is still used. The Taiwan government and the mainland Chinese government do not always agree with each others. Disagreements between the two exist and in certain areas are irreconcilable. In the area of citizenship, language reforms, and other educational and cultural issues the two governments have different policies. The attitudes and policies of a mother country toward her immigrants does affect the ethnic identity of those immigrants.

Since 1957 with the exception of the period of the Cultural Revolution from 1966 to 1976, Beijing's policies toward the overseas Chinese (including Chinese Americans) have been relatively consistent (Fitzgerald 1972). But the PRC's policies toward overseas Chinese differ significantly from those of the ROC. While the Taiwan government still considers overseas Chinese citizens of the ROC and prefers to maintain that relationship, the PRC began as early as 1954 to encourage its overseas Chinese to respect the local customs, abide by the laws, and become, if possible, citizens of their countries of residence. Premier Chou En-lai in 1954 pointed out the differences between the PRC and ROC concerning the problem of nationality:

> For our past, we are willing to urge the overseas Chinese to respect the laws of the local governments and local social customs. It is worth pointing [out] that in the past, reactionary Chinese governments never made any attempt to solve the problem of overseas Chinese nationality. This not only placed the overseas Chinese in a difficult position, but was often the cause of discord between China and the countries of residence. In order to improve this situation, we are prepared to solve this problem, beginning with those Southeast Asian countries with which we have diplomatic relations. (Chou En-lai, Report to the First Session of the First National People's Congress, September 23, 1954, in Fitzgerald 1972, 102)

In 1957 the Chinese Communist Party explicitly advocated that overseas Chinese acquire nationality in their countries of residence. The following joint statement was made during the Fifth Session of the First National People's Congress, and it spells out the stand of the PRC on the matter of nationality:

> The broad masses of overseas Chinese residents abroad must now put aside any reservation, and on the principle of free choice, choose local nationality. The must live and work in peace in the countries of residence, actively cooperate and coexist with the local people, and strive for the peace, happiness, and prosperity, of the countries in which they live. This will be of assistance in promoting friendly relations between China and the countries of residence. (*Kuang-tung Ch'iao-po*, May 1, 1958, in Fitzgerald 1972, 142)

This policy of encouraging the overseas Chinese to acquire local citizenship and participate actively in the social life of their country of residence differs significantly from that of the Taiwan government, which claims the overseas Chinese as nationals of the ROC (B. Wong 1986). Currently, the PRC does not accept dual nationality. When a Chinese becomes naturalized in the United States, he or she is no longer a citizen of the PRC. This policy differs from that of Taiwan. Even after becoming a U.S. citizen, one can still be a citizen of the ROC. However, for those who return to Taiwan to assume public office above the departmental head level, they have to give up their foreign citizenship. The major of Taipei and the president of the Academia Sinica, for instance, had to give up their U.S. citizenship.

Although the Taiwanese government does not specifically instruct its emigrants to identify with their adopted country, in Silicon Valley there are more Taiwanese Chinese than mainland Chinese who are active in local politics. This is presumably due to the fact that the Taiwanese Chinese have been in Silicon Valley longer and have become more familiar with its political system.

But whether they are from mainland China, Hong Kong, or Taiwan, the Chinese in Silicon Valley grasp the first opportunity they have to become naturalized citizens of the United States. Being an American citizen has responsibilities but also practical advantages. A citizen can vote and demand legal protection within the larger society. Citizenship opens up more economic opportunities, and is sometimes required for employment, especially for federal jobs. It allows individuals to run for political office and to sponsor their relatives to come to the United States. A citizen travels with a passport rather than a green card, which often invites unfair treatment from immigration officials around the world. From interviewing my informants in Silicon Valley, I learned that officials in the PRC are more courteous to Chinese visitors with U.S. passports than to those with green cards. For the Chinese, citizenship in America also means that their permanent home is the United States.

Taiwan-China Squabbles and Their Impact

Occasionally international conflicts between Taiwan and China can cause disagreements in the Chinese community in Silicon Valley. At one point Taiwan, over the protest of China, was interested in the purchase of military hardware and technology from the United States. Taiwan argued that the military equipment was mainly for defensive purposes. China's argument was that the sale of weaponry to Taiwan represented American disregard of the One China principle. The sale also represented, according to the PRC, interference in the internal affairs of China. These debates were reported in the local Chinese newspapers and had repercussion in the local community. How a Silicon Valley Chinese American views debates such as this one often depends on several factors. Those Chinese Americans with American citizenship feel more protected because they are no longer citizens of the PRC or the ROC. Because of this, they know that their homes are in the United States and that they will not be vulnerable if war should break out between mainland China and Taiwan. But those who are not citizens and who have relatives in Taiwan may feel that it is the obligation of Taiwan to protect their interests in Taiwan. At the same time, those Chinese Americans who are from mainland China and who promote the unification of China and Taiwan may feel that the sale of certain weapons to Taiwan poses an obstacle to the eventual unification of the two countries. In general, those Chinese Americans who have become citizens of the United States are not affected by the sale and therefore have little or no interest in the debate.

There are disagreements on cultural issues. In the Chinese schools of Silicon Valley there have been heated debates on the use of textbooks issued by the Overseas Chinese Commission of the ROC in Taiwan. Some think that the contents of the books and their information about the Chinese Communist Party, the Nationalist Party, and current events are not objective enough. In terms of the use of phonetic systems, the PRC uses a standard pinyin system to indicate the sounds of the Chinese characters in Mandarin. But Taiwan prefers to use the Taiwanese-style general pinyin system, which transliterates the local dialect as well as Mandarin. Furthermore, the PRC uses simplified Chinese characters, but Taiwan is vehemently against the use of them. The latter accuses the former of destroying in this way Chinese cultural heritage. The former would call those who want to use the Taiwan-style phonetic system *Tai Du fen zi* (Taiwan independent elements). These accusations also extend to the Chinese in Silicon Valley. Even those who have become U.S citizens can be unwittingly involved in acrimonious debates over the cultural policies of their mother countries.

First-generation Chinese immigrants in Silicon Valley celebrate one or more national days depending on where they came from and where they were born. These are celebrated on July 4 (United States), October 1 (PRC), and October 10 (Taiwan). Independence Day on July 4 is a day for many families and friends to go on a picnic or go with their children to watch the parade. October 1 is the Foundation or National Day of the PRC. Immigrants from mainland China have lobbied Santa Clara County to have a flag ceremony in city hall to commemorate the National Day of the PRC. The pro-ROC group similarly asked the county city hall to fly the flag of the ROC. The city hall of Milpitas does this for both the PRC and ROC. Some pro-PRC organizations invite officials from the Chinese consulate in San Francisco to join them in the celebration of the National Day of the PRC on October 1. The Taiwanese do the same, inviting government officials from the Taipei Economic and Cultural Office of San Francisco on October 10. These national day celebrations offer an emotional display of the ties of the Silicon Valley Chinese to the countries of their origin.

There are often sensitive discussions about a current regime in Taiwan. The PRC at times has been concerned that the government of Taiwan was for Taiwan independence, and just as in the debate over the Taiwan-style phonetic system, it calls the leadership and highly ranked officials of such an administration *Tai Du fen zi.* In Silicon Valley there are also followers of the Taiwan independence movement. Typically, these are the native Taiwanese (*bendi*) who still have relatives in Taiwan. As mentioned earlier, the native-Taiwanese Chinese feel that they are different from the mainland-born Chinese from Taiwan. Although the two groups are from Taiwan, they belong to different subcultures. The native Taiwanese have a stronger interest in the Taiwan independence movement. They also follow the elections of Taiwan closely. Taiwanese political parties like the Democratic Progressive Party and the Taiwanese Solidarity Union for an Emerging Taiwanese Nation also engage in "long distance" nationalism in Silicon Valley. This phenomenon occurs in other ethnic communities (Appadurai 1998; Basch, Schiller, and Blanc 1994). There is a Chinese TV talk show called *Cross Talk* on KTSF in the Bay Area and it has many fans among the Chinese from Taiwan. The show is often dedicated to Taiwanese politics and Taiwan-China relations. Most of the mainland Chinese in the valley are not interested in the show at all. Those Chinese who are interested in the show are often those who still have close ties to Taiwan and are not American citizens yet. In fact, some of them continue to participate in Taiwanese elections, forming clubs to support their favorite candidates in Taiwan. However, those who have become American citizens tend to lose their interest in the politics of Taiwan. Suffice it to say that only a small number of Taiwanese Americans are influenced by the politics of Taiwan.

In the case of the mainland Chinese, there is a small number of immigrants who are interested in establishing democracy in China. However their organization, Silicon Valley Chinese for Democracy in China, is not extensive and its influence is limited. Interestingly, one of the founders of this organization is an American citizen. He is also a member of the Committee of 100, which is committed to protecting the civil rights of Chinese Americans and which encourages their participation in American politics.

Factionalism in the Chinese American community and political squabbles between Taiwan and China have another effect. Through these disagreements many immigrants realize that they are no longer citizens of either Taiwan or China and that their true home is in America. The debates over Taiwan independence and the unification of China help sharpen the sense of belonging of many of the Chinese in America. They become keenly aware of the political maneuvering in their mother countries, and they come to the realization that they are actually far away from these maneuverings and that they have become part of America. "Whether we like it or not, we are here. We have made our decision to come here and our careers, our businesses, and our homes are in America." This is the sentiment of a vast majority of the Chinese in Silicon Valley.

Nationality and Cultural Heritage

Many Chinese also separate the issue of nationality from their ethnic heritage. One can, they say, keep one's Chinese heritage and be an American citizen at the same time. As a naturalized citizen or citizen by birth, a Chinese American needs to fulfill his or her duties as a citizen. One informant was adamant about this responsibility, stating that:

I made the distinction between cultural heritage and passports. Passports are just travel documents. One can keep one's cultural heritage and be [a] citizen of America. The Chinese in America who are citizens should realize that they are Americans. They are part of America. They are citizens of America. One can eat Chinese food and have one's culture at home. But in the public, in the work place and in interaction with a foreign country, they are Americans. To participate in American politics is good. To participate in American through the voting box is a necessity. (Informant L, interview with author, September 19, 2001)

Does participation in the global economy make one less a citizen of the United States? My informants are very clear on this issue. They do not believe that working overseas will necessarily make one less patriotic. GM, Ford, and other large American companies have many white employees working overseas. My informants believed that Americans are uncomfortable about Chinese Americans working overseas and that there is a double standard. George Koo of Deloitte and Touche in Silicon Valley also made a similar argument:

One can keep one's native culture and American culture. Bicultural background could be an asset in building bridges between two cultures. There is not necessarily a problem of divided loyalty, provided that one knows that as a citizen, he is an American. This priority should be clear. As a citizen, loyalty is here. But you could have knowledge of two cultures and use them to help Americans understand China's policy and vice versa. (George Koo, interview with author, October 6, 2001)

Citizenship and cultural heritage need not be in conflict with each other. Another of my informants, Mr. Mo, said he loves Chinese culture but he also loves the United States. He came to San Jose many years ago as an immigrant. After finishing his education, he worked as a flower grower and later as a realtor. He has since lived in Milpitas for more than ten yeas. He has served in the U.S. military and made numerous donations for the victims of the September 11 terrorist attacks and to other charitable organizations in the United States. He feels that as a citizen he needs to fulfill his obligation to serve this country. Furthermore, he said that one needs to pay back his community for what he receives. Bicultural heritage and a love for one's native culture need not be in conflict with one's allegiance to one's adopted country. In other words, ethnicity and citizenship need not be coterminous. This is particularly the case in multicultural America. Many first-generation immigrants still have emotional or cultural ties to their birthplaces in their home countries. It is natural that an Englishman, an Italian, or a New Zealander will continue to show interest in the culture and development of his ancestral land. They may be American citizens, but ethnically they may have emotional connections to the countries of their origin. This is part of their identity, this combination of American citizenship and ethnic culture. American citizenship and an Anglo-cultural heritage is quite common. This kind of hybridization has become more acceptable in the case of Anglo-Americans but less so in other ethnic groups. When the hybridization involves an ethnic minority, it creates an uneasy feeling among many white Americans (Rosaldo 1993).

A mother country exerts its influence on the assimilation and participation of an ethnic group in an adopted country. The PRC's citizenship policy encourages the overseas Chinese in Silicon Valley to become U.S. citizens, while the ROC allows dual citizenship for the Taiwanese Chinese. But after they have been naturalized, the Chinese in Silicon Valley tend to identify with the United States politically and with China culturally They call themselves *Mei Ji Hua Ren* (American citizens of Chinese descent).

Technology and Cultural Identity Maintenance

The Silicon Valley Chinese community is a globalized community. It is linked with China, Taiwan, Hong Kong, and the rest of the world by modern communication technology and jet travel. There is a daily transnational flow of the members of this community traveling back and forth between Silicon Valley and the rest of the world. They carry cultural and political currents in both directions. High-tech engineers and business executives come back from China with the latest information on Chinese fashion, food, housing, interaction patterns, aspirations, and values. Conversely, in returning to China they bring back information about the American way of life, the latest political and social events there, and its material culture.

E-mail, Internet websites, Chinese TV programming, and Chinese newspapers help keep Chinese culture alive in Silicon Valley. Taiwanese and mainland Chinese TV companies supply cultural and entertainment programs and broadcast their daily news for their audience in the Bay Area. They present special programs in Chinese communities in different parts of the world. A popular TV series, *Story from Afar*, focuses on the lives of the overseas Chinese in Africa, Latin America, the Middle East, and Europe. And Sina.com offers news, e-mail, chat, dating clubs, and financial and shopping services. Its news coverage includes international news, U.S. news, and news from different Chinese communities around the world. (With more than 700,000 registered users, sina.com is the most popular website among the Chinese in Silicon Valley. It aims to be the equivalent of America Online and Netscape combined, and it serves approximately 1.5 billion Chinese speakers worldwide.) Chinese Americans in Silicon Valley do indeed get global knowledge about the Chinese diaspora. Technological developments help the valley Chinese maintain their connection to Chinese culture and Chinese communities around the world. Technology in this sense guides the maintenance of Chinese culture.

The ethnic Chinese in general are aware of the existence of global and local perspectives, and they are international in their orientation. Many of them travel extensively for a living. They are eager for political or economic analysis of the news. They want to know the different points of views for the same news event. The NATO bombing of the Chinese Embassy in Belgrade in 1999 and the collision of the American spy plane and the Chinese fighter jet over the South China Sea in 2001 were events for which the Chinese in the valley wanted to know the point of view from both the American side and the Chinese side, so much so that they practically overloaded Sina.com's servers in Beijing. The same goes for news stories concerning the Chinese in different parts of the world. Chinese viewers are hungry for news from the point of view of the native country as well as from an international perspective. Some scholars of overseas Chinese communities opine that the internet actually helps the Chinese obtain justice. They say that the circulation of news through the internet has helped the Chinese in Indonesia in the past several years. The anti-Chinese riots that took place there were brought quickly under control and the host country took action swiftly. Hence, the use of the internet can be beneficial in promoting social justice and human rights—a positive impact of technology.

The use of technology to enhance one's quality of life is common among the Chinese all over the world. China alone is expected to have 37 million Internet users by 2005 (*San Jose Mercury News* May 17, 1999). In general, Asian Americans are fond of the Internet. According to Forrester Research and Jupiter Communications, 69 percent of Asian American households in 2000, which translates to about 2.2 million households, had Internet access. Among white households, the number was only 54 percent (*San Francisco Chronicle* June 19, 2000). Asians and Chinese Americans constitute a large group of internet users. In Silicon Valley there were at least two computers in every Chinese home I visited during my fieldwork. Some families have one for each person who speaks English. Parents are concerned about computer literacy and are willing to invest in this area. For these parents, they do not want their children to be left behind. All fifty of the family homes I visited were wired to access the web.

Aside from sina.com, another popular Internet site used by the Silicon Valley Chinese is huren.org, which is run by a global organization called the World Huren Federation (www.huren.org/mission). *Huren* literally means Chinese. It was established to serve as a forum for Chinese around the world for the discussion of issues relevant to the Chinese diaspora. It is a nonprofit, nonpolitical, and nonreligious organization, like a one-stop meeting place for Chinese overseas around the world, who are estimated to number around 50 million dispersed in 130 countries (*Straits Times* August 20, 1998). The World Huren Federation does not support or encourage Chinese chauvinism. Nor does it encourage global citizenship without commitment or loyalty to a country. On the contrary, it advocates that the Chinese be responsible citizens in their adopted country, and that they participate actively in the mainstream of the larger society.

Huren.org has been instrumental in awakening the consciousness of the Chinese to the plight of the Indonesian Chinese. The report of Huren.org on the rape of 160 ethnic Chinese women in Indonesia led to many public demonstrations and protest rallies around the world. Letters of protest poured into the offices of the Indonesian government and its embassies. In the San Francisco Bay Area there was candlelight vigil on Union Square and an exhibition of photographs of the anti-Chinese riots in Indonesia. California Senator Dianne Feinstein quickly introduced legislation to condemn the mass rape and racial violence.

Huren.org also played an important role in initiating the campaign for the exoneration of Dr. Wen Ho Lee. In its community forum, huren.org had newspaper clippings on the case. It also had a link to the Wen Ho Lee Foundation in Fremont, which likewise sought redress for Dr. Lee. The Chinese community in Silicon Valley was particularly interested in his case due to its ethnic and occupational resonance: like many of the Chinese in Silicon Valley, he is a scientist.

The use of e-mail to fight discrimination is also common among the Chinese in Silicon Valley. Scrupulous merchants and discriminatory store keepers are identified and the relevant information passed on throughout the e-distribution list. I have mentioned the salesperson in an automobile dealership in Serramonte in the South Bay who used racial slurs against a Chinese customer and his family. The news traveled quickly via e-mail to other Chinese families in the valley. Many contacted the dealership and asked it to reprimand or dismiss the salesman. The dealership manager quickly apologized and resolved the dispute. The use of technology to seek collective support, to maintain one's cultural identity and to resolve conflicts has been quite successful in the Silicon Valley Chinese community. This is due to the fact that the valley is a high-tech community in which many Chinese households possess computers and use the latest information technology.

CONCLUSION

Contrary to what some scholars have said about the negative impact of globalization on ethnic identity, I found that the Chinese in Silicon Valley are not a rootless, unpatriotic mass without commitment to any nation-state. They are not an ungrounded empire, nor are they a stateless people. The majority of them are not multiple passport holders or opportunistic flexible citizens. From the data available, I found that a global flow of transnational migrants keeps Chinese culture alive in Silicon Valley. Instead of developing a homogeneous Chinese culture, I found the emergence of a heterogeneous population composed of many regional Chinese cultures. With immigrants from diverse areas of Asia, the creation of an Asian American identity is fostered. As Silicon Valley draws talent from different regions of China, one sees the emergence of many subethnicities. The ethnoscape, technoscape, and ideoscape in Silicon Valley are now driven by diversity, technology, and political ideology. From my field research, it became clear that the Silicon Valley Chinese now have more options in their selection of identity. They also have a greater opportunity to create hybrid identities.

The regional culture and customs of a migrant's ancestral land provide reinforcement as well as constraints in the migrant's creation of a suitable cultural identity. Thus, the transnational migrant may claim an Asian American, Chinese American, Taiwanese American, or Hong Kong American identity. The migrant is also free to create a Taiwanese, Hong Kong, or mainland Chinese culture in Silicon Valley. Therefore, globalization does not homogenize; it diversifies.

Amid cultural diversity, there is a need for unity. Globalization pushes forward some of these unifying elements. Ethnic pride (China's winning bid to host the 2008 Olympics), common tragedy (discrimination against the Chinese in Indonesia, the Wen Ho Lee incident), and international politics (the unification debates) can come to the forefront because modern communication tools quickly unify the Chinese in Silicon Valley. Even though the transnational flow of information and people in the modern world can create differences as well as unity, from my study it is this far obvious that among the Chinese there is a great deal of shared interest in maintaining a Chinese culture in Silicon Valley. Yet theirs is not a diaspora in the strictest sense of the word, because the common outcome is a hybridization of American life-style and Chinese culture. The Chinese want to have material affluence, and to enjoy the benefits of the American political system, but they prefer Chinese interaction patterns. *Luo di sheng gen* (establishing roots) in America is the desire of the majority of the Chinese in Silicon Valley.

This study found that the Chinese in Silicon Valley, are not sojourners like their forebears from the past. This is due to the fact that the present-day Chinese population differs from that of the nineteenth century. Today's Chinese are more educated and work in wholly different fields. They consciously made their decision to come to Silicon Valley to participate in the economy of the United States. Their identification with the United States has been driven by their countries of origin and the policies of those countries, and by the educational opportunity, political stability, and free enterprise system of the United States. External factors can cause significant changes in an ethnic community. Chinese Americans differ from their counterparts in Southeast Asia where the host societies often treat the Chinese unfairly. As a result, many of the Chinese in Southeast Asia are noncommittal to their host societies. Local citizenship may be awarded to them but they develop skeptical attitudes toward the local government. The overseas Chinese businessmen there treat then their citizenship as a matter of convenience. For security, they may acquire multiple citizenships and become multiple-passport holders. However, this is not the case for the majority of the Chinese immigrants in Silicon Valley. Hence, data obtained from different parts of the world should not be applied indiscriminately to the Chinese in the United States. The concepts of flexible citizenship (Ong 1999) and ungrounded empire (Ong and Nonini 1996), therefore, need to be examined with a critical eye.

Contemporary approaches to identity in this transnational world should go beyond the confines of a national state. The identities of the Chinese in Silicon Valley are influenced by their homelands and host country as well as by regional cultures and subcultures. A person can assume more than just one identity. The transnational migrant may have to rethink the issues of citizenship, nationalism, nation, and cultural identity while refiguring his or her relation to a host country and mother country in this global community. Hybridization of culture forms is common in Silicon Valley. Multiple identities and cultural hybridity are the result of social interactions and are a necessary by-product of cultural and economic flows in the transnational world.

8

Conclusion: Globalization, Citizenship, Social Networks, and Identity

How globalization affects the high-tech transnational Chinese migrant has been the central question of this book. Within the scope of this general question, I addressed a number of related questions, while focusing on the ways in which globalization affects the social and personal lives of the transnational Chinese migrants and their families, economic activities, identity, and community and interaction patterns with the larger society. This has been an ethnography with a focus on the impact of globalization. My study has furthermore found that the Chinese community in Silicon Valley exists as an unique transnational community, and I have sought to improve our understanding of the many complex theoretical issues surrounding the overall concepts of globalization and transnationalism. Many of the theories addressing the transnational community have not been grounded on empirical data. The current muddle in theoretical formulations on globalization, citizenship, diaspora, entrepreneurship, and ethnic identity are the result of incomplete ethnographical data or empirical bases. Theoretically, the present study finds that globalization does not necessarily lead to homogenization of social differences, identities, citizenship, and culture. Nor does it lead to the disappearance of informal social relationships such as kinship, friendship, and social networks. Globalization intensifies the use of social networks for the creation and maintenance of social identities as well as for economic and technological innovation and goal-seeking activities. Globalization helps localization via a process of heterogeneous combination of identities and an involved process of social and economic transactions among individual actors. Contrary to the claims of many global studies scholars, contemporary diaspora is neither a middle ground of essentialized identity nor a place for homogenized, transnational, cosmopolitan personalities. It is a place that is highly heterogeneous and through which a process of contestation is conducted by transnational social connections. It is also a place through which the individual actor hopes to achieve multicultural citizenship and to learn how to adapt to the changing global economy for the sake of his or her survival. In this sense, the Chinese community in Silicon Valley is not just a home away from home; rather it provides a framework and the mechanism through which a diasporan can successfully survive in a modern and complex world.

GLOBALIZATION AND THE TRANSNATIONAL COMMUNITY: CITIZENSHIP AND DIASPORA

Studying the Chinese community in Silicon Valley, I have found that globalization does not eliminate the transnational migrant's commitment to an adopted country. The constant crossing of national borders, and participation in an economy that extends beyond a single national border do not automatically create seamless borders between nations, nor do they produce rootless citizens. Flexible citizenship has been studied but it does not yet have universal applicability. There is a constant flow of immigrants into the United States, all of them with a great enthusiasm to be part of the United States and part of the Silicon Valley Chinese community. These migrants want to become permanent residents and, as soon as possible, U.S. citizens. They differ from other European nationality groups such as the English, the Dutch, or the Germans, many of whom may have green cards but do not want to give up their citizenship. During my research I found very few multiple passport holders. The mainland Chinese, by PRC laws, can possess only one passport; dual nationalities are not permitted. The majority of Taiwanese Chinese, though they are able to have dual citizenship, also want to participate in the United States as citizens. The same can be said of most of the Chinese from Hong Kong and other parts of the world. Empirically, the idea of multiple passport holding and of flexible citizenship have not caught the imagination of the Chinese. The major concern for them is how to be accepted professionally, politically, and economically by mainstream American society, a process they refer to as *luo di sheng gen* (establishing roots). For this reason they are tirelessly fighting to be part of their local communities by participating in PTA meetings, voting, becoming elected community officials, or joining community civic organization. This is contrary to the ways in which the overseas Chinese are perceived as acting in other parts of the world. Many of our common assumptions about the overseas Chinese as unassimilable foreigners have been derived from limited data on Southeast Asia. There is no intrinsic anti-assimilation philosophy among the Chinese people. Historically and empirically, one can find the integration of the Chinese with non-Chinese. The development of Chinese civilization is a case in point. From the nucleus of the Yellow River district to the inclusion of territories in the northern, southern, and western parts of China, there has been throughout China's history an integration of many different peoples and material cultures. The Chinese in Central and South America are highly integrated with their local communities. They are particularly assimilated in the general populations of Cuba, Trinidad, Peru, and Ecuador (Pan 1996). Some are of the Chinese are less integrated with the local populations than others; the Malaysian Chinese are one such example. Thus, all the Chinese diasporas are not the same. Perhaps it is more accurate to say that there is more than one single Chinese diaspora in the world, the Chinese in the United States differing from those in other countries.

The Chinese community of Silicon Valley is an American community whose members live in different municipalities and participate in the economic, political, and social life of America. This community is composed of people of shared Chinese cultural and historical heritage as well as of shared occupational background. It is different from most other ethnic enclaves in which the members usually participate in ethnic businesses. The Chinese high-tech personnel are professionals and entrepreneurs participating in the computer industry and other information-related businesses. This community, formed principally in the 1980s, originated at a time when American society was transitioning from the melting pot model to the multicultural model. This explains why the Chinese community, on the one hand, emphasizes *luo di sheng gen*, while on the other hand, it keeps its cultural heritage. It is a social movement that has developed in the special historical and social context of the United States. In the past twenty years, there has been a greater emphasis on multiculturalism in all aspects of American life. Although the process of assimilation is continuing, American people of different heritages are no longer hiding their ethnicity. This is particularly the case in the San Francisco Bay Area. The Silicon Valley Chinese feel that they are part of America and yet they identify with the Chinese culture. Wanting to be U.S. citizens, many apply for naturalization as soon as they qualify. The impression that the Chinese have divided loyalties is a figment of the imagination of a xenophobic political establishment that particularly fears latecomers from Asia. As a kind of self-fulfilling prophecy, this establishment created a scapegoat in the person of Dr. Wen Ho Lee. Its temporary success points to the fragility of the social experiment of multiculturalism. Non-white ethnic groups, it would seem, can have their culture but not their citizenship rights. They have been profiled, scrutinized, and held in isolation cells, all without pretext.

The Chinese in Silicon Valley have spoken out on their desire to be treated as other Americans. Their actions have proven that they want to participate in their neighborhoods, cities, schools, and communities. In Silicon Valley, Chinese entrepreneurs and engineers serve on the boards of public and private universities. They contribute to organizations for the aged and the helpless.

Their generosity is reflected in their donations to relief funds following the September 11 terrorist attacks.

In terms of cultural retention activities, the Chinese in Silicon Valley behave in a way similar to other ethnic groups. While Latinos celebrate Hispanic Heritage Month and blacks celebrate African American Heritage Month, the Chinese celebrate Asian Pacific Heritage Month. While Latinos celebrate Cinco de Mayo, the Irish, St. Patrick's Day, and the Jewish, Yom Kippur, the Chinese celebrate the Chinese New Year. In fact, in Silicon Valley these different ethnic groups freely attend each other's festivals. Keeping old-world traditions alive in multicultural America enriches the cultural life of contemporary America. However, this should not be confused with divided loyalty or resistance to full-fledged American citizenship. In a country like the United States with a long history of immigration by diverse ethnic groups, there are people from many cultures. They are *all* Americans in their own way, whether Anglo-American, African American, Iranian American, Jewish American, Irish American, Japanese American, or Chinese American.

In multicultural America, first-generation immigrants are bound to have cultural connections with their homeland. People are not raised in a vacuum, and they will have been enculturated. If they are recent immigrants, they are likely to be enculturated in more than one culture. Early childhood experiences and memories of the past will bring back thoughts of their old culture. Within the global economy, when immigrants become transnationals residing in new homes in adopted countries intermittently, many old-world cultural traditions become revitalized. At the same time, new-world cultural traditions flow back and forth between the two countries. The new and old cultures become mixed and hybridized. New immigrants to the United States may become nostalgic for their old-world conditions and culture. At the same time, upon returning temporarily to the home country, they may miss their adopted land, the United States. This "grass is always greener" kind of sentiment is not unique to the Chinese. Diasporic communities exist for many ethnic groups. Many Americans find it difficult to accept the diasporic cultural practices of the Chinese Americans even though these transnationals are newcomers to America and arrive with fresh memories of their home culture. But we now live in a different time when multiculturalism and a transnational existence have become facts of life in the fast-paced and sophisticated world of twenty-first-century technology. High-tech immigrants exist in a mode that many ordinary Americans have not experienced. The idea of a diaspora weighs more heavily on these transnational immigrants than on any established, second- or third-generation American. As time goes by, the diasporic experience of the Chinese Americans will change as well. Data obtained from this study indicates that the ABC have only limited knowledge about their old-world culture. Some intermarry with different ethnic groups or have been completely integrated into mainstream American society.

The Chinese community in Silicon Valley is an American community, but paradoxically it is also a diaspora. It has three homelands: Taiwan, Hong

Kong, and China. It is connected to these homelands in both nostalgic memory and by constant contemporary travel and business interaction. The Chinese of this community have certain nostalgic and emotional ties to their lands of origin. They may have relatives and friends there who are still part of their active social networks. These immigrants may surely have different political ideologies regarding their homelands. In this transnational community, one finds political contestations. Heterogeneity in political attitude toward a homeland, disharmony within the community, and political squabbles about affairs of that homeland are real. Many scholars who write of the urban-ethnic community as a homogeneous population with a common ethnic identity exaggerate this aspect of ethnic solidarity. In the transnational community of the Chinese in Silicon Valley, one sees the differences between class, subethnicity, and opposing political view even though all of the members of the community share a common language and a knowledge of Chinese culture. To what extent this phenomenon is shared by other contemporary urban-ethnic groups in America is an empirical question that waits to be answered by scholarly research.

The Mother Country and Ethnicity

The Silicon Valley Chinese diasporic community differs significantly from other communities that participate in the politics of a homeland. In fact, many of the Chinese American organizations in Silicon Valley, emphasize that they do not participate in the politics of the homeland. Furthermore, they indicate that they want rather to participate in American politics, and they encourage their members and others to run for political office so that they can be an important part of the United States. This position differs from that taken by other ethnic groups. For instance, the Cubans in Miami or the Afghans in California often would like to participate in what is going on in their homeland and even want to eventually return there. The mainland Chinese in Silicon Valley, however, want to maintain a political distance from their motherland. This is due in part to the fact that the PRC encourages its overseas Chinese citizens to "forge" blood with their host country and its citizens. Moreover, the PRC does not recognize dual citizenship. The mainland Chinese immigrant must choose between being a citizen of the United States or of China, but not of both. Thus, the PRC's policy toward the overseas Chinese plays a role in the decision of the mainland Chinese to establish roots in America. Public policies may thus affect one's ethnic affiliation and allegiance.

Regional Cultures

The Chinese community in Silicon Valley is not a monolithic one. Globalization has created an influx of Chinese immigrants from different states, nations, and continents. Their unity or solidarity is both organic and mechanic.

They depend on each other for survival and for better treatment in the United States, which they try to ensure by forming various kinds of professional associations. They also need each other's products, capital, and service. Thus, in the Durkheimian sense, theirs is an organic solidarity resulting from mutual needs. What Durkheim called mechanical solidarity results from similarities of lifestyle, occupation, and immigration experience as well as career path. The sameness that these groups share creates a unity or solidarity. However, ethnic solidarity does not imply the absence of conflict or social difference. As demonstrated in this study, social and cultural differences do exist. There are social inequalities as well as contestations in this high-tech professional community.

The concept of a Chinese culture is not shared equally by all Chinese. Although each is of ethnic Chinese extraction, their diversity arises from the fact that they have been drawn to Silicon Valley from different regions of Asia. There are different local dialects, values, and traditions among the different groups. The high-tech economy has drawn them together, but it meanwhile allows them to keep their diversity. This is another case of how universalism has perpetuated particularism.

This community of professionals differs from other Chinese communities in the United States because it is composed of highly educated Chinese. The most important organizations in Silicon Valley are no longer based on family name, hometown, or district. What is important here are modern, professional organizations like engineering, manufacturing, and computer software associations. The priorities for these immigrants are their careers, their families, and their children's education in the United States. When it comes to a permanent home, though these immigrants may travel around the globe and work in different parts of the world, they are firmly rooted or plan to soon establish roots in America. Their permanent home has changed from Asia to America. Their old homelands have become overseas business destinations and, ironically, a home away from home. It is a complete reversal of the old immigration systems. These locations are linked by fax, e-mail, telephone, and other modern communication systems. Even the concept of diaspora needs to be changed. As a concept, diaspora traditionally implies a group of people who are exiled and exclusive. They keep a distance from their host society and enclose themselves morally, geographically, or both. They long to return to their original homeland. In the case of the Chinese in Silicon Valley, they long to return to their adopted homeland, and at the same time to keep selected Chinese traditions from their homeland. They did not want to sever their ties with their motherland either, for that land continues to support them economically in this global economy. The situation is thus a complicated one. In terms of political allegiance, however, there is no divided loyalty. Chinese Americans made their choice clear when they became naturalized. From my research I have found that the commitment in this community to the American system is very strong; these people are no longer merely sojourners. Thus, the social science literature and its existing theories and concepts needs to be enlarged and reworked to accommodate this new social phenomena. The global economy has created a new social group that has to cross many borders and has to locate and relocate its social and economic existence. Its activities are configured by social and technological networks. It is a network society in a special way. The members of this group are linked by *guanxi* and by technology. The traditional idea of the diaspora as a moral community characterized by dispersion from the homeland and separation from and exclusion from the larger society needs to be modified. What is important here is the transnational connection of this community to its home cultures. This key element in the diaspora community is also emphasized by Jonathan Okamura (1996, 1998) and other scholars (Braziel and Mannur 2003; Werbner 2002). The aspects of dispersion, exclusiveness, and separation may not necessarily be essential features of all diasporas. The Chinese in Silicon Valley are a case in point.

To participate in a global economy as an expatriate, as an immigrant, and as a Chinese businessperson requires connections or social networks. Contrary to the arguments of scholars and writers on Chinese transnational communities, a social network is neither mysterious nor exclusive. Studies exemplified by books like *Lords of the Rim* (Seagrave 1995) and *The Bamboo Network* (Weidenbaum and Hughes 1996) have made the concept of social networking a muddle. A social network is an egocentric web of social actors. This network is formed for a common goal or a special social action. A person may have several social networks for different purposes that may or may not overlap. Common ethnicity is not an automatic requirement for inclusion. Common interest, common sentiment, and common goals are far more important than just common ethnicity. The social network has to be achieved and is not to be prescribed. My research on the overseas Chinese in Asia (B. Wong 2001b, 2001c), Latin America (B. Wong 1978), and the United States (B. Wong 1988, 1998a, 2001a, 2001b) indicates that networks have to be formed, maintained, and activated with certain goals in mind. There is no such thing as an intrinsic overseas Chinese or "bamboo" network. A Chinese person is not automatically a member of a Chinese social network. In fact, it is sometimes easier for a Chinese person to form a network with a non-Chinese person. We have seen in this study the case in which a Chinese colleague cooperated with an Indian colleague in order to organize a start-up company. They did so because there was a spirit of camaraderie existing between them. They had known each other for a long time and had learned from previous experience that they got along well, so they decided to be partners. This network had a common goal, and that goal became the basis for a new company. Therefore these social networks of the Chinese do not necessarily exclude the non-Chinese. Sometimes the participation of the non-Chinese is even a requirement, especially when the non-Chinese possess valuable experience and talent. Non-Chinese lawyers, accountants, marketing specialists, technical experts, and managerial talent are deliberately recruited to be part of these social networks. Again there is no mysterious bamboo network that monopolizes the world. It is precisely this kind of unfounded prejudice that is not only detrimental to world peace but also perpetuates racial profiling. Stereotyping and overgeneralization promote a racist society, and create conflict by pitting group against group and people against people.

GLOBALIZATION, TECHNICAL ENTREPRENEURSHIP, AND SOCIAL NETWORKS

The use of social networks for entrepreneurial activities has new meaning in this transnational community. Alejandro Portes (1998), Saskia Sassen (1991), and many others have written about the importance of these networks. As this study demonstrates, social networks go beyond traditional kinship and local ties. There are other elements to consider, one being talent, the second being trustworthiness, and the third being the ability of the network's members to work together for a common goal. Not all of one's kin can meet the above requirements. In the high-tech Chinese community of Silicon Valley, talented *tongxie* (classmates), *tongshi* (colleagues) from the same companies, and peers from the same universities, can be more important than the individuals available through one's traditional kinship or hometown origin ties. Outsiders and non-Chinese will be accepted in a Chinese-dominated company, provided that these outsiders have something to offer and are willing to work with the group. The social networks among these high-tech Chinese are thus open to non-Chinese ethnic groups. This emphasis departs from that of the Chinese in various Chinatowns in America where the principles of clanship and locality of origin are still used heavily in organizing social relations (B. Wong 1982, 1988). This is reflected in the large number of family name associations and regional or hometown associations to be found in American Chinatowns. One of the reasons why colleagues and alumni relations are important in Silicon Valley is the class, business, and professional interest of the high-tech business. In this community one sees the transitioning of a traditional culture emphasis on blood and locality ties to class concerns. For goal-seeking activities in the global economy, resources like educational achievement, creativity, and professional knowledge are more effective than anything else.

In entrepreneurial pursuit, local knowledge of the opportunity structure of both host and guest countries is of utmost importance. People who have local knowledge are resources. Immigrants who have language skills developed in their sending countries can now use them to conduct business. Their social ties and connections turn out to be advantageous for economic globalization. In this way social networks continue to function in the global economy. Similarly, white Americans who are familiar with business management and the laws of their own country are important assets for Chinese entrepreneurs. Mutual help and mutual needs dictate the formation of multi-ethnic partnerships. Hence, social networks may not necessarily be ethnically based. From data obtained, it seems that non-Asians may have to adapt to the Asian way of doing business in predominantly Chinese-controlled companies. Asianization or "sinicization" does take place. Social relations are important in all businesses. There is an American way of social relations management and an Chinese way of social relations management. Culture plays a role in business. The handshake, the toast, and the Christmas party may be important for Americans. But for the Chinese, the process of developing *guanxi* is important and slowly obtained. Seeking common ground, entertaining, giving gifts, developing mutual trust, sipping tea, and going out to recreational places may be important in creating the *guanxi* that can then be used in entrepreneurial pursuits. All people use social networks for goal-seeking activities. Thus, social networking is not the exclusive domain of the Chinese. Many books and articles have been written about the social networks of the Chinese, giving them the mysterious qualities mentioned above. There should not be any mystique about it. In the United States these networks are called old-boy networks. In Latin America, they may be patron-client, friendship, or *compadrago* networks. The Jewish people use their own network systems. The English, the Hindus, and the Muslims similarly use networks. In the case of the Chinese, it is called *guanxi*. While the ways of developing networks vary, the purpose of these networks are identical— they are meant for the accomplishment of specific goals.

Guanxi is contracted with ease between people who know each other intimately. Local knowledge and language ability is important, but a non-Chinese can develop *guanxi* with a Chinese and use it for entrepreneurial activities. In general, such connections can be facilitated by a common ground whether it be language, school, or company, professional, or business interest. The emergence of international communicative networks, linking immigrants and returnees to their countries of origin through a variety of family, kinship, friendship, and economic and emotional ties, has become significant in the process of globalization. These informal social ties facilitate not only economic globalization but also the development of a new social order and institution. The astronaut syndrome, the feasibility of travel between politically hostile regions for economic purposes, and the protocol for property acquisition and investment by the Chinese in China, Hong Kong, and Taiwan have become possible. Thus, social networks have political and economic significance in the process of globalization. Other authors have recognized this. Stephen Castles (1998) and others have shown how social networks, special programs, and public policies facilitate the return of immigrant workers to their homeland. The use of informal and formal social networks to connect returnees and the homeland has become a feature of the global economy.

Globalization and Localization

The process of globalization requires an extensive use of local networks. The flow of capital, people, and networks that this flow creates are not one-directional. It is not a departing from one point and an ending up at another but rather, it is a cyclical or zigzagging movement. The theories of Wallerstein (1980, 1990) and Frank (1967) concerning center and periphery relations between developed and underdeveloped economies and between colonizing countries and their colonies are no longer applicable. The centers are fluctuating and transitional; so are the peripherals. Hong Kong was an important center for commerce in the latter half of the twentieth century but is now being replaced by Shenzhen (the new Special Economic Zone outside of Hong Kong), and Shanghai. Beijing, Shanghai, and Suzhou have become more important centers than Taipei, Hsinchu (in Taiwan), and even Silicon Valley when it comes to the production of certain goods and services. Products are moving out of China to the United States and other parts of the world. The flow of capital is moving along with the goods and services in a non-unilineal fashion. The development of high-tech products has become multicentric. Semiconductor chips are produced in Taiwan but the software they use is produced in Silicon Valley. Parts are transported from one area of the world and assembled in another. Economic development is specialized in different localities. Similarly, venture capitalists no longer focus on one geographical area. Investment as well has become multicentric and globalized. Hence, world systems theory has lost its applicability in the postmodern world. Globalization implies decentralization and localization. International itinerants have to transverse national borders and penetrate local business networks and production systems. They need to create and foster local connections. Globalization requires localization; universalism and particularism go hand in hand.

Fostering local connections requires a change of mindset as well as behavioral patterns among the Chinese. First, they have to learn how to deal with the larger society. A certain familiarity with social etiquette and American custom is required. The ways of American entertaining or doing business have to be mastered. In mainland China, personal relationships may outweigh legal agreement; in the United States the Chinese have to pay special attention to the contractual and legal aspects of business relations. In mainland China, people may insist on *li yao* (reasonableness); in the United States businesses may emphasize legal procedure. Thus, local knowledge is pivotal in business transactions. In this regard, the ABC as well as the Taiwan Chinese, when compared to the mainland Chinese, are more in tune with American practice. All Chinese entrepreneurs, however, sooner or later must and do develop some sophistication in business transactions with the dominant society.

The Chinese in Silicon Valley have acquired a number of practical strategies for their survival in the community. As indicated earlier, they have changed their traditional pattern of staying with the same company for years. To improve their working conditions and to achieve social mobility, they have adapted and learned from other American workers to change jobs frequently. Social mobility may necessitate a change of jobs or a relocation. Traditionally the Chinese did not change their jobs frequently out of a desire for stability and in order to show loyalty to their company. In Silicon Valley they quickly learn that they have to modify their attitudes toward their jobs. Some will change their jobs four times in two years. The recession of 2001 produced quite a few unemployed Chinese in the high-tech industry. These unemployed individuals learned from other Americans to seek retraining in fields for which workers were in demand, such as business management and real estate. Changing one's occupation in order to survive by meeting the demand of the local economy is indeed an adaptation. Another strategy for social mobility is to become an entrepreneur. This step is harder for the mainland Chinese engineer than it is for the engineer from Hong Kong or Taiwan. The knowledge of Western capitalism among the mainland Chinese is limited. Furthermore, for a long period of time the mainland Chinese were not taught to appreciate or aspire to be entrepreneurs. To correct this lack of understanding and motivation among Chinese high-tech professionals, many Chinese professional organizations have established seminars, workshops, and discussion groups to teach Chinese transnational immigrants how to organize start-up companies and how to be owners, financiers, and CEOs of high-tech companies in Silicon Valley.

Return migration is also used by the Chinese to participate in the global economy. While they are in Silicon Valley, they learn how to enhance their earnings by tapping into low-cost manufacturing resources in Asia. Some establish transnational corporations in Asia and the United States. Others may return to Asia to obtain high-paying employment. These returnees, whether they are entrepreneurs or professionals, tend to ground themselves in Silicon Valley. They have houses or a family living in the United States. Their permanent home is the United States and their home away from home is Asia, and as we've seen, this phenomenon is sometimes misunderstood and misinterpreted as noncommitment to the Unites States. In reality, it is a strategy that the Chinese transnational migrants use to establish themselves economically in the United States. In order to achieve the American Dream many return trips to their old country, or a pattern of circular migration between the United States and their home countries may be required. This frequent travel practice has given rise to what the Chinese call astronaut syndrome. The astronaut has to spend a considerable amount of time flying for the sake of economic grounding. But circulation migration or frequent flying has social costs. The impact it has on the lives of the astronaut as well as his or her family is often significant.

Impact on Family and Social Life

As indicated in this study, the new astronaut life style has broken up many families. Some families have to suffer frequent separation from a wage earner who leaves the family up to seven times a year. Some of these astronaut wage earners spend as many as eight months a year away from their permanent home. An absentee husband or wife can produce marital strain and may do harm to parent-child relations. These nearly single-parent households put undue pressure on the supervising parent who stays behind to run the household. This is particularly the case if the supervising parent is also a wage earner. His or her work schedule will be frequently disrupted because of family emergencies or child-care obligations. Many of these households have to resort to the hiring of caretakers or au pairs to care for the children.

Men who are overseas may develop connections or extramarital relations with local women. Even those who do not go astray bear their social costs as well. These include loneliness, jet lag, and an undisciplined social schedule. Then there are those who have an overseas assignment and who travel with their family. They may have to uproot their lives in Silicon Valley and transplant those lives to an overseas location. This may be an opportunity and a refreshing experience. On the other hand, it can be an enormous sacrifice for the children who have to adjust to a new educational system and a new set of friends. There is also the situation of the so-called parachute children. These are the ones who are dropped off in Silicon Valley to live by themselves. They have to take care of their own schooling, the family house, and the family cars while their parents travel back to Taiwan, Singapore, China, or Hong Kong for business. Many are the untold sufferings of these separated families.

For the unmarried transnational migrant, frequent travel is not conducive to the establishment of permanent social relations in the first place. In the high-tech Silicon Valley economy, the ratio between male and females is highly skewed, and men face great difficulty in finding a suitable mate. To offset the imbalance between men and women, many strategies have been developed. Some Chinese men and women advertise in local Chinese papers to seek potential marriage partners. Entrepreneurs may organize dating services. Or professional organizations may create social events to attract women from Taiwan and Hong Kong to parties or mixers in the valley. But even if two people get the opportunity to meet each other, it is still difficult for them to establish a permanent relationship due to the frequent travel necessitated by overseas assignment. Some have lost their loved ones in this manner. Therefore a new bachelor society has formed that is not dissimilar to those societies of the old days when Chinese railroad workers and miners left their families to come to the United States to seek their fortune. These men became bachelors or lived the lives of bachelors. Will this phenomenon create a problem in reproduction? This is a question to be pondered.

Globalization in the high-tech industry creates a working schedule that makes it difficult for workers to have a normal social life. Many of them have to work according to the time zones of the headquarters overseas. For some, the busy hours are from 5 pm to midnight—the time that their head office has its normal daytime operation hours in Asia. During the daytime hours, many of the high-tech people who work for transnational corporations sleep. And when they have free time, other people are at work. Therefore they have difficulty meeting other people, which creates loneliness. The global economy has done harm to the social lives of its workers.

GLOBALIZATION AND IDENTITY FORMATION: HYBRIDITY, CONTESTATION, AND NEGOTIATION

The ethnic identity of the Chinese in Silicon Valley is not a given. They have to create, negotiate, and even hybridize elements from their home region, mother country, and host society. Chinese Americans in Silicon Valley are different from the American Chinatown Chinese, or even the Chinese from other countries. But global competition and the enlargement of economic activities beyond national borders do not eliminate ethnic tradition or the importance of place and localism. The Silicon Valley Chinese, having gone to work for multinational corporations and having perhaps returned to Asia to work temporarily, may continue to be influenced by the their host or adopted country. Thus, modern communication has increased rather than diminished the importance of a place's accessibility. While they are away on overseas employment, they still maintain close ties with their homes and their relatives and friends in America. For the ABC who are transnational workers, their ties to America are one-way because their forebears have been in America for generations. Yet the Chinese immigrants who are traversing continents and national borders may have many sets of networks within which to work. Their family and friends may be in Silicon Valley while their relatives and associates are in ancestral places like Taiwan, Hong Kong, mainland China, and Singapore. Their position in the global economy in this sense has as much to do with occupational and class background as it does with regional and subethnic networks. Globalization does not eliminate their ethnic networks. On the contrary, it sharpens their awareness of their ethnic resources. There is a quest for identity accompanying the instrumentality of these ethnic resources. Are we Chinese? Are we American? Are we Chinese Americans or Asian American? What are we? These questions of identity are intimately linked with work, ideology, cultural tradition, and citizenship.

As immigrants living in an area with a heterogeneous population, just like white, African American, Hispanic, and other Asian-Pacific groups, the Chinese feel that they are different from other populations. Global forces and the impersonality of the marketplace may also pose a threat to these immigrants. Modern technology, consumerism, and capitalism seem to swamp their local traditions. Lacking universal acceptance from white Americans drives them to flock together to seek support from each other. It is not difficult to understand the rationale behind the formation of ethnic associations in Silicon Valley.

However, the formation of an ethnic identity is by no means the result of just ethnic differences in the face of heterogeneity and globalization. The process is far more complicated than previously thought. Fragmentation, hybridization, syncretism, deterritorialization, and diasporization can all take place at the same time. The Chinese in Silicon Valley simultaneously possess unity and diversity. The development of regional culture into Taiwanese, Hong Kong, and mainland Chinese culture is a case in point. There are professional associations that cater to professionals from different places and different universities. Hybridization takes place in interracial and interregional marriage. The Hong Kong Chinese marry Taiwanese Chinese. The children from this union may speak both Mandarin and Cantonese. Hybridization also occurs in diet. And syncretism occurs when two or more cultural practices are carried out. For instance, some Chinese use both American medicine and Chinese herbal medicine at the same time. Furthermore, there is a sense that all the Chinese are alike and that they need to develop solidarity through community organization. The various Chinese political groups are a case in point. Then there is the sense that Asians should develop unity, and hence Asian coalitions are formed. In this sense, deterritorialization takes place. Chinese Americans in this way give up national differences for the strength of a coalition.

Another phenomenon is diasporization. On huren.com and a number of internet websites, there are discussions of the overseas Chinese networks. However, the consciousness of having a universal overseas diaspora is not strong. When the massacre of the ethnic Chinese in Indonesia occurred, the Chinese in America showed their sympathy and rendered their support. However, there is a big difference between the Chinese in Indonesia and the Chinese in other parts of the world. There is no single identity among them. The overseas Chinese are not a single diaspora. Rather, there are multiple diasporas among the Chinese living in different parts of the world. Even within America the Chinese in Silicon Valley differ from those living in the American Chinatowns. Furthermore, fragmentation within the Chinese community in Silicon Valley takes place. Hong Kong Chinese and the ABC see themselves as different from each other. Politically in the valley, there are pro-Taiwan and pro-PRC segments. Among the immigrants from Taiwan there are Pro-KMT and pro-Taiwan independence factions, and within each faction there are smaller units who in turn disagree with each other. In the PRC group, there are those who are for reforms and liberalization. Among them, there are some who want to see more democracy and religious freedom in mainland China. In the Hong Kong group, some are unhappy with the chief executive administrator, Tung Chee Hua, while others support him. Thus, political differences and disagreements exist, especially during the time of local elections in Taiwan and Hong Kong. But a remarkable phenomenon in this community is that a certain accommodation exists. For instance, at the Bay Area Chinese Athletic Meet, people from Taiwan, Hong Kong, and mainland China get together strictly for athletic competition. Flags representing Taiwan, Hong Kong, and China are used to designate geographical origins. However, there is a tacit agreement among the spectators and competitors that they will not let political differences spoil their fun. Everybody abides by this rule: "Only talk athletics, do not talk politics." When Beijing won its bid to host the Olympics, all the Chinese whether they were from Hong Kong, Taiwan or mainland China expressed their ethnic pride. Together they participate in the Chinese New Year Parade or the Dragon Boat Race. A certain unity exists, but it is more a cultural unity than a political unity. Nevertheless, one sees politically a certain tolerance of the groups toward each other. This mutual respect for political difference is a highly unusual phenomenon among the Chinese in Silicon Valley. It is like a multiculturalism within the community. But members of this community do not hesitate to assert their regional and subcultural differences. A case in point is the debate over the use of phonetic systems. Some want to use the PRC's pinyin system. Other wants to use Taiwan's *Tong Yong* pinyin system. Some want to send their children to Chinese schools to learn Mandarin, some want them to learn Taiwanese, and still others, to learn Hakka or Cantonese. Chinese culture is Silicon Valley is not a monolithic culture. There are subcultural differences, and discussions of differences are tolerated. It is therefore heterogeneity amidst unity. This is perhaps due to the influence of Silicon Valley which is already a very heterogeneous society with white, Hispanic, Indian, African American, Vietnamese, and other minority groups participating in it.

The formation of an ethnic identity for the Chinese in Silicon Valley has taken place under the reinforcement and constraint of the opportunity structure of the global and regional economy, and it has been governed as well by mainstream society and the ability of each individual Chinese making up the community. The Chinese in Silicon Valley possess different sets of resources. They are not like the overseas Chinese trading communities in Southeast Asia where the actors are merchants who have been in their host countries for many generations. Many of these are not highly educated. They worked mostly in colonial societies until recently. Their mind-set and adaptive strategies differ entirely from those of the Chinese in Silicon Valley. The Chinese in Silicon Valley are mostly high-tech people who are highly educated. They came to the United States as students and culminated their careers as well-paid engineers and scientists. Some became CEOs of start-up companies that turned into financial empires. They are highly urban and cosmopolitan in their outlook. Additionally, they are mostly new immigrants with the intention of staying in the United States permanently. While establishing their roots in America, they would like to retain a certain sense of Chinese-ness.

In the present globalized world, in order to better position themselves as bridge makers and entrepreneurs, the Chinese in Silicon Valley are encouraged to forge *guanxi* with their ancestral lands because *guanxi* are resources important for economic globalization. These social ties and social networks are instrumental in their economic activities. Old friendship, kinship, locality ties, and alumni connections require nurturing and provide a background for the articulation of the new identity of Chinese Americans. This by no means implies that the Chinese in Silicon Valley are motherland oriented. On the contrary, their connecting with the motherland is more instrumental than substantial. They prefer to settle in the United States and establish roots in America. They identify themselves as "Americans of Chinese descent" when they are in mainland China.

In the United States these Chinese would like to participate in American social and political life. To this end they have formed interest groups and associations as well as coalitions with other Asians to fight for their place in U.S. society. They vote and they send their children to the best educational institutions in the hope that they in turn will be fully accepted by mainstream society. On the other hand, the Chinese are deeply interested in retaining their Chinese culture. Furthermore, their effort for and interest in their culture are made possible in the new social climate that is being created as mainstream Americans espouse the idea of multiculturalism. In the previous generation, the melting pot ideology, which emphasized assimilation and conformity to an Anglo-American culture, was the main policy. It was considered subversive to be bicultural. The old-world culture was often thought to be baggage, a negative factor to be gotten rid of in the process of Americanization. Today, the atmosphere has changed. Multiculturalism has been embraced. It is possible to be an American and at the same time to retain one's cultural heritage. The idea of multiculturalism has been encouraged, although in certain sectors of the population multiculturalism is still attacked as subversive. For instance, Patrick Buchanan (2001) has criticized the practice of bilingualism and multiculturalism. He considers these to be obstacles to assimilation and even harmful to a strong and unified America. His view of the policy of bilingualism is highly erroneous. Instead of seeing it as a strength and as an instrument to help minorities to fully participate in modern American life, he sees it as a weakness. Scientifically and pragmatically, more language skills and more cultural knowledge will help rather than impede participation in American life. Immigrant children whose English is limited will find it difficult to study politics, science, and other subjects unless the concepts are explained in their native language. Thus, the bilingual policy will help them make a rapid adjustment to the American school system and will assist them in the process of becoming desirable citizens. These bilingual skills are also helpful in securing American affluence in this global world. They position the new American citizen to better participate in the global economy.

The identity of the Chinese in Silicon Valley is constructed and negotiated with global, national, and multicultural "bricks." This echoes the assertion of Robin Cohen (1997) when he says that the new diasporic identity is an integration of the universal with the particular. It is a fusion of cosmopolitanism with localism and a synthesis of "home" with "a home away from home." Thus, identity is no longer totally grounded in one particular location. It flows with time and space. The Chinese in the United States differ from the Chinese elsewhere, and within this Chinese American identity there are sub-identities: the ABC, the Chinese Americans who migrated from Taiwan, the Chinese Americans who migrated from Hong Kong, the Chinese Americans who migrated from mainland China, and the Chinese Americans who migrated from elsewhere. Based on data from this study, it is safe to say that in all these different subgroups, the overwhelming ideology is to establish roots in the United States. They do so with social as well as economic resources from their adopted as well as their ancestral countries. The Chinese in Silicon Valley were drawn from different regions of China and different parts of the world. Many of them came with hyphenated or regional identities such as Hong Kong Chinese, American Chinese, Taiwan Chinese, mainland Chinese, Singapore Chinese, Philippine Chinese, or Peruvian Chinese. They were recruited to work in Silicon Valley because of their high-tech training or high-tech connections. Some of the Chinese came to Silicon Valley via Canada, England, or other parts of the world. When people from diverse regions and diverse cultural experiences come together, they are bound to show differences in their creation of an identity or identities, and so it is in the Chinese community of Silicon Valley. The global economy does contribute to the diversity of the Chinese population and the formation of multiple identities in Silicon Valley. Thus common ethnicity should not necessarily imply common identity. Some have argued that it does not make sense to develop a Chinese American identity. This school of thought advocates the development of an Asian American identity, for in doing so, a larger voting block can be created that will have more political influence and thus help increase Asian participation in the resource distributions of the larger society. This will benefit all Asians, including the Chinese. Another school of thought suggests that all Chinese share one cultural identity since there is only one Chinese culture. They argue that there is one common history and one common cultural core shared by all Chinese whether they are from mainland China, Taiwan or Hong Kong. Still others argue that regional differences in dialect and tradition truly separate the Chinese. They prefer to develop an umbrella identity called Chinese American. Within that identity, they want to have their subcultural identity recognized. They believe that the community would allow regional expressions. They would like to see Chinese schools teaching Hakka, Taiwanese, Mandarin, or Cantonese to the children of families from different regions of China. They would like see Chinese shops, restaurants, churches, temples, TV stations, or newspapers that serve people who still keep their regional identities. Thus we find a form of multiculturalism within the Chinese population.

The traditional concept of assimilation is unrealistic and dogmatic. The assimilation melting pot suggests the loss of cultural baggage and the wholesale adoption of the institutions and cultural traits of the host society. Minority ethnic groups are "melted" into the dominant group. In reality, one sees a continuity of ethnic cultures in America. The idea of multiculturalism has been experimented with recently. Voting rights, affirmative action programs, revised work schedules to accommodate the religious or ethnic holidays of an immigrant group, bilingualism as a tool in the transition to the official language, and ethnic schools have been tried. The Chinese in Silicon Valley, as indicated here, have de facto implemented and pushed for the implementation of these multicultural practices. However, the traditional concept of multiculturalism misses the transnational ties and the global flows of cultural influences. Thus, what is going on in the ancestral land may have an impact on an ethnic community. Language reforms, the use or nonuse of simplified Chinese characters, the use of the mainland Chinese pinyin system or the Taiwan *Han Yu* pinyin system, the adoption by schools of certain textbooks, the celebration of national holidays, the flying of flags, the debate over the unification of China, and the other policies of the ancestral lands may continue to influence an ethnic community. These transnational ties need to be taken into consideration. Transnational ties are important ingredients in new identity formation, a point that has been made by many of the scholars of transnationalism including Walter Anderson (1999) and Arjun Appadurai (1996). However none of these scholars have attempted to integrate the concepts of transnationalism and multiculturalism. To integrate the local with the global, the multicultural with the transnational, and the particular with the universal remains a challenging task for social scientists. Data obtained from this study suggests that the bounded concepts of assimilation and multiculturalism need to be modified in order to make the presentation of social reality possible.

Globalization, we have seen, does not erase cultural differences, nationalism, regionalism, racism, sexism, ethnic identity, or localism. Transnational migrations have constructed and negotiated new forms of identification. The Chinese transnational migrants have assumed and created new identities with input from both host and ancestral societies. They have used these new hybrid identities as Americans of Chinese descent, as Asian Americans. They have used these new identities in strategic ways to better position themselves in the globalizing world. Transnational migrants, therefore, should not be depicted as helpless individuals in exile or as traumatized victims. They are decision makers, doers, and shapers of their own destiny. Perhaps the concept of diaspora and its implications of home and away, exile and sojourn, and trauma and safety needs to be revised and updated because it does not take into account that people are capable of developing a hybridized identity to adjust to a new world.

The Silicon Valley Chinese community has many paradoxes and contradictions. It is a high-tech community participating fully in the global economy, while at the same time it is a community taking advantage of traditional Chinese culture, informal social networks, and flexible modes of accumulation. The members of the Silicon Valley Chinese community want to enjoy a hybridization of both cultures, Chinese and American. They want to establish roots in America but to live with Chinese culture as well as their own regional cultures. It is perhaps the latest experiment in a transnational existence to be found in modern multicultural America.

Glossary

COMMON CHINESE WORDS AND PHRASES USED IN THE BOOK

An Ju Le Ye 安居樂業
Beijing Dai Xue 北京大學
Bendi 本地
Biao Da Fang Fa Bu Yi Yang 表達方法不一樣
Che Zi 車子
Cheng Kung Dai Xue 成功大學
Cheng-du 成都
Chuang Ye 創業
Chuang Ye Jia 創業家
Chungshan (Zhongshan) 中山大學
Da Gong 打工
Da Guanxi 打關係
Da Lu Wen Hua 大陸文化
Da Men Ye You Zhuang Qing 大門也有壯青
Dong Ya Bing Fu 東亞病夫
Dui Shi Bu Dui Ren 對事不對人
Fa Cai Guang Rong 發財光榮
Fa Lun Gong 法輪功
Fang Zi 房子
Feng Shui 風水
Fu Dang Da Xue 復旦大學
Fujian Hua 福建話

Gan Qing (Kan chin) 感情
Gan Xiong Di 乾兄弟
Gao Guanxi 搞關係
Gao Ji Hua Gong 高級華工
Gao Ji Zhi Shi Fan Zi 高級知識份子
Ge Mo 隔膜
Guanxi 關係
Guo Jia Pei Yang 國家培養
Guo Ji Y i Bao 國際日報
Hai Zi 孩子
Hakka (Keijia) 客家
Han Yu Pin Yin 漢語拼音
Hen Xiao de Sheng Huo Quan Zi 很小的生活圈子
Hen Ze de Sheng Huo Quan Zi 很乍的生活圈子
Hong Bao 紅包
Hsinchu (Xin Zhu) 新竹
Jian Shi Yi Xia 見識 一下
Jian Ye 建業
Jiaotong Da Xue 交通大學
Jin Shan Shi Bao 金山時報
Li Shi (Cantonese) 利是
Li You 理由
Liang Di Tou Zi 兩地投資
Luo Di Sheng Gen 落地生根
Mei Guo Hua Ren 美國華人
Mei Guo Sheng Huo, Zhongguo Wen Hua 美國生活，中國文化
Mei Ji Hua Ren 美籍 華人
Mei You Li You 沒有理由
Mianzi 面子
Min Nan Hua 閩南話
Ming Bao 明報
Mo Di 摸底
Name Hoi (Nan Hai) 南海
Nanjing Da Xue 南京大學
Ning Wei Ji Tou Bu Wei Niu Hou 寧爲雞頭不爲牛後
Ngp Pu (or E Bu) 惡補

Nu Qiang Ren 女強人

Nuey Keung Yan 女強人 *(Cantonese)*

Pien Ren 騙人

Putonghua 普通話

Qi Zi 妻子

Qiao Bao 僑報

Ren Qing Wei 人情味

Ren Qing 人情

Sam Yap (Sanyi) 三邑

Shandong 山東

Sze Yap (Siyi) 四邑

Ta Men Ye You Zhuang Qing 大門也有壯青

Tai Da 台大

Tai Du Fen Zi 台獨份子

Tai Ji Quan 太極拳

Tai Kong Ren 太空人

Tai Yu 台語

Taiwan Ren 台灣人

Taiwan Da Xue 台灣大學

Taiwan wen hua 台灣文化

Tanggu 塘沽

Tianjin 天津

Tiochew (Chaozhou) 潮州

Tong Shi 同事

Tong Xue Ji Mei 同學姐妹

Tong Xue Xiong Di 同學兄弟

Tong Xue 同學

Tong Yong Pin Yin 通用拼音

Qing Hua Da Xue (or Tsing-Hua University) 清華大學

Wai Sheng Ren 外省人

Wen Hua Zai Zhong Guo, Zheng Zhi Zai Mei Guo 文化在中國，政治在美國

Wen Hua 文化

Wu Bu (Ngo Pu) 惡補

Wu Zi Deng Ke 五子登科

Xin Yong (or Shin Yung) 信用

Xiang Geng Wen hua 香港文化

Xingdao Yi Bao (or Sing Tao Daily) 星島日報

Xiao Yu Shan 小玉山
Xue Xiong Di 學兄弟
Ya Li Bu Dai 壓力不大
Yi Guo Liang Zhi 一國兩制
Yi Qi (Yee Chi) 義氣
Yin Zi 銀子
Ying You Jin You 應有儘有
You Heng Hao de Guanxi 有很好的關係
Yu Shan 玉山
Zhao Guanxi 找關係
Zhejiang Da Xue 浙江大學
Zhi Du Hua 制度化
Zhong Guo Tong Yi 中國統一
Zhong Guo Wen Hua 中國文化
Zhong Guo Zheng Qian 中國掙錢
Zhong Guo Zheng Qian, Mei Guo Sheng Huo 中國掙錢，美國生活
Zhongguo Daily 中國日報
Zhong – Li (Taiwan) 仲立

Bibliography

Allan, Graham. 1996. *Kinship and Friendship in Modern Britain*. New York: Oxford University Press.

Amyot, Jacques. 1993. *The Manila Chinese*. Quezon City: Institute of Philippine Culture.

Anderson, Benedict. 1991. *Imagined Communities: Reflections on the Origins and Spread of Nationalism*. London: Verso.

Anderson, Walter T. 1999. "The Self in Global Society." *Futures* 31 (8):804–12.

Anthias, Floya. 1999. "Beyond Unities of Identity in High Modernity." *Identities* 6 (1):121–44.

Appadurai, Arjun. 1995. "The Production of Locality." In *Counterworks: Managing the Diversity of Knowledge*, ed. Richard Fardon, 205–25. London: Routledge.

———. 1996. *Modernity at Large: Cultural Dimensions of Globalization*. Minneapolis: University of Minnesota Press.

———. 1998. "Dead Certainty: Ethnic Violence in the Era of Globalization." *Public Culture* 10 (2):225–47.

———. 1999. "Grassroots Globalization and the Research Imagination." *Public Culture* 12 (1):1–19.

Arensberg, Conrad. 1954. "The Community Study Method." *American Journal of Sociology* 60:109–24.

Auster, A., and H. Aldrich. 1984. "Small Business Vulnerability, Ethnic Enclaves, and Ethnic Enterprise." In *Ethnic Communities in Business: Strategies for Economic Survival*, ed. R. Ward and R. Jenkins. Cambridge: Cambridge University Press.

Avenarius, Christine. 2003. "Work and Social Network Composition among Immigrants from Taiwan to Southern California." *Anthropology of Work Review* 23 (3–4):3–15.

Banks, Erik. 2000. Think Locally, Act Globally. *Social Policy* 30 (3):36–40.

Barnes, J. A. 1954. "Class and Committees in a Norwegian Island Parish." *Human Relations* 7:39–58.

Basch, Linda, Nina Glick Schiller, and Christina Szanton Blanc. 1994. *Nations Unbound: Transnational Projects, Postcolonial Predicaments and Deterritorialized National-States*. Amsterdam: Gordon and Beach.

Barsook, Paulina. 2000. *Cyberselfish: A Critical Romp through the Terribly Libertarian Culture of High-Tech*. New York: Public Affairs.

Barth, Fredrik, ed. 1969. *Ethnic Groups and Boundaries*. Boston: Little, Brown.

Beaverstock, Jonathan, Richard Smith, and Peter Taylor. 2000. "World-City Network: A New Metageography?" *Annals of the Association of American Geographers* 90 (1):123–34.

Beck, Ulrich. 2000. "The Fight for a Cosmopolitan Future." *New Statesman* 130 (November):33–34.

Benedict, Burton. 1968. "Family Firms and Economic Development." *Southwestern Journal of Anthropology* 24 (1):1–19.

Benhabib, Seyla. 1999. "Citizens, Residents, and Aliens in a Changing World: Political Membership in the Global Era." *Social Research* 66 (3):709–44.

Bernstein, Steven, and Benjamin Cashore. 2000. "Globalization, Four Paths of Internationalization and Domestic Policy Change." *Canadian Journal of Political Science* 33 (1):67–99.

Blau, Peter M. 1995. *Inequality and Heterogeneity*. New York: Free Press.

Blim, Michael. 2005. *Equality and Economy: The Global Challenge*. Walnut Creek, Calif.: Altamira Press.

Bonacich E., and J. Modell. 1980. "A Theory of Middleman Minorities." *American Sociological Review* 37:583–94.

Bosco, Joseph. 2004. "Orientalism vs Nationalism." In *East Asian Anthropologists' Discussion*. www.easianth@Listserve.Temple.edu (accessed February 2, 2004).

Bott, Elizabeth. 1971. *Family and Social Networks*. London: Tavistock.

Bourdieu, Pierre. 1997. *Outline of a Theory of Practice*. Cambridge: Cambridge University Press.

Braziel, Jana Evans, and Anita Mannur, eds. 2003. *Theorizing Diaspora*. Malden, Mass.: Blackwell Publishers.

Bronson, Po. 1999. *The Nudist on the Late Shift*. New York: Random House.

Brown, Melissa. 2004. *Is Taiwan Chinese?* Berkeley: University of California Press.

Buchanan, Patrick. 2001. *The Death of the West: How Dying Populations and Immigrant Invasions Imperil Our Country and Civilization*. New York: Thomas Dunne.

Burawoy, Michael et al. 1991. *Ethnography Unbound: Power and Resistance in the Modern Metropolis*. Berkeley: University of California Press.

———. 1999. *Global Ethnography*. Berkeley: University of California Press.

Cameron, David, and Janice Gross Stein. 2000. "Globalization, Culture and Society: The State as Place amidst Shifting Spaces." *Canadian Public Policy* 26:S15–S34.

Carly, Christian. 2000. "The Citizens of Nowhere in Arabia's Hong Kong." *New Statesman* 129 (4480):32–33.

———. 1999. "Globalization and Citizenship: An Australian Dilemma." *Patterns of Prejudice* 35 (1):91–109.

Castells, Manuel. 1996a. *The Power of Identity*. Malden, Mass.: Blackwell Publishers.

———. 1996b. *The Rise of the Network Society*. Malden, Mass.: Blackwell Publishers.

———. 2000a. *End of Millennium*. Malden, Mass.: Blackwell Publishers.

———. 2000b. "Toward Sociology of the Network Society." *Contemporary Sociology* 20 (5):693–99.

Castells, Manuel, and Peter Hall, eds. 1994. *Technopoles of the World: The Making of Twenty-first-century Industrial Complexes.* New York: Routledge.

Castles, Stephen. 1998. *New Migrations, Ethnicity and Nationalism in Southeast and East Asia.* www.transcomm.ox.ac.uk/working_papers.htm (accessed May 27, 2005).

Cha, Ariana. July 28, 2000. "Immigrant Brain-Drain." *San Jose Mercury News.* 1A, 16A.

Champlin, Dell and Paulette Olson. 1999. "The Impact of Globalization on U.S. Labor markets: Refining the Debate." *Journal of Economic Issues* 33 (2):443–51.

Chan, Kwok-bun. 1997. "A Family Affairs: Migration, Dispersal, and the Emergent Identity of Chinese Metropolitan." *Diaspora* 6 (2):195–213.

Chan, Sucheng. 1991. *Asian Californian.* San Francisco: Boyd and Fraser.

Chen, Tien-Shi. 2001. *Chinese Diaspora: The Networks and Identities of Chinese Entrepreneurs* [in Japanese]. Tokyo: Akashi Co.

Cheng, Lucie. 1996. "Globalization and Women's Paid Labour in Asia." *International Social Science Journal* 51 (2):217–28.

Cleveland, David B. 2000. "Globalization and Anthropology: Expand the Options." *Human Organization* 59 (3):370–74.

Clifford, James. 1994. "Diasporas." *Cultural Anthropology* 9(3):302–38.

Clifford, James and George E. Marcus. 1986. *Writing Culture.* Berkeley: University of California Press.

Cohen, Robin. 1997. *Global Diasporas: An Introduction.* London: UCL Press.

Cunningham, Hilary. 1996. "The Ethnography of Transnational Social Activism: Understanding the Global as Local Practice." *American Ethnologist* 26 (3):583–604.

Curry, Lynne. 1995. "Global Grasp: Hong Kong's Li and Fung Looks beyond China." *Far Eastern Economic Review* 160 (April):48–49.

Denemark, Robert A., Jonathan Friedman, Barry K. Gills, and George Modelski. 2000. *World System History.* New York: Routledge.

Dirks, Robert. 1972. "Networks, Groups, and Adaptation in an Afro-Caribbean Community." *Man* 7 (4):565–85.

Dirlik, Arif. 1997. "Diasporas in Global and Place-Based Perspectives." A presentation at the Second International Conference on Contemporary Diaspora. Tsukuba, Japan.

———. 1998. *What Is in a Rim?* 2nd ed. Boulder, Colo.: Rowman and Littlefield.

Echeverria, Rafael. 1999. "The Observer and the Changing Self." *Futures* 31 (8):818–21.

Ehrentraut, Adolf. 1994. "Cultural Nationalism, Corporate Interests and the Production of Architectural Heritage in Japan." *Canadian Review of Sociology and Anthropology* (32):215–42.

Elkins, David. 1997. "Globalization, Telecommunication, and Virtual Ethnic Communities." *International Political Science Review* 18:139–52.

Emmott, Bill. 1999. "A Semi-integrated World." *Economist* 352 (8136):41–42.

England, Sarah. 1999. "Negotiating Race and Place in the Garifuna Diaspora: Identity Formation and Transnational Grassroots Politics in New York City and Honduras." *Identities* 6 (1):5–53.

English-Lueck, J. A. 2002. *Cultures@Silicon Valley.* Stanford, Calif.: Stanford University Press.

Enriquez, Juan. 1999. "Too Many Flags?" *Foreign Policy* 116 (Fall):30–32.

Escobar, Arturo. 2001. "Culture Sits in Places: Reflections on Globalism and Subaltern Strategies of Localization." *Political Geography* 20 (2):139–74.

Evans, Peter. 1999. "Fighting Marginalization with Transnational Networks: Counter-Hegemonic Globalization." *Contemporary Sociology* 29 (1):230–41.

Faist, Thomas. 1999. "Transnationalization in International Migration: Implications for the Study of Citizenship and Culture." www.transcomm.ox.ac.uk/working_papers.htm (accessed May 27, 2005).

Fallers, L. A., ed. 1964. *Immigrants and Associations.* The Hague: Mouton.

Fan, Maureen. June 2, 1999. *San Jose Mercury News.*

Featherston, Mike. 2000. "Public Life, Information Technology, and the Global City: New Possibilities for Citizenship and Identity Formation." In *Identity and Social Change,* ed. Joseph E. Davis, 53–79, New Brunswick, N.J.: Transaction.

Fisher, William F. 1996. "Doing Good? The Politics and Antipolitics of NGO Practices." *Annual Review of Anthropology* 26:439–64.

Fitzgerald, Stephen. 1972. *China and the Overseas Chinese: A Study of Peking's Changing Policy, 1949–1970.* Cambridge: Cambridge University Press.

Fong, Timothy P. 1994. *The First Suburban Chinatown.* Philadelphia: Temple University Press.

Forte, Maximilian. 1998. "Globalization and World-Systems Analysis" *Review: Fernand Braudel Center* 21 (1):29–99.

Foucault, Michel. 1973. *The Order of Thing: Archaeology of the Human Sciences.* Trans. Alan Sheridan. New York: Vintage.

———. 1982. "The Subject and Power." In *Beyond Structuralism and Hermeneutics,* eds. Herbert Dreyfus and Paul Rabinow. Chicago: University of Chicago Press.

Frank, Andre. 1967. *Capitalism and Underdevelopment in Latin America.* New York: Monthly Review Press.

Friedman, Jonathan. 2002. "Globalization and Localization." In *The Anthropology of Globalization,* eds. Johnathan Xavier Inda and Renato Rosaldo. Malden, Mass.: Blackwell Publishers.

Friedman, Thomas L., and Ignacio Ramonet. 1999. "Dueling Globalizations: A Debate between Thomas L. Friedman and Ignacio Ramonet." *Foreign Policy* 116 (Fall):110–27.

Fugita, Stephen S., and David J. O'Brien. 1991. *Japanese American Ethnicity: The Persistence of Community.* Seattle: University of Washington Press.

Fulchere, James. 2000. "Globalization, the Nation-State and the Global Society." *Sociological Review* 48 (4):522–43.

Galbraith, John Kenneth. 1977. *The Age of Uncertainty.* Boston: Houghton Mifflin.

Gallo, Miguel A., and Jannicke Sveen. 1991. "Internationalizing the Family Business: Facilitating and Restraining Factors." *Family Business Review* 4 (2):181–90.

Gans, Herbert. 1963. *Urban Villagers: Group and Class in the Life of Italian-Americans.* New York: Free Press.

Garbher, Gernot, and David Stark. 1998. "Organizing Diversity." In *Theorizing Transition,* ed. Adrian Smith and John Pickles. London: Routledge.

Geertze, Clifford. 1963. "The Integrative Revolution." In *Old Societies and New States,* ed. Clifford Geertze, 105–57. New York: Free Press.

Giddens, Anthony. 1991. *Modernity and Self-Identity.* Stanford: Stanford University Press.

———. 1999. *Runaway World.* London: Routledge.

Gilley, Bruce. 2000. "Pulling Away." *Far Eastern Economic Review* 163 (February):42–45.

Ginsburg, Martin. April 14, 2000. *San Francisco Chronicle.*

Gladney, Dru. 1999. *"Ethnic Identity in China."* Fort Worth, Tex.: Harcourt Brace.

Glassman, Jim. 1996. "State Power beyond the 'Territorial Trap': The Internationalization of the State." *Political Geography* 18 (6):669–96.

Glazer, Nathan. 1983. *Ethnic Dilemma 1904–1982.* Cambridge: Harvard University Press.

———. 2000. "Two Cheers for 'Asian Values.'" *National Interest* 57 (Fall):27–34.

Glazer, Nathan, and Patrick Moynihan. 1970. *Beyond the Melting Pot: The Negros, Puerto Ricans, Jews, Italians and Irish of New York City.* Cambridge, Mass.: Harvard University Press.

Godet, Michel. 1996. "Towards Flexibility with a Human Face." *Futures* 28 (November):879–84.

Gordon, Milton. 1964. *Assimilation in American Life: The Role of Race, Religion, and National Origins.* New York: Oxford University Press.

Greeley, Andrew. 1971. *Why Can't They Be Like Us?* New York: E.A. Dutton.

Guest, Kenneth. 2003. *God in Chinatown.* New York: New York University Press.

Guldin, Gregory. 1977. "Overseas at Home: The Fujianese of Hong Kong." Diss., University of Wisconsin, Madison.

Gupta, Akhil, and James Ferguson. 1997. *Anthropological Locations: Boundaries and Grounds of a Field Science.* Berkeley: University of California Press.

Hackenberg, Robert. 1996. "Advancing Applied Anthropology: Joe Hill in Cyberspace: Steps Toward Creating 'One Big Union.'" *Human Organization* 59 (3):365–69.

———. 1999. "Globalization: Touchstone Policy Concept or Sucked Orange?" *Human Organization* 58 (2):212–15.

Haley, Tan, and Haley. 1998. In *Markplus Quarterly* (October-December).

Hall, Stuart. 1990. "Cultural Identity and Diasporas." In *Identity: Community, Culture, Difference*, ed. Jonathan Rutherford, 222–37. London: Lawrence and Wishart.

Handley, John. 2001. *Toward the Golden Mountain: The History of the Chinese in the Santa Clara Valley.* Cupertino, Calif.: Cupertino Historical Society and Museum.

Handlin, Oscar. 1972. *Uprooted: The Epic Story of the Great Migrations that Made the American People.* 2nd ed. Boston: Little, Brown.

Hannerz, Ulf. 1990. "Cosmopolitans and Locals in World Culture." *Theory, Culture and Society* 7 (2–3):237–51.

———. 1993. "The Withering Away of the Nation?" *Ethnos* 58 (3–4):377–91.

———. 1996. *Transnational Connections: Culture, People, Places.* New York: Routledge.

———. 1997. "Scenarios for Peripheral Cultures." In *Culture, Globalization and the World System: Contemporary Conditions for the Representation of Identity*, ed. Anthony D. King, 107–28. Minneapolis: University of Minnesota Press.

Hannerz, Ulf, and Orvar Lofgen. 1994. "The Nation in the Global Village." *Cultural Studies* 8 (2):198–207.

Held, David, Anthony McGrew, David Goldblatt, and Jonathan Perraton. 1996. *Global Transformations.* Stanford, Calif.: Stanford University Press.

Hermans, Hurbert J. M, and Harry J. G. Kempen. 1996. "The Moving Cultures: The Perilous Problems of Cultural Dichotomies in a Globalizing Society." *American Psychologists* 53 (10):111–20.

Hilsum, Lindsey. 2000. "No Revolution, Thanks, We're Czech." *New Statesman* 129 (October):13–14.

Hoefler, Don. 2000. "History of Silicon Valley." www.intervalley.com.

Holston, James, and Arjun Appadurai. 1996. "Cities and Citizenship." *Public Culture* 8 (2):187–204.

Holton, Robert. 2000. "Globalization's Cultural Consequences." *Annals of the American Academy of Political and Social Science* 570 (July):142–52.

Hossfeld, Karen. 1988. "Divisions of Labor, Divisions of Lives: Immigrant Women Workers in Silicon Valley." Diss., University of California, Santa Cruz.

Hsu, Francis L. K. 1971. *The Challenge of the American Dream: The Chinese in the United States.* Belmont, California: Wadsworth Publishing.

———. 1981. *Americans and Chinese.* Honolulu: University Press of Hawaii.

———. 1983. *Rugged Individualism Reconsidered.* Knoxville: University of Tennessee Press.

Huang, Shirlena, Peggy Teo, and Brenda S. A. Yeoh. 2000. "Diasporic Subjects and Identity Negotiations: Women in and from Asia." *Women's Studies International Forum* 23 (4):391–98.

Ibarra, Robert. 1976. "Ethnicity Genuine and Spurious: A Study of a Norwegian Community in Rural Wisconsin." Diss., University of Wisconsin, Madison.

———. 2001. "Shaping American Values: The Legacy of Social Organization in a Norwegian American Farm Community." In *Family, Kin and Community: A Contemporary Reader,* ed. Bernard Wong, 169–87. Dubuque, Iowa: Kendall/Hunt.

Inda, Jonathan Xavier, and Renato Rosaldo. 2002. *The Anthropology of Globalization: A Reader.* Malden, Mass.: Blackwell Publishers.

Issacs, Harold R. 1980. *Scratches on Our Minds.* Armonk, N.Y.: M.E. Sharpe.

Jacobson, David. 1996. *Rights across Borders: Immigration and Decline of Citizenship.* Baltimore: Johns Hopkins University Press.

Jenkins, Richard. 1996. "Ethnicity Etcetera: Social Anthropological Points of View." *Ethnic and Racial Studies* 19 (4):807–22.

Joint Venture: Silicon Valley Network. 2000. *Silicon Valley Network Internet Cluster Analysis 2000.* San Jose, Calif.: Joint Venture: Silicon Valley Network.

———. 2001. *Index of Silicon Valley.*

Jones. T. P., D. McEvoy, and G. A. Barrett. 1994. "Labour Intensive Practices in the Ethnic Minority Firm." In *Employment, the Small Firm and the Labour Market,* ed. J. Atkinson and D. Storey. London: Routledge.

Ju, Yanan. 1996. *Understanding China.* Albany: State University of New York Press.

Kastoryano, Riva. 1998. "Transnational Participation and Citizenship: Immigrants in the European Union." www.transcomm.ox.ac.uk/working_papers.htm (accessed May 27, 2005).

———. 2002. "Settlement, Transnational Communities and Citizenship." *International Social Science Journal* 52 (3):165, 307–12.

Kearney, Michael. 1995. "The Local and the Global: The Anthropology of Globalization and Transnationalism." *Annual Review of Anthropology.* 24:542–65.

———. 1999. "Transnational Oaxacan Indigenous Identity: The Case of Mixtecs and Zapotecs." *Identities* 7 (2):173–95.

Keister, Lisa A. 2001. "Exchange Structures in Transition." *American Sociological Review* 66, no. 3 (June):336–60.

Kessler, Clive S. 2000. "Globalization: Another False Universalism?" *Third World Quarterly* 21 (6):931–42.

King, Anthony. 1995. *Culture, Globalization and the World-System.* Minneapolis: University of Minnesota Press.

Kipnis, Andrew. 1997. *Producing Guanxi: Sentiment, Self and Subculture in a North China Village.* Durham, N.C.: Duke University Press.

Kloosterman, Robert, and Jan Rath, eds. 2003. *Immigrant Entrepreneurs.* Oxford: Berg.

Koh, Shi Jin. 2003. *From Zero to One Hundred Billion* [Chun Lin Dao Yeh Ba Yeh]. Taipei: Prophet Press.

Kondo, Seiichi. 1999. "Advancing Globalization." *Far Eastern Economic Review* 162 (44):30.

Koo, George. October 6, 2001. Speech given during the annual meeting of the Silicon Valley Chinese Engineers at Sunnyvale, California.

Koopmans, Ruud, and Paul Statham. 1999. "Challenging the Liberal-State? Postnationalism, Multiculturalism and the Collective Claims Making of Migrants and Ethnic Minorities in Britain and Germany." *American Journal of Sociology* 105 (November):652–96.

Kotkin, Joel. 1993. *Tribes: How Race, Religion, and Identity Determine Success in the New Global Economy.* New York: Random House.

Kraidy, Marwan. 1999. "The Global, the Local, and the Hybrid: A Native Ethnography of Glocalization." *Critical Studies in Mass Communication* 16 (4):456–76.

Krasner, Stephen D. 2000. "Sovereignty." *Foreign Policy* 122 (January–February):20–29.

Lai, Him Mark. 1997. "Huangliang Du (Wong Leung Do) Community in Northern California." In *Hee Shen Benevolent Association Centennial Celebration: 1895–1995,* ed. Francis Wong. Santa Clara: Evergreen.

Lashman, Paul. 1994, "Feel-Bad Factor." *New Statesman and Society* 8 (June):26–7.

Laxer, Gordon. 2000. "Surviving the Americanizing New Right." *Canadian Review of Sociology and Anthropology* 37 (1):55–75.

Lee, Lester. October 6, 2001. Speech given during the annual conference of the Silicon Valley Chinese Engineers Association.

Lessinger, Johanna. 1996. *From the Ganges to the Hudson: Indian Immigrants in New York City.* Boston: Allyn and Bacon.

Lewellen, Ted. 2002. *Anthropology of Globalization.* Westport, Conn.: Bergin and Garvey.

Light, Ivan. 1971. *Ethnic Enterprise in North America: Business and Welfare among Chinese, Japanese and Blacks.* Berkeley: University of California Press.

———. 1979. "Disadvantaged Minorities in Self-Employment." *International Journal of Comparative Sociology* 20:31–45.

———. 1984. "Immigrant and Ethnic Enterprise in North America." *Ethnic and Racial Studies* 7:195–216.

Little, Kenneth. 1965. *West African Urbanization: A Study of Voluntary Associations in Social Change.* London: Cambridge University Press.

Liu, Xio-li. 1995. *The Ultimate Winners* [in Chinese]. Millbrae, Calif.: Think Big Publishing.

Lowe, Lisa. 1998. *Immigrant Acts: On Asian American Cultural Politics.* Durham, N.C.: Duke University Press.

Lydon, Sandy. 1985. *Chinese Gold: The Chinese in the Monterey Bay Region.* Capitola, Calif.: Capitola Book.

Lyman, Stanford, and William Douglas. 1973. "Ethnicity: Strategies of Collective and Individual Impression Management." *Social Research* 40 (2):345–65.

Malinowski, Bronislaw. 1961. *Argonauts of the Western Pacific.* New York: E.P. Dutton.

Mangin, William. 1965. "The Role of Regional Associations: Adaptation of Rural Migrants to Cities in Peru." In *Contemporary Cultures and Societies of Latin America.* eds. Dwight B. Health and Richard N. Adams. New York: Random House.

Mannur, Anita. 2003. "Cyberscapes and the Interfacing of Diasporas." In *Theorizing Diaspora,* ed. Jana Evans Braziel and Anita Mannur. Malden, Mass.: Blackwell Publishing.

Marcus, George. 1998. *Ethnography through Thick and Thin.* Princeton, N.J.: Princeton University Press.

Mathews, Gordon. 2000. *Global Culture/Individual Identity.* London: Routledge.

Mauss, M. *The Gift.* 1990. New York: W.W. Norton.

Mayer, Philip. 1961. *Townsmen and Tribesmen.* Capetown: Oxford University Press.

McClellan, Janet, and Anthony H. Richmond. 1993. "Multiculturalism in Crisis: A Postmodern Perspective on Canada." *Ethnic and Racial Studies* 17:662–83.

McCorquodale, Robert, and Richard Fairbrother. 1996. "Globalization and Human Rights." *Human Rights Quarterly* 21 (3):735–66.

McKeown, Adam. 2001. *Chinese Migrant Networks and Culture Change.* Chicago: University of Chicago Press.

McLuhan, M., and B. R. Powers. 1992. *The Global Village: Transformations in World, Life and Media in the 21st Century.* New York: Oxford University Press.

McPherson, Miller J., Pamela A. Popielarz, and Sonja Drobronic. 1991. "Social Networks and Organizational Dynamics." *American Sociological Review* 57 (2):153–70.

Mesiner, Maurice. 1999. "The Habit of Distrust." *Los Angeles Times.* May 30.

Mele, Christopher. 1996. "Globalization, Culture, and Neighborhood Change: Reinventing the Lower East Side of New York." *Urban Affairs Review.* 32:3–22.

Miller, Matt. 1998. "New Gold Mountain." *Far Eastern Economic Review* 161 (28):76–77.

Min, Pyong Gap, and Mehdi Bozorgmehr. 2000. "Immigrant Entrepreneurship and Business Patterns: A Comparison of Koreans and Iranians in Los Angeles." *International Migration Review* 34:707–38.

———. 2003. "United States: The Entrepreneurial Cutting Edge." In *Immigrant Entrepreneurs,* ed. Robert Kloosterman and Jan Rath. Oxford: Berg.

Mortland, Carol A. 1998. *Diasporic Identity: Selected Papers on Refugees and Immigrants.* Arlington, Va.: American Anthropological Association.

Murata, Lynn. 2001. *Transnationalism: The New Kinship Structure of Hong Kong Chinese.* San Francisco: Center for Urban Anthropology.

Murdock, George Peter. 1965. *Social Structure.* New York: Free Press.

Naisbitt, John. 1995. *Megatrends Asia.* New York: Simon and Schuster.

New York Times. February 21, 1995. "Skilled Asians Leaving U.S. for High-Tech Jobs at Home."

Ng, Franklin. 1988. *The Taiwanese Americans.* Westport, Conn.: Greenwood Press.

Ng, Michele, and Lloyd Wong. 1998. "Chinese Immigrant Entrepreneurs in Vancouver: A Case Study of Ethnic Business Development." *Canadian Ethnic Studies* 30 (1):64–85.

Ng, Wing Chung. 1995. *The Chinese in Vancouver, 1945–80.* Vancouver: University of British Columbia Press.

Novak, Michael. 1972. *The Rise of the Unmeltable Ethnics.* New York: Macmillan.

Okamura, Jonathan Y. 1996. "Writing the Filipino Diaspora: Roman R. Cariaga's *The Filipinos in Hawaii.*" *Social Process in Hawaii* 37:36–56.

———. 1998. *Imagining the Filipino American Diaspora: Transnational Relations, Identities and Communities.* New York: Garland.

Okongwu, Anne Francis, and Joan Mencher. 2000. "The Anthropology of Public Policy: Shifting Terrains." *Annual Review of Anthropology* 29:107–24.

Olds, Kris. 1995. "Globalization and the Production of New Urban Spaces: Pacific Rim Mega-Projects in the Late 20th Century." *Environment and Planning* 27:1713–43.

Ong, Aihwa. 1996a. "A Better Tomorrow? The Struggle for Global Visibility." *Sojourn* 12 (2):192–225.

———. 1996b. "Cultural Citizenship as Subject-Making: Immigrants Negotiate Racial Boundaries in the United States." *Current Anthropology* 37:731–51.

———. 1996c. "Southeast Asian Refugees and Investors in Our Midst." *Positions* 5 (3):806–13.

———. 1999. *Flexible Citizenship.* Durham, N.C.: Duke University Press.

Ong, Aihwa, and Donald Nonini. 1996. *Ungrounded Empires.* London: Routledge.

Palinkas, Lawrence. 1990. *Rhetoric and Religious Experience: The Discourse of Immigrant Churches.* Fairfax, Va.: George Mason University Press.

Pan, Lynn. 1996. *The Encyclopedia of the Chinese Overseas.* Cambridge, Mass.: Harvard University Press.

Park, Edward Jang-Woo. 1994. "Asian Americans in Silicon Valley: Race and Ethnicity in the Postindustrial Economy." Diss., University of California, Berkeley.

———. 1995. "Asian Matter: Asian American Entrepreneurs in the Silicon Valley." In *Reframing the Immigration Debate,* eds. Bill Ong Hing and Ronald Lee, 155–77. Los Angeles: Leadership Education for Asian Pacific and UCLA Asian American Studies Center.

Park, Robert. 1950. *Race and Culture.* Glencoe, Ill.: Free Press.

Park, Robert, Ernest Burgess, and Rodrick Makenzie. 1925. *The City.* Chicago: University of Chicago Press.

Parrenas, Rhacel Salazar. 2001. *Servants of Globalization: Women, Migration and Domestic Work.* Stanford, Calif.: Stanford University Press.

Pasternak, Burton, Carol R. Ember, and Melvin Ember, eds. 1997. *Sex, Gender, and Kinship.* N.J.: Prentice Hall.

Peng, Dajin. 2000. "Ethnic Business Network and the Asian Pacific Economic Integration." *Journal of Asian and African Studies* 35, no. 2 (May):229–50.

Peterson V. Spike. 1996. "The Politics of Identification in the Context of Globalization." *Women's Studies International Forum* 9:5–15.

Pieke, Frank. 1995. "Bureaucracy, Friends, and Money: The Growth of Capital Socialism in China." *Comparative Studies in Society and History* 37:494–518.

Pieterse, Jan Nederveen. 1999. "Globalization and Human Integration: We Are All Migrants." *Futures* 32 (5):385–98.

Portes, Alejandro. 1996. "Global Villagers: The Rise of Transnational Communities." *American Prospect* 25:74–77.

———. 1997. "Globalization from Below: The Rise of Transnational Communities." www.transcomm.ox.ac.uk/working_papers.htm (accessed May 27, 2005).

Portes, Alejandro, Manuel Castells, and Lauren A. Benton. 1991. *The Informal Economy*. Baltimore: Johns Hopkins University Press.

Poston, Dudley, Michael X. Mao, and Mei-ya Yu. 1992. "Patterns of Chinese Global Migration." Paper presented at the *Luo Di Shen Gen* International Conference on Overseas Chinese, San Francisco.

Preyer, Gerhard, and Mathias Bos. 2001. "Introduction: Borderlines in Time of Globalization." *Protosociology* 15:4–13.

Ramu, G. N. 2001. "Kinship Structure and Entrepreneurship: An Indian Case." In *Family, Kin and Community: A Contemporary Reader*, ed. Bernard P. Wong. Dubuque, Iowa: Kendall/Hunt.

Redding, S. G. 1990. *The Spirit of Chinese Capitalism*. Berlin: Walter de Gruyter.

Redfield, Robert. 1941. *The Folk Culture of Yucatan*. Chicago: University of Chicago Press.

———. 1947. "The Folk Society." *American Journal of Sociology* 52:293–306.

Riley, Jennifer. 1999. "Grass-Roots Globalism." *Hispanic* 12 (12):36–38.

Rosaldo, Renato. 1989. *Culture and Truth*. Boston: Beacon Press.

———. 1993. "Borderlands of Race and Inequality." Paper presented at the spring meeting of the Society for Cultural Anthropology, Washington, D.C.

Rouse, Roger. 1996. "Mexican Migration and the Social Space of Postmodernism." *Diaspora* 1 (1):8–23.

Safran, William. 1991. "Diasporas in Modern Societies: Myths of Homeland and Return." *Diaspora* 1 (1):83–99.

Sahlins, Marshall. 1993. "Goodbye to Tristes Tropes: Ethnography in the Contest of Modern History." *Journal of Modern History* (65):1–25.

San Francisco Examiner. April 20, 1989. "New Money Elite."

———. April 21, 1989. "Asia Influence Comes of Age."

San Jose Mercury News. August 22, 1993. "Time of Opportunities Turns for Taiwanese Engineers."

Sassen, Saskia. 1991. *The Global City*. Princeton, N.J.: Princeton University Press.

———. 1996a. "Cities and Communities in the Global Economy: Rethinking Our Concepts." *American Behavioral Scientist* 39 (March–April):629–39.

———. 1996b. *Cities in a World Economy*. Thousand Oaks, Calif.: Pine Forge Press.

Saxenian, AnaLee. 1999. *Silicon Valley's New Immigrant Entrepreneurs*. San Francisco: Public Policy Institute of California.

———. March 25, 2002. Personal communication.

Saxton, Alexander. 1971. *The Indispensable Enemy: Labor and the Anti-Chinese Movement in California*. Berkeley: University of California Press.

Schumpeter, Joseph. 1961. *The Theory of Economic Development*. London: Oxford University Press.

Scudder, Thayer. 1999. "The Emerging Global Crisis and Development Anthropology: Can We Have an Impact?" *Human Organization* 58 (4):351–64.

Seagrave, Sterling. 1995. *Lords of the Rim*. New York: G.P. Putnam's Sons.

Sennett, Richard. 1996. "Cities without Care or Connection." *New Statesman* 129 (June):25–7.

Serrie, Hendrick. 1996. "Training Chinese Managers for Leadership: Six Cross-Cultural Principles." *Practicing Anthropology* 21 (4):35–41.

Settles, Barbara. 2001a. "Being at Home in a Global Society: A Model for Families' Mobility and Immigration Decisions." *Journal of Comparative Family Studies* 32 (4):627–45.

———. 2001b. "Conflicts between Family Strategies and State Policy in a Global Society." *Journal of Comparative Family Studies* 32 (2):147–66.

Sexton, Jean Deitz. 1992. *Silicon Valley Inventing the Future: A Contemporary Portrait.* Hong Kong: Windsor Publications.

Simon, Denis. 1996. "Charting Taiwan's Technological Future: The Impact of Globalization and Regionalization." *China Quarterly* 148 (December):1196–223.

Sklair, Leslie. 1996. "Transnational Practices and the Analysis of the Global System." www.transcomm.ox.ac.uk/working_papers.htm (accessed May 27, 2005).

Smart, Alan. 1998. "*Guanxi*, Gifts, and Learning from China." *Anthropos* 93:559–63.

Smart, Alan, and Josephine Smart. 1999. "Failures and Strategies of Hong Kong Firms in China: An Ethnographic Perspective." In *Globalization of Chinese Business Firms*, eds. Henry Wai-chung Yeung and Kris Olds. New York: St. Martin Press.

Southall, Aidan. 1998. *The City in Time and Space.* London: Cambridge University Press.

Soyal, Yasemin. 1994. *Limits of Citizenship: Migrants and Postnational Membership in Europe.* Chicago: University of Chicago Press.

Stack, Carol B. 1974. *All Our Kin.* New York: Harper and Row.

Stephen, Lynn. 1996. "Globalization, the State and the Creation of Flexible Indigenous Workers." *Urban Anthropology and Studies of Cultural Systems and World Economic Development* 30 (2/3):189–214.

Storper, Michael. 2000. "Lived Effects of the Contemporary Economy: Globalization, Inequality, and Consumer Society." *Public Culture* 12 (2):375–409.

Takaki, Ronald. 1989. *Strangers from a Different Shore.* New York: Penguin Books.

———. 1993. *A Different Mirror.* Boston: Little Brown and Company.

Tan, Joe. 2001. Editorial. www.huaren.org.

Tapinos, Georges Photios. 2000. "Globalization, Regional Integration, International Migration." *International Social Science Journal* 52 (3):297–306.

Tehranian, Katherine Kia. 1998. "Global Communication and Pluralization of Identities." *Futures* 30 (2/3):211–17.

Teng, Hai Jew. 1998. *Outstanding Stories in Silicon Valley* [Jeh Gu Chuang Chi]. 2 vols. Taipei: Yuan-Shen Press.

Thurow, Lester C. 2000. "Globalization: the Product of a Knowledge-Based Economy." *Annals of the American Academy of Political and Social Science* 570:19–31.

Tien, Ju-kang. 1953. The Chinese of Sarawak: A Study of Social Structure. London: London School of Economic Monograph of Social Anthropology. No. 12.

Tomlinson, John. 1996. *Globalization and Culture.* Oxford: Polity.

Turner, Bryan S. 2001. "The Erosion of Citizenship." *British Journal of Sociology* 52 (2):189–209.

Tu, Weiming. 1996. "Cultural Identity and the Politics of Recognition in Contemporary Taiwan." *China Quarterly* 148 (December):1115–40.

Vargas-Llosa, Mario. 2001. "Golden Globe." *New Statesman* 130 (March):42–6.

Walby, Sylvia. 1996. "Analyzing Social Inequality in the Twenty-first Century: Global-ization and Modernity Restructure Inequality." *Contemporary Sociology* 29 (6):813–18.

Waldinger, Robert, Howard Aldrich, and Robin Ward. 1990. *Ethnic Entrepreneurs.* Newbury Park: Sage Publications.

Wallerstein, Immanuel. 1974. *The Modern World-System.* New York: Academic Press.

———. 1980. *The Modern World-System II: Mercantilism and the Consolidation of the European Economy 1600–1750.* New York: Academic Press.

———. 1990. "Culture as the Ideological Battleground of the Modern-World System." In *Global Culture*, ed. Mike Featherstone. London and Newbury Park: Sage.

Walt, Stephen M. 2000. "Fads, Fevers and Firestorms." *Foreign Policy* 121 (November/December):34–42.

Wang, Gungwu. 2000. "Ethnic Chinese: The Past in their Future." *Chinese America: History and Perspectives 2000.* San Francisco: Chinese Historical Society of America.

———. Forthcoming. "A Single Chinese Diaspora?" *Imagining the Chinese Diaspora: Two Australian Perspectives.* Canberra: Centre for the Study of the Chinese Southern Diaspora, Research School of Pacific and Asian Studies, Australian National University.

Wang, Jenn-hwa. 2004. "Transnational Co-evolution of Technology and Institutions: The Development of Taiwan's PC Industry." Paper presented at the Center of Chinese Studies. Berkeley: University of California.

Wang, Ling-chi, and Wang Gungwu. 1996. *The Chinese Diaspora: Selected Essays.* 2 vols. Singapore: Times Academic Press.

Wang, Shaoguang. 1996. "The Social and Political Implications of China's WTO Membership." *Journal of Contemporary China* 25 (November):373–405.

Watson, James L. 1997. *Golden Arches East: McDonald's in East Asia.* Stanford, Calif.: Stanford University Press.

———. 2000. "China's Big Mac Attack" *Foreign Affairs* 79 (May/June):120–34.

Weatherford, Jack McIver. 1988. "The Clans on Capital Hill." In *Contemporary Cultural Anthropology*, ed. Michael Howard, 322–25. Boston: Scott, Foresman and Company.

Weber, Max. 1951. *Religion of China.* New York: Macmillan.

———. 1958. *The Protestant Ethnic and the Spirit of Capitalism.* New York: Charles Scribner's Sons.

Weidenbaum, Murray, and Samuel Hughes. 1996. *The Bamboo Network.* New York: Free Press.

Werbner, Pnina. 2002. *Imagined Diasporas among Manchester Muslims.* Santa Fe, N. Mex.: School of American Research.

Whyte, Martin K. 1988. "The Chinese Families and Economic Development: Obstacle or Engine?" *Economic Development and Culture Change* 45 (1):1–30.

Wilkinson, John. 1997. "A New Paradigm for Economic Analysis?" *Economy and Society* 26:305–39.

Winland, Daphne N. 1988. "Our Home and Native Land?" *Canadian Review of Sociology and Anthropology* 35 (4):555–77.

Wirth, Louis. 1938. "Urbanism as a Way of Life." *American Journal of Sociology* 44:1–24.

Wolf, Eric. 1966. "Kinship, Friendship and Patron-Client Relations in Complex Societies." In *The Social Anthropology of Complex Societies*, ed. Michael Banton, 1–35.
London: Tavistock.

———. 1982. *Europe and the People without History*. Berkeley: University of California Press.

Wong, Bernard. 1978. "A Comparative Study of the Assimilation of the Chinese in
New York City and Lima, Peru." *Comparative Studies in Society and History* 20
(3):335–58.

———. 1979. *A Chinese American Community: Ethnicity and Survival Strategies*.
Singapore: Chopmen Enterprises.

———. 1982. *Chinatown*. New York: Holt, Rinehart and Winston.

———. 1985. "Family, Kinship and Ethnic Identity of the Chinese in New York City,
with Comparative Remarks on the Chinese in Lima, Peru and Manila, Philippines."
Journal of Comparative Family Studies 16 (2):231–54.

———. 1986. "The Impact of Changing U.S.–China Policies on Chinese Americans."
Asian Profile 14 (1):1–11.

———. 1987. "The Role of Ethnicity in Enclave Enterprises: A Study of the Chinese
Garment Factories in New York City." *Human Organization* 46 (2):120–31.

———. 1988. *Patronage, Brokerage, Entrepreneurship and the Chinese Community
of New York*. New York: AMS Press.

———. 1994. "Hong Kong Immigrants in San Francisco." In *Reluctant Exiles?* ed.
Ronald Skeldon, 235–54. Armonk, N.Y.: M.E. Sharpe.

———. 1997. "Globalization, Anthropology and the Chinese Diaspora." Keynote
speech presented at the Second International Conference on Contemporary Diaspora. Tsukuba, Japan: Tsukuba University.

———. 1998a. *Ethnicity and Entrepreneurship: The New Chinese Immigrants in the
San Francisco Bay Area*. Boston: Allyn and Bacon.

———. 1998b. "Transnationalism and New Chinese: Immigrant Families in the United
States." In *Diasporic Identity*, ed. Carol A. Mortland, 158–74. Arlington, Va.: American Anthropological Association.

———. 2001a. *Family, Kin and Community: A Contemporary Reader*. Rev. ed.
Dubuque, Iowa: Kendall/Hunt.

———. 2001b. "From Enclave Small Businesses to High-Tech Industries: The Chinese
In the San Francisco Bay Area." In *Manifest Destinies: Americanizing Immigrants
and Internationalizing Americans*, eds. David Haines and Carol A. Mortland,
111–30. Westport, Conn.: Praeger.

———. 2001c. "The Role of Kinship in the Economic Activities of the Chinese in the
Philippines." In *Family, Kin and Community: A Contemporary Reader*, ed.
Bernard Wong, rev. ed. 188–215. Dubuque, Iowa: Kendall/Hunt.

———. 2005 "Chinese Diasporas." In *Immigration and Asylum: From 1900 to the
Present*. ed. Mathew Gibney. Oxford: ABC-Clio.

Wong, Bernard, Becky McReynolds, and Wynnie Wong. 1992. "The Chinese Family
Firms in the San Francisco Bay Area." *Family Business Review* 5 (4):355–72.

Wong, Lloyd. 1997. "Globalization and Transnational Migration: A Study of Recent
Chinese Capitalist Migration from the Asian Pacific to Canada." *International Sociology*, 12 (3):329–51.

Wu, David Y., H. McQueen, and Y. Yamamoto. 1997. *Emerging Pluralism in Asia and the Pacific*. Hong Kong: Hong Kong Institute of Asia-Pacific Studies, Chinese University of Hong Kong.

Yamashita, Shinji, Kadir H. Din, and J. S. Eades. 1996. *Tourism and Cultural Development in Asian and Oceania*. Bangi: Penerbit Universiti Kebangsaan Malaysia.

Yan, Yunxiang. 1996. *The Flow of Gifts: Reciprocity and Social Networks in a Chinese Village*. Stanford, Calif.: Stanford University Press.

Yang, Mayfair. 1994. *Gifts, Favors and Banquets: The Art of Social Relationships in China*. Ithaca, N.Y.: Cornell University Press.

———. 2004. "Agrarian Sovereignty vs Coastal Economy." Paper presented at the Center for Chinese Studies, University of California, Berkeley.

Yeoh, Brenda S. A., and T. C. Chang. 2001. "Globalising Singapore: Debating Transnational Flows in the City." *Urban Studies* 38 (7):1025–44.

Yeoh, Brenda S. A., and Shirlena Huang. 1963. "'Home' and 'Away': Foreign Domestic Workers and Negotiations of Diasporic Identity in Singapore." *Women's Studies International Forum* 23 (4):413–29.

Yeoh, Brenda S. A., and Katie Willis. 1996. "Singapore Unlimited: Configuring Social Identity in the Regionalisation Process." www.transcomm.ox.ac.uk/working _papers.htm (accessed May 27, 2005).

Yeung, Henry Wai-chung. 1997. "Business Networks and Transnational Corporations: A Study of Hong Kong Firms in the ASEAN Region." *Economic Geography* 73 (11):1–25.

———. 2000. "Economic Globalization, Crisis and the Emergence of Chinese Business Communities in Southeast Asia." *International Sociology* 15, no. 2 (June):265–87.

Yeung, Henry Wai-chung, and Kris Olds, eds. 1999. *Globalization of Chinese Business Firms*. New York: St. Martin Press.

Yu, Connie Young. 1986. *Profiles in Excellence: Peninsular Chinese Americans*. Palo Alto, Calif.: Stanford Area Chinese Club.

———. 1993. *Chinatown San Jose, U.S.A.* San Jose, Calif.: San Jose Historical Association.

Zachary, G. Pascal. 2000. "Get Over It." *Foreign Policy* 120 (September):62–63.

Zhang, Wei Tian. 2000. *Silicon Valley's Red Guards* [Jeh Gu Hung Wei Bin]. Taipei: Bookzone.

Index

political organizations, 74–75
political participations, 120–24
population of San Francisco, 3; of the
nine counties of, 3; of the Chinese in
California, 4
Portes, Alejandro, 7, 230
prestation, 54, 181. See also Mauss, M.
primordial feeling, 34
professional organizations. *See*
associations
protectionist backlash, 48
putonghua, 73
PTA. *See* Parent Teacher Association

racism, 10, 153, 156–57
racial profiling, 8, 153–54
Ranch 99, 146, 202, 203
real-estate, 184–85, 204–206
reasonable: philosophy of being, 56–58
reasonableness: concept of, 57; lack of,
57
reciprocity, 49; in employer-employee
relations, 49. See also *social
relations*
regional cuisines, 146–90
regional culture, 32, 139–42, 158, 227
regionalism and social networks, 71–72
ren chin or *renqing* (human feeling),
46, 96, 101
residence, length of, 203
restructuring of the U.S. economy, 2, 5
return migration, 35, 101–102, 107,
163–67; to China, 162–64; motives
for, 168; to Taiwan, 162–63
Rosaldo, Renato, 9

Safran, William, 9
San Jose, 31, 33
Santa Clara, 24
sanyi, 28
Sassen, Saski, 7, 230
Saxenian, AnaLee, 4, 12, 26
school problems, 173–74; in Asia, 173;
cram sessions, 173
Seagrave, Sterling, 2, 11
September 11, 2001 (9/11), 157
sex ratio, 199

Shanghai Circle, 191
Shenzhen, 52
shin yung or *xin yong* (trust), 46, 54
Silicon Rush, 19
"Silicon Soup," 112
Silicon Valley culture, 112, 113
Sina.com, 27, 161
sinicization, 231
"sister cities, " 30–31
siyi, 28
social class, 24, 158, 167
social clubs, 8
social mobility: problems of, 97–101,
114–17. *See also* glass ceiling
social network: and modern
technology, 72–74; studies, 7–8
social relations, informal, 48, 164; and
globalization, 69–71; in high-tech
businesses, 48–58
social tension, 33, 34, 41
sojourners, 196
Solectron, 20
stereotypes, 115–16, 151
Story from Afar, 217
subethnicities, 190–201, 220
Sunnyvale, 24

Tai Du, 34. See also Taiwan
Independence Movement
tai kong ren, 167. See also astronaut
Tainan, 31
Taipei Drive, 190
Taipei Economic and Culture Office, 14,
143
Taiwan, 31; -born Chinese
professionals, 25; Chinese, 22;
returnees, 163
Taiwanese, 193; entrepreneurs, 131–33.
See also bendi
Taiwan Independence Movement, 34,
120
Taiwan wen hua, 143, 194
Tai yu, 194
Takaki, Ronald, 155
tongshi (colleague), 230
tongxie (classmate), 65, 230
tong yong pinyin, 237

About the Author

Bernard Wong, PhD, is professor of anthropology at San Francisco State University. In the course of his studies he has conducted field research on the Chinese communities in the Philippines, Singapore, New York City, San Francisco, Silicon Valley, Lima (Peru), Kobe, and Yokohama, Japan. His research interests include the family, ethnic identity and ethnic subcultures, cultural citizenship, globalization, and ethnic entrepreneurship.

Dr. Wong is the author of five scholarly books and numerous journal articles. He has presented papers at the meetings of many professional societies and given speeches at universities across the globe including Keio University (Japan), Tsukuba University (Japan), Academia Sinica (Taiwan), the University of Singapore, Yonsei University (Korea), the University of Amsterdam, and the University of California, Berkeley.